W9-DDC-235

# ABUSE AND NEGLECT OF OLDER CANADIANS:
## STRATEGIES FOR CHANGE

Michael J. MacLean, Editor

CANADIAN ASSOCIATION ON GERONTOLOGY

*Ottawa*

THOMPSON EDUCATIONAL PUBLISHING, INC.

*Toronto*

# ABUSE AND NEGLECT OF OLDER CANADIANS:
## STRATEGIES FOR CHANGE

Michael J. MacLean, Editor

CANADIAN ASSOCIATION ON GERONTOLOGY
*Ottawa*

THOMPSON EDUCATIONAL PUBLISHING, INC.
*Toronto*

Copyright © 1995 Thompson Educational Publishing, Inc.

All rights reserved. No part of this publication may be reproduced or transmitted in any form or by any means, electronic or mechanical, including photocopy, recording, or any information storage and retrieval system, without permission in writing from the publisher.

Requests for permission to make copies of any part of the work should be directed to the publisher.

**Canada**

14 Ripley Avenue, Suite 105

Toronto, Ontario

M6S 3N9

Tel (416) 766–2763

Fax (416) 766–0398

**Canadian Cataloguing in Publication Data**

Main entry under title:

Abuse and neglect of older Canadians : Strategies for change

Includes bibliographical references.

ISBN 1-55077-068-3

1. Abused aged - Services for - Canada. 2. Aged - Abuse of - Canada. 3. Aged - Abuse of - Canada - Prevention. 4. Aged - Crimes against - Canada -Prevention. 5. Violence - Canada - Prevention. I. MacLean, Michael J., 1947-   . II. Title: Abuse and neglect of older Canadians.

HV6626.3.A38 1995   362.88'084'6   C94-932670-4

Book and text designed by: Danielle Baum

Cover designed by: Danielle Baum and Mike McAuliffe

Printed and bound in Canada.

1 2 3 4     98 97 96 95

# TABLE OF CONTENTS

# ACKNOWLEDGEMENTS

This book is part of a multi-faceted project entitled "Abuse and Neglect of Older Canadians: Consolidation and Strategies for Change" that the Canadian Association on Gerontology undertook in 1992 with funding from the Family Violence Prevention Division of Health Canada. Beginning with the encouragement and support of Katalin Kennedy, FVDP Program Development Consultant in the initiation of the project, this book is the product of the generous cooperation and committed collaboration of many, many people.

First and foremost are the twenty-seven authors, and the resource persons with whom they consulted in writing the chapters, including the participants at a pre-conference workshop in Montreal in October 1993 where the authors shared their preliminary findings for open discussion. These discussions were enriched also by the reflections of seniors across the country who were unable to attend the workshop but whose voices were heard thanks to the efforts of the provincial Gerontology Associations in coordinating written summaries of these seniors' contributions. The Sovereign and Military Order of Malta, Canadian Association, helped make this workshop possible through its financial support. Nine persons, whose expertise on the topic spanned academic, government, community, and senior perspectives, generously shared their thoughts and suggestions as external readers of the book. The ten members of the CAG Project Advisory Committee - John Bond, Thérèse Darche, John Gray, Jean Kozak, Michael MacLean, Lynn McDonald, Daphne Nahmiash, Elizabeth Podnieks, Michael Stones, and Blossom Wigdor - have overseen its production, along with CAG Director of Programmes, Benita Langdon, and Rosemary Williams, the Project Officer. Danielle Baum of Ottawa and Keith Thompson of Thompson Educational Publishing have offered us their ongoing encouragement along with technical expertise for the production of the book.

To all of these people from different disciplines and walks of life, practitioners, policy-makers, educators, researchers, students and older Canadians, the Canadian Association on Gerontology extends sincere appreciation and thanks.

## WAIVER

Findings and opinions expressed in this book are those of the authors and not necessarily those of the Canadian Association on Gerontology, nor of Health Canada.

# FOREWORD

*Sr. St. Michael Guinan, Ph.D.,*

*Professor Emeritus, Brescia College, London, Ontario*

In the 1960s when I first sent students to investigate elder abuse, their findings shocked me. Current research has intensified that shock. It is now recognized that abuse and neglect of older people occurs world-wide. In Canada, not only are more situations of such mistreatment being uncovered, but with the growing proportion of seniors in our society and the widespread social problems brought on by current high levels of unemployment, this problem is predicted to increase.

As a senior, this troubles me. But it is not an issue just for older people. Through friends, family, and acquaintances, or through our own aging, we are all connected with older persons. We may be part of the problem, but we can also be part of the solution. It may be a matter of how we treat our parents and grandparents, how we provide care at home or in institutions, what resources we provide and how we offer them to seniors who need support. None of us can feel at ease knowing that senior members of our society are being abused and neglected—often "behind closed doors", or as a matter of "normal" interaction with the very persons they ought to be able to trust.

Knowing about elder abuse is an important step in acting against it. With this book, the Canadian Association on Gerontology brings together the accumulated knowledge of people who have been working on this issue from quite diverse standpoints—researchers and educators, policy-analysts and practitioners. A picture emerges of elder abuse and what can be done about it which shows that strides are being made in acknowledging and dealing with the issue. It also shows that we must proceed with caution, for there are no quick, ready-made solutions.

Students, educators, professionals in gerontology, health and social services, law and security, community workers, seniors, and members of the public at large, I urge you to read this book. I especially recommend that you look to the sections whose perspective may be outside your usual familiarity. With deepened understanding, then, we must all work to undertake strategies for change, and together build a society where seniors are accorded the respect and care that we all desire.

# INTRODUCTION

*Michael J. MacLean and Rosemary M. Williams*

The Canadian Association on Gerontology has undertaken to join with the growing number of Canadians striving to do something about the outrage that older members of our society are being abused and neglected. In this book we bring together the analysis and reflections of twenty-seven authors, many of whom have themselves long been engaged in confronting this issue. Their recommendations for future action reflect the wisdom that springs from experience as well as knowledge derived from systematic evaluation of current efforts to address the problem.

Our goal must be action to stop this abuse and neglect, to support older people who have been mistreated, and ultimately to prevent abuse and neglect of older persons from happening. But action can take many forms. In fact, as several authors underline, success in fighting this complex problem will require the combined efforts of people from many disciplines and many points of contact within our society.

## FOUR PERSPECTIVES

In this book we have focussed on four perspectives from which to examine what we know and what we are doing about the abuse and neglect of older Canadians. These are: practice, policy, education, and research.

By "practice", we understand direct front-line intervention with seniors who have been abused and neglected. In this book, "practice" refers mainly to workers within the health and social services system who intervene to deal with and alleviate this abuse. Insofar as any of us may be in positions to offer assistance to older persons whom we suspect are being abused or neglected, however, we too will be engaged in "practice".

"Policy" refers to the establishment of regulations and guidelines for acknowledging and dealing with elder abuse and neglect. A government's, institution's or community organization's policies may determine, for example, what kind of services are provided, in what quantity, and under what conditions. Content of educational programs may depend on policies about the inclusion of issues on the topic. In this book, policy development with regard to elder abuse is discussed. One author in the section also engages in policy analysis, examining the basic premises on which Canadian policies and programs are based.

"Education" in this book includes not only formal academic programs, but also public education programs developed by community organizations, continuing education within the workplace, and ongoing learning throughout one's life. The authors show the importance of formal and informal educational efforts in challenging many aspects of abuse and neglect of older Canadians.

"Research" refers to studies or investigations seeking to test out beliefs and to establish knowledge about a subject. How the study is designed and carried out affects the validity of its findings. In this book, authors scrutinize current research on abuse and neglect of older persons and evaluate the soundness of the findings.

These fields are closely interconnected. Authors from one section, for example, often refer to chapters in other sections. The front-line field where practice takes place is also a field for research. The knowledge established by research can help practitioners know how effective their interventions are. Education helps practitioners to be informed and to develop skills and sensitivity for their work. Practitioners' activities are influenced by government and workplace policies, and policy-makers need to hear from front-line practitioners in order to develop sound policies. Undertakings in research and education are likewise affected by government or institutional policies. Research findings can have direct application for education programs and for policy development and review. And in each of these fields, the voices of older Canadians must be heard.

These four perspectives bring different approaches and methods, different modes of action. Interconnected as they are, dialogue and collaboration is essential. This book, we hope, will advance that dialogue and that collaboration, as we affirm the value of partnerships and multi-disciplinarity in our quest to address abuse and neglect of older persons in Canada, and ultimately to prevent it from happening. We recognize that what has been accomplished within these individual domains is often unknown to those outside the groups engaged in particular programs, or is beyond the readership of the respective academic or professional journals in which the accomplishment has been presented. Such material needs to be shared with the wide audience of persons in diverse contexts who are concerned about the issue, and this book aims to facilitate this wide sharing.

## HISTORICAL OVERVIEW [1]

In order to situate the authors' analysis of current efforts, we first trace some landmarks in the Canadian history of addressing the issue. It was in 1989 that the emergence of the *Journal of Elder Abuse and Neglect*, published in New York, signalled the coming-together of abuse and neglect of older persons as a specialty topic drawn from gerontology, law, family studies, and the helping disciplines. In the United States, attention to the issue dates from the late 1970s, where it developed quickly, to the effect that by 1986, for example, all the states had adult protection laws (Johnson, 1989). By comparison, action in Canada has moved at a more considered pace. The topic became recognized as a social issue in Canada mainly during the 1980s.

An early initiative was Newfoundland's *Neglected Adults Welfare Act* of 1973, in which reporting became compulsory for cases of known or suspected neglect. This Act preceded developments in the United States, where fewer than one-third of the states had enacted adult protective legislation even a decade later (Johnson, 1989). Other regions with adult protective laws include the maritime provinces of Nova Scotia (1985) and Prince Edward Island (1988), and the prairie province of Saskatchewan (1989-90). Other provinces protect seniors with programs administered under family services laws (e.g. New Brunswick, 1980).

The Manitoba Association on Gerontology in 1979 was the first of the provincial gerontology associations to become involved in addressing the issue of elder abuse. Others began in the early 1980s, and some provincial associations produced publications. Examples include Quebec (Bélanger, 1981), Manitoba (Shell, 1982), Newfoundland (G.A.

Frecker Association on Gerontology, 1983), and Alberta (Stevenson, 1985). These early efforts mainly aimed to identify the kind and extent of the abuse and neglect of seniors.

The next developments concerned funding, programming, and education. An early federal initiative was the discussion of abuse in a federal government working paper (Health & Welfare Canada, 1987). In 1988, the Seniors Independence Program funded projects directly addressing senior mistreatment (Health & Welfare Canada, 1990). The funding in seven provinces was for programming, educational and resource materials, and the development of a screening tool. Beginning around 1990, the Family Violence Prevention Division began to sponsor or to fund projects. A recent survey of 307 groups involved with senior mistreatment found that about 90% received funds from government sources (Health & Welfare Canada, 1992).

Although some Canadian researchers previously published in the academic journals (e.g. Bristowe & Collins, 1989), the landmark work must be Podnieks' national prevalence study (Podnieks, 1990). This study included a modified random sample of two thousand seniors living in private dwellings. Although aspects of the measurement of abuse and neglect have been questioned (Kozma & Stones, this volume), this study was the first to be national in scope, and marks an important step for understanding the extent of the problem in Canada.

## TERMINOLOGY

Abuse and neglect of older persons is commonly called "elder abuse", a phrase which includes the notion of neglect. Other terms such as "senior mistreatment" may also be used, or even the outmoded slang phrase "granny bashing". The terms themselves bear thinking about: "elder", for instance may connote particular meaning within aboriginal and religious communities, and some people find the term "senior" patronizing. At the present time, there is no generally agreed-upon way to refer to the issue, and this itself becomes a significant problem for research in the area. In this book, although different authors call it by different names, they are all focussed on the same phenomenon: the fact that older Canadians are abused and neglected in diverse ways.

"Victim" presents another controversial term. As much as possible we have avoided using it in this book, and have chosen instead "abused senior". We believe that a person's identity—how we think of and refer to that person, or to ourselves—should not be bound to his/her/our having been subjected to violence or other injustice. Certainly, abuse and neglect should not be glossed over or denied, but to refer to the person primarily as "victim" is to overstress the passivity which "victim" connotes, and to undervalue the strength and dignity that he/she retains as an autonomous individual.

From an empowerment perspective, "abused senior" offers a better ground than does "victim" as a position from which to respond in strength. If persons who have experienced abuse understand themselves as "victims", they then may well understand themselves as passive, needing the assistance of someone else to rescue them. If, on the other hand, they see themselves as "abused seniors", the abuse is named, its injustice, far from being covered over, is clearly highlighted when juxtaposed with "senior", and their primary identification is as an older person—one who has been abused, but who can react against it. This consideration has application also for how service providers working with abused persons think about the older person, and about themselves and their own role.

The words we use for naming experience and identifying people are crucial to how we think and act. We are, however, limited by the language at our disposal: until better terms are developed, current terms such as "elder abuse" and "senior" will continue to be used for communicating on this topic, and are indeed used in this book. We urge only that the readers, and indeed all people working on the issue of the abuse and neglect of older people, be sensitive to the meanings and connotations of the terms we use.

## GROUNDWORK FOR ACTION

As people become aware of abuse and neglect of older persons, the questions arise, "What can be done to stop it?" "What can *we* do to stop it?" Front-line intervention and provision of support to abused older persons, and to abusers, is one way. Introduction of policies for detection of abuse and follow-up attention, professional and public education and sensitization of members of our society to this problem, and research towards better understanding of elder abuse and neglect are other ways.

Action takes place on many fronts. We hope that this book, in its multi-faceted analysis and recommendations, will be informative and thought-provoking, both for personal reflections on how we treat older persons, and for our collective response to the abuse and neglect that is a very real part of life for some older Canadians.

---

[1]    We are indebted to Michael Stones for his contribution to this historical overview.

# SECTION 1:
# PRACTICE

# INTRODUCTION:

# PRACTICE ISSUES IN THE ABUSE AND NEGLECT OF OLDER CANADIANS

## Daphne Nahmiash

This section analyzes some key issues to be considered from the perspective of the practitioner or service provider in the area of abuse and neglect of seniors. Examples are offered of models for interventions in community and institutional settings, reflection on particular concerns, and approaches used in practice with abused and neglected seniors.

One of the main problems Canadian practitioners have experienced as they develop models for intervening on abuse and neglect of seniors is the dearth of conclusive research on intervention. The available research on abuse and neglect comes primarily from the United States (Pillemer & Moore, 1989). When it does address intervention programs, the examples are not always relevant for Canada because of the differences in the health and social service systems. Thus, in the area of abuse and neglect of older Canadians, even though a number of innovative practice models have begun to be developed (Health & Welfare, 1992), Canadian practitioners have been obliged to create their own programs without the benefit of evaluative research on existing models or of appropriate "how-to" manuals. At present, however, several models, including the Manitoban and British Columbian ones discussed by McKenzie, Tod and Yellen in this section, are in the process of being evaluated.

Another major problem in this area has been the lack of reliable and validated tools, protocols and basic definitions for abuse and neglect. A myriad of tools and definitions are being formulated across Canada as a starting point for intervention programs. This may represent a rediscovery of the wheel and a waste of time, funds, energy and resources for practitioners and researchers. In this context, the coordination and effective dissemination of available research and program evaluation information is essential.

Also, practitioners working in the area of abuse and neglect of seniors may have difficulty in deciding among approaches to be used in service delivery. There is no consensus with regard to approaches to be used, and as research offers little conclusive evidence on this subject, a selection of approaches may be the solution. What may be effective in some situations may not be effective in others. Currently, however, the choice of approach may spring from the particular philosophies of individual service providers or practitioners, whereas what is needed is an informed selection of approaches according to the particular situation. For example, the empowerment approach has been defined by Health and Welfare Canada (1993a) as "the process of helping individuals to maximize their confidence, skills, and abilities in order to take control of their lives, and to make informed decisions that are in their best interests. Empowerment also involves the element of choice and available, accessible options" (p. 4). This empowerment approach may be most influential with abused seniors who are able to take steps to solve their own problems. On the other hand, intervention based on a protection approach may be better suited to those who are unable to take such steps, such as those who suffer from dementia. The adult protection approach is described in McDonald, Hornick, Robertson and Wallace (1991), as "characterized by special powers of investigation and intervention, and mandatory reporting. The intervention strategies associated with adult protection programs may include the power of removal, and compulsory custody and services" (p. 68). It is important for practitioners to reflect on their choice of approaches.

It is within this context that the authors of this section address particular issues for practitioners working with abused seniors. In the first chapter, McDonald, Pittaway and Nahmiash discuss ethical issues, multicultural concerns, and the provision of services and resources to abused seniors. In the second chapter McKenzie, Tod and Yellen review the literature pertaining to abuse and neglect in community-based settings and provide examples of Canadian practice models and programs for working with abused and neglected older persons living in community settings. In the third chapter, Beaulieu and Bélanger consider interventions on senior mistreatment from the perspective of institution-based settings. As with the former chapter, the authors describe particular Canadian programs currently in operation.

All three chapters demonstrate that there are no easy answers nor sure solutions for practitioners who encounter these issues when intervening in abuse and neglect situations with older people. The authors highlight the fact that practitioners' judgement in at-risk situations is crucial. Front-line workers provide a major contribution to the prevention and treatment of elder abuse and neglect. This section points to the need for a partnership among practitioners, researchers, policy-makers, educators, and seniors, whose domains clearly have an impact on one another. Such collaboration and communication may well be the key to effective action against abuse and neglect of older people.

# 1-1

## ISSUES IN PRACTICE WITH RESPECT TO MISTREATMENT OF OLDER PEOPLE

*Lynn McDonald, Elizabeth Pittaway and Daphne Nahmiash*

## INTRODUCTION

In this chapter we examine some of the fundamental issues faced by practitioners working in the area of mistreatment of older persons. Being familiar with these issues expands the choices of the practitioner and underscores the fact that there is no one "correct" approach to each situation. In the first section of this chapter, we consider the basic issues of the right to protection versus the right to privacy, the competence/incompetence of the older person, and the problem of confidentiality. The second section addresses an important set of issues hitherto neglected in the literature but frequently encountered by the practitioner—the multicultural dimensions of practice with mistreated elderly people. The third section of the chapter explores the issues pertaining to service delivery. Should new services be developed and/or existing services be enhanced to meet the challenge of mistreatment of older adults? What gaps are there in service delivery and are services accessible to those most needing them? Are services co-ordinated and are complaint mechanisms available and effective?

## THE ETHICS OF EVERYDAY PRACTICE

In this discussion we make the assumption that most practitioners face the same dilemmas in dealing with mistreatment of older people, whether or not they practice in a jurisdiction covered by adult protective legislation. Adult protective legislation, particularly legislation that has mandatory reporting provisions, simply magnifies the ethical dilemmas faced by most practitioners and makes the issues more vivid. As Gordon and Tomita (1990) have noted in their list of objections to mandatory reporting, "In any given situation, the principles of beneficence, autonomy and non-maleficence must be weighed carefully before a decision is made, since they may well conflict." (1990, p. 3). Mandatory reporting simply compounds these conflicts because it forces the practitioner to take action or face legal consequences (see Robertson, this volume).

These three ethical principles are commonly found in the code of ethics of most health and social service professions. According to the principle of beneficence, professionals should act in a manner that will do good for other people; for example, removing and preventing harm, and providing benefits (Gilbert, 1986). The principle of autonomy is the bedrock of the helping professions—to respect the self-determination of others through acting only with consent and respecting confidentiality. The application of this principle usually presumes that the person can act autonomously because he or she is mentally competent or has reached the age of majority. The non-maleficence principle is generally limited in meaning to the avoidance of unintentional harm since the goals of all helping professions preclude inflicting intentional harm (Gilbert, 1986). A related ethical principle is that of limited benevolent intervention wherein the state recognizes an adult's right to receive and the state's duty to provide the least restrictive and intrusive form of care.

In maltreatment situations, practitioners strive to weigh the benefits of following one principle against the costs of abandoning another principle, while recognizing that the balance will be weighted differently in every case. Following Gilbert (1986), we discuss some of the fundamental dilemmas experienced by most practitioners in their work to end mistreatment of older persons.

## Ending the Mistreatment Versus Obtaining Consent

When mistreatment is confirmed but the older person refuses service, beneficence collides with autonomy. Does the practitioner violate self-determination and deliver the services to end the harm, or not deliver the services and respect the person's right to self-determination? Most practitioners acknowledge an ethical, if not a legal, duty to end the mistreatment. However, many practitioners express frustration because a large proportion of their clientele do not consent to the receipt of services even when the abuse has been confirmed (Health & Welfare, 1992).

Several studies in the United States have found that about 36 to 40 percent of mistreated elderly people refuse intervention services (Gilbert, 1986; Vinton, 1991). The reasons cited for refusing service were that the older person was ashamed, feared retaliation, feared nursing home placement and/or the breakdown of valuable family ties (Dolan & Blakely, 1989). The dilemma is particularly disturbing because the maltreated persons most likely to refuse services were older women who had been abused by their sons. This finding is particularly disturbing because the sons were more likely to resort to physical violence than were spouses or daughters (Vinton, 1991).

Thus, the practitioner is truly in a quandary. He or she must simultaneously balance the customary professional goal of stopping the mistreatment while respecting the person's right to make his or her own decisions, assuming the person is competent. The dilemma is, of course, exacerbated by mandatory reporting. Using legal powers to force oneself into an older person's home, and attempting to respect that person's right to self-determination while conducting an assessment is almost as troublesome as accepting the person's refusal of service in the face of blatant mistreatment.

The arguments in favour of giving primacy to supporting the self-determination of the older abused person over protecting him or her from harm are many. There is no evidence to suggest that advanced years or physical disability render a person incapable of making his or her own decisions. The person may purposely choose to live with a greater risk than others would choose for him or her. Intervening against the wishes of the older person will, in most cases, destroy the professional relationship and the practitioner will have no recourse in monitoring the situation. Intervention presumes that the older person will benefit from the services offered. However, older persons have a realistic chance of being removed from their homes (Gordon & Tomita, 1990) and may understandably resist. In a study of protection workers in the United States, changing the living circumstances of the mistreated person was perceived to be the most effective intervention (Dolan & Blakely, 1989). What is more, forcing an intervention has the potential of alienating, if not generating resentment in, the caregiver, thereby further endangering the older person.

While these are compelling arguments, the other side of the debate is equally convincing. By favouring intervention over self-determination, the practitioner has the potential to reduce the amount of harm caused to the older person; the abuser may be deterred by the presence of a service intervention, and the practitioner may lessen the suffering of older adults who may be accused of disrupting family/friend relationships (Gilbert, 1986; Gordon & Tomita, 1990). By being held responsible, the practitioner could save face for the older person who may be coerced into refusing services by the abuser. Although the practitioner may experience a hostile relationship with the caregiver, the older person will still be protected.

## Competency Versus Limited Benevolent Intervention

What happens when we suspect that the mistreated person is incompetent to make decisions regarding his or her own care? How do we challenge the competency of an older adult to care for him or herself, and pretend to maintain self-determination? The principle of autonomy is often considered to be less useful when persons are not able to act autonomously, and in such cases, the principle of limited benevolent intervention takes on more weight (Gilbert, 1986). The two principles can easily clash, however. The right of the adult to receive, and the state's duty to provide, the least restrictive and intrusive form of care (i.e., limited benevolent intervention), while respecting the individual's autonomy is a formidable task. The inability to achieve a reasonable balance can be seen in cases of self-neglect where eccentric and harmless behaviour is labelled self-neglect and the person deemed incompetent (Gilbert, 1986). Perhaps even more grave is the tendency of some professionals to use the person's refusal to consent as an indication of mental incompetency, a flagrant affront to self-determination. At the other extreme, some agencies have reported using the complete withdrawal of services as a strategy to precipitate a crisis in the senior's life so that services will be accepted. This could be construed as placing too much emphasis on the autonomy principle (Office for Senior Citizen's Affairs, 1991).

The fundamental problem for the practitioner is the fact that incompetency has not been clearly defined even in jurisdictions where there is legislation to that effect (Gordon, Verdun-Jones & MacDougall, 1986). The fact that some provincial laws provide for limited, rather than total, incompetence highlights the harm that may result in establishing incapacity. And it comes as no surprise that some legislation in Canada attempts to link the responses to abuse with the concept of guardianship. The lack of clarity in the legislation is often reflected in policies, thereby, leaving the practitioner with few guidelines for establishing the competency of the older person.

Amplifying the problem is the fact that the practitioner is making judgements about a person's mental competency in one or two meetings, often in an environment strange to the client. If the practitioner has the luxury of using some type of assessment instrument, it is probably less than reliable (McDonald, Hornick, Robertson & Wallace, 1991). Then there is a problem of defining the nature of the least intrusive intervention because, presumably, intervention measures should be different for each person.

To add a twist to the already complex predicament of the practitioner, recent research findings suggest that it is not the functional or cognitive impairment of the abused older person that directly or necessarily results in severe abuse. Rather, the depression of the caregiver can lead to abuse in situations where the older person is mentally incapacitated (Homer & Gilleard, 1990; Paveza, Cohen, Eisdorfer, Freels, Semla, Ashford, Gorelick, Hirschman, Luchins & Levy, 1992). As well, a larger than expected proportion of the caregivers described a mutually violent relationship with the older person. Although abusive behaviour of the aged person is no excuse for mistreatment at the hands of the caregiver, the situation becomes complicated. Currently, the debate about who is dependent on whom, and whose characteristics should be assessed—the caregiver's or the older person's—is gaining momentum as new research is generated (Pillemer, 1993). While some practitioners believe that it is possible to advocate for both the caregiver and the abused person, others do not, raising yet another issue as to who is to be the target of intervention.

The advantage of limited benevolent intervention with older persons experiencing mental and physical impairment is that the older person is likely to receive immediate assistance that will help put an end to the mistreatment. The disadvantage is that there is a danger that the older person will forfeit his/her due process rights. Effectively disempowered, the person may feel humiliated because he/she, allegedly, can no longer care for him/herself. This stigmatization could take on a case life of its own in agency and medical files and would be difficult to reverse. Another potential disadvantage of limited benevolent intervention is that it encourages the practitioner to focus on caregiving rather than on the abuse, and to offer supports that may not be related to the problem. In other words, if the practitioner is concerned about being intrusive, especially in ambiguous situations, he or she will be less likely to launch a full scale investigation. That the older person is mentally incompetent ensures that there would be few repercussions for the practitioner. At the same time, support services for the caregiver may offer an opportunity to maintain contact.

## Removing Harm Versus Protecting Confidentiality

The ethical and legal necessity to remove harm frequently interferes with the abused person's right to confidentiality. The slightest suspicion of abuse usually necessitates an investigation triggering the involvement of the service network. Finding the balance between releasing enough information to effectively access help, and protecting the abused older person's and the caregiver's right to confidentiality, is not straightforward. For example, a practitioner, out of concern for confidentiality, refused to share any information with an out-of-town relative who independently discovered the abuse of her relative, and thus precluded any help that relative may have been prepared to give. In a study of practitioners in Ontario, the respondents indicated that confusion about the rules of confidentiality limited their effectiveness in specific abuse cases (Office for Senior Citizen's Affairs, 1992).

There are trade-offs between removing harm and honouring confidentiality. Sharing information has a number of positive possibilities. The less sketchy the information offered to other professionals, presumably the better the fit between the identified needs of the older person and the services offered. A multidisciplinary team can function only with the sharing of confidential information (McDonald et al., 1991). As well, sharing information could improve coordination amongst the community agencies needed to respond to the abuse. To enlist the help of other family and/or friends, information would also have to be shared.

Protecting confidentiality conveys to the abused older person and his or her family that the practitioner can be trusted. Furthermore, protecting confidentiality could make it more likely that the older person and the perpetrator would seek assistance. The confidentiality of recorded information is another issue. Files, reports of abuse or, as in the case of mandatory reporting, databases of information, are supposed to be protected by limited access. Despite precautions, it is unavoidable that errors will be made and the risks and the consequences are probably higher in smaller cities and rural areas where social networks are smaller and more tightly linked. In such regions, the keeping of records for set time periods could mean that the individuals involved, including the older person, may be stigmatized by ongoing suspicion.

The practitioner could easily become paralysed by inaction when confronted with the moral issues related to mistreatment. Yet decisions have to be made and actions taken. Awareness of the many dimensions of the issues would indicate that a cautious stance is needed on the part of the practitioner. By cautious, we mean erring in favour of empowering the older person to make his or her own decisions.

## MULTICULTURAL PRACTICE ISSUES

Research and knowledge linking abuse and neglect of older people and ethnic diversity is sparse. A review of the literature found few references regarding abuse and neglect related to ethnic diversity. Ethnicity refers to sharing a common national origin, race, culture and/or language. This section will focus on practice issues pertaining to abuse and neglect as it relates to older people from ethnocultural communities.

### Canada: An Ethnically Diverse Nation

Our population is not only aging, but it is also changing significantly in racial and ethnic composition. Canada has become a multicultural nation (Driedger & Chappell, 1987; Ontario Advisory Council on Senior Citizens, 1989) with a growing number of older people from ethnocultural communities. Twenty-two percent of seniors in Canada report an ethnic origin other than British or French; approximately 17% of seniors are born outside Canada; approximately 6,000 seniors immigrate to Canada each year; approximately 24% of all those in Canada who speak neither English or French are seniors; and among seniors, twice as many women as men speak neither English nor French (Secretary of State, 1988).

Moreover, each ethnocultural group is not homogeneous. Whereas aboriginal people are often considered a homogeneous population, in Canada the diversity of First Nations peoples is great. Aboriginal people include Indians, Metis and Inuit. There are ten major aboriginal groups in British Columbia alone, with different languages and cultures (Ministry of Native Affairs, 1990). Asian-Canadians likewise are comprised of several different Asian groups and many Pacific Islander groups. Homogeneity within similar ethnocultural groups differs according to whether the members are born in Canada, are longer-term immigrants, or new immigrants arriving with a history of oppression and abuse from the country from which they have immigrated. Each will likely experience their "ethnicity" differently and may hold varying values, attitudes or beliefs. Furthermore, people who are, for example, third generation may have assimilated the mainstream values into their own belief systems.

The demographic changes in ethnocultural communities in relation to aging have implications for practice in the area of abuse and neglect of seniors. The assumption of North America being a homogeneous, English speaking, mainly white population, with relatively similar needs, is no longer relevant (Wray, 1991), but it often leads to the marginalization of people of different ethnic origins.

### Differences in Language

Practice is often guided by new knowledge from research; however, because elderly people from different ethnocultural backgrounds are often not included in research studies, there exists a significant gap in this knowledge. Many elderly people from ethnocultural communities are often excluded from research samples because of communication difficulties. Translation is frequently restrictive and, therefore, often avoided. In one study of senior abuse and neglect, Pittaway and Westhues (1993) found that although translation was available for some participants, 11.2% of non-participants had difficulty communicating because of language differences. Samples from ethnocultural communities may not be considered large enough in some studies and are excluded from analyses.

Services are not always available in different languages. Family members often accompany elderly members to appointments to interpret for their relatives. However, if the family member is an abuser, the abuse is unlikely to be disclosed, or the family member may not interpret exactly what the elderly person has said. Therefore, services should be made accessible in languages which reflect the growing reality of the older population in ethnically diverse communities. For example, cultural interpretation services have been developed (Information London, 1990) which match trained interpreters with requests from professionals or service organizations. This type of service offers training programs for bilingual and bicultural individuals as well as training for service providers in ways to work more effectively with the interpreters. Education and training pertaining to abuse and neglect for this type of organization might alleviate some of the difficulties in communication in practice.

## Professional Preparation

More social service and health care professionals need curricula that focus on race, ethnicity, age, and gender (Watson, Kelley, MacLean & Meredith, 1992). The study of ethnicity and race is not central in curriculum and, if offered, is often not mandatory. Professionals do need to be critically reflective of policies and practices which contribute to the marginalization of "invisible populations" (Carniol, 1990) such as minority ethnic groups and aboriginal people in Canada. Racism is a combination of stereotyping, prejudice and discrimination which is oppressive to individuals, their cultural communities and to society as a whole. Social service and health care professionals could benefit by exploring their attitudes possibly through "unlearning racism" workshops in order to intervene more appropriately in culturally-sensitive ways. The majority of professionals in health and social services are representative of mainstream society and they need to encourage and facilitate more students of ethnic and racial minority communities to enter professional schools.

Many social service and health care professional schools do include the study of aging in their curricula (Watson et al., 1992). However, courses on aging are often offered mostly as electives, and as a result do not provide all students with the opportunity to reflect upon ageist attitudes that prevail. Lucas (1991) suggests that health professionals' ability to recognize abuse depends somewhat on their understanding of the normal aging process and the professionals' own attitudes about older people.

Although most social service and health care professional training includes some aspect of family violence, because of the influence of the women's movement, most feminist literature has ignored the experience of older abused women (Vinton, 1991; Friedan, 1993). Social service and health care professionals need to recognize that the structure of the family in many cases continues to exploit women (Friedan, 1993) and in some instances makes them vulnerable to abuse or neglect.

## Service Experience of Culturally-Diverse Clients

The culture, beliefs and values held within any ethnic group will influence perceptions and utilization of social and health care services for elder abuse and neglect. While Canadian literature is sparse, the limited American studies that do exist tend to focus on comparisons between blacks and whites. For example, in one study it was found that blacks were more likely to use services than whites (Tatara & Rittman, 1991). Although the authors acknowledge that blacks utilize informal social support networks more often than whites, their finding may be more a reflection of lower poverty levels among the blacks in their study who require service. The experiences of different cohorts within an ethnic group may also be reflected in their use of services for abuse and neglect of seniors. Newquist, Berger, Kahn, Martinez and Burton (1979) found that health care providers and facilities were less available to older minorities than older whites; that access to health care providers and facilities was more difficult for older blacks and Mexican-Americans than whites; and that health care providers and services were less appropriate and acceptable to minority elderly people than to white older adults. In a study by Korbin, Anetzberger, Thomasson and Austin (1991), older persons' responses to abuse ranged from suffering in silence, seeking help from social service agencies, or getting legal intervention. They found that abused seniors who utilized legal services were younger and more likely to be African-American than other abused clients identified within the agencies.

Immigration has become a political issue, as frequently immigrants or refugees have been abused prior to their arrival. Abuse in older years may be connected with previous experience of abuse, and hence there is a need for practitioners to be sensitive to the cultural and political climates from which immigrants and refugees have come. Canada is experiencing a growth in the diversity of its population, and increased immigration in the United States in the 1980s has accounted for more than a third of that country's population growth (Gelfand & Yee, 1991). Social and health care services may be needed, but be difficult for elderly immigrants and refugees to access. In one multicultural health centre study (Roche & Doumkou, 1990) older people from different cultural backgrounds stated that they had difficulty communicating, they did not have transportation, they had few or no financial resources because of poverty, and they were expected to care for grandchildren. Formal services are sometimes intimidating for those who are accustomed to relying solely on family members for support. In addition, the bureaucratic system may be overwhelming.

In summary, the service experience of culturally-diverse clients may be related not only to their own beliefs and values regarding service utilization, but may also be affected in some instances by the availability of social support networks, economic status, prior abuse, difficulty in accessing unfamiliar services, and systemic racism. Practitioners need to increase their awareness and sensitivity to these potential barriers which could impede access to and appropriate delivery of services.

## Cultural Knowledge and Myths

In practice, we need to recognize that the extended cultural family system as a caring network is a stereotype. While this may be the reality for most, we cannot deny that abuse occurs for some ethnic older persons in the privacy of their home (Watson, 1991). Again drawing from American studies since Canadian material is limited at present, Watson (1991) reports that homicide rates among people 55 years of age or older are increasing and that physical assault was higher for immigrant elderly people in urban centres, where abuse frequently occurs within the home. In Kratcoski's study (1990), 72% of the abusers over 60 years of age were African-Americans. Their abuse had resulted in deaths following quarrels. In 89% of the cases the abuser and abused person knew each other; 82% were male abusers; and the home was where the abuse took place. While these studies cannot be generalized to Canada, as there is more violence and apparent tolerance for violence in the United States, this potential trend is one to monitor in Canada. On the other hand, Hall (1986) found little difference between ethnic-racial minority and non-minority abused persons in his work.

Certain living arrangements have been noted as a risk factor of abuse of older persons in ethno-cultural communities (Pittaway, 1993). Social service and health care professionals must also assess whether older people from ethnic backgrounds live in a cultural community where they can communicate freely, or whether they live in an English or French speaking community in which they may be isolated if they do not speak either of these languages.

Gender, combined with ethnic differences, has a profound impact on practice. Women in some cultural communities are more oppressed than in mainstream society. Some women from ethnocultural backgrounds working as homemakers or care aides in facilities are often subjected to racial and verbal abuse by those for whom they are caring (Tellis-Nayak & Tellis-Nayak, 1989). Vinton (1991) found that mothers who had been abused by sons were significantly less likely to accept help, than either mothers or fathers who had an abusive daughter. Often sexist and racist attitudes are observed and presented within the context of an individual situation but these attitudes are well entrenched in society. In order for practitioners to achieve social change, it may be more effective if they address these issues at a macro level of intervention using structural analysis, education and advocacy. Otherwise, the status quo likely will be maintained.

The question often arises whether abuse in one culture is really abuse in another. Conflicts can arise when behaviour which is considered abusive in Canadian society appears to be accepted in ethnocultural communities within Canada. Different cultural values may exist between abusers and abused people. Within the Canadian context, there are many inter-racial and inter-ethnic marital relationships. Most mainstream agencies focus on services to the abused seniors, with some providing service to abusers. In some native communities, abuse and neglect is seen as a health problem of the community, rather than of individuals (Maxwell & Maxwell, 1992). Social service and health care professionals must be aware of their own values and their clients' cultural differences.

In summary, Canada is a diverse nation. The multicultural composition of our society impacts social service and health care professionals' work with older persons, particularly with regard to language and communication, provision and use of services, and culturally diverse and potentially conflictual value systems. Sensitivity to the impact of ageism, racism, and sexism is essential in training for better knowledge in order to intervene appropriately in a culturally-sensitive way.

## SERVICE UTILIZATION AND RESOURCES

In a recent document entitled *A Shared Concern* (Health & Welfare, 1992), the types of programs and services offered in Canada to prevent or intervene in abusive situations involving seniors have been described in detail. These programs and services are provided through health and social service agencies, legal agencies, community organizations, seniors' groups, and government programs.

McDonald et al. (1991), identifying types of programs as adult protection programs, domestic violence programs, crisis intervention programs and advocacy programs, pose the questions: What services should be provided? Who should deliver them? What type of organizations? There has not yet been enough Canadian research to provide definitive answers to these questions. We can, however, make a few general assumptions. Most of the programs take a broad-based approach to family violence, and offer services mainly to abused seniors and not to abusers (Health & Welfare, 1992). Other programs focus more on the caregiver stress model, offering services to abused seniors and also to their abusers or potential abusers. Some services and programs take a protective approach to intervention, while others stress empowerment of seniors. Although protective programs have been described extensively (McDonald et al., 1991; Bond, Penner & Yellen, 1992), most empowerment programs do not appear to spell out the process or principles which have been defined by numerous authors such as Rappaport (1985), Health and Welfare (1993a) and Myers (1993). Some programs encompass both empowerment and protection approaches, putting more emphasis on one aspect or the other, depending on the needs and abilities of abused seniors. If seniors are able to solve their own problems with accompanying help, the empowerment approach is used; if they are not able to go through the problem-solving process, a protective approach is used, employing such mechanisms as public guardianship. Little research exists which has evaluated the effectiveness of Canadian models, approaches or interventions and protocols (see Spencer, this volume). Another chapter in this volume (McKenzie, Tod & Yellen) will describe in detail two Canadian models which have been evaluated. Two other Canadian models are now in the process of being evaluated: the Synergy Project model, developed at the Kerby Centre in Calgary, and the Project Care model, developed in Montreal. Several Canadian provinces have produced intervention guides and protocols, (Nahmiash & Shrier, 1991; Council on Aging of Ottawa-Carleton, 1987); however, as yet there are no Canadian standards or guidelines for development of protocols for dealing with elder abuse and neglect.

With regard to developing and implementing services to respond to abuse and neglect of older people, there seems to be general agreement on several issues among Canadian and American analysts. The first issue pertains to the introduction of new resources to combat abuse and neglect, versus the development and expansion of existing resources. McDonald et al. (1991) state that new or unique services are not necessarily required. Rather, the problem to be addressed is the provision of variation in the type of services and their availability.

Services, which include both intervention teams and programs or strategies, are sometimes specific to abuse intervention and prevention. Others are based on existing multidisciplinary health and social service teams, such as homecare teams. The home-care teams, such as those working with Project Care in Montreal, have been trained to identify cases of abuse and neglect of seniors. Such teams, as already mentioned, may or may not use protocols and guidelines to intervene. In the authors' opinion, guidelines and protocols are important for practitioners to base their interventions on, even though each situation may be unique. Practitioners should use the guidelines flexibly, and adapt them to the individual circumstances. Bond et al. (1992) conclude that effective interventions require a broad, multidisciplinary network of services and professionals.

McDonald et al. (1991) point out that intervention strategies are based on diverse theoretical concepts. Other Canadian research (Gold & Gwyther, 1989; Gottlieb, 1991) suggests that to reduce stress in caregivers and to improve their coping skills, strategies are needed that are specifically oriented to abuse and neglect situations. They suggest interventions for mobilizing support to family caregivers to prevent abuse, conflicts or stress. Harshbarger (1993) suggests victim-oriented strategies, such as setting up a Community Crimes Bureau and an Elder Issues Group. Several authors, including those of this chapter, agree that there is no correct approach to be used in terms of providing preventative or intervention services (National Advisory Council on Aging [NACA], 1991; Bond et al., 1992; Health & Welfare, 1992), and advocate the development of a variety of intervention strategies to combat abuse and neglect of seniors.

## Barriers to Service Utilization, and Service Gaps

The most common barrier to effective intervention was found to be the reluctance of abused seniors and abusers to seek out services to ameliorate their situation (Wolf & Pillemer, 1989; Foekler, Holland, Marsh & Simmons, 1990). A Health and Welfare report (1993) provides insight into why seniors fail to report abuse and neglect. There are emotional reasons for this, such as fear of reprisal from the abuser, shame or embarrassment. There are situational reasons as well, such as isolation, an inability to contact help, and service availability/accessibility including the lack of emergency shelters. The same report urges specific strategies that focus on utilizing existing seniors' networks and which promote the active involvement of seniors in every aspect of programs and projects. The report also highlights the potential for involvement of trained retired professionals. Creative solutions which are simple and stress positive ways to encourage abused or neglected persons to reach out for help are recommended. For example, it is suggested that community dialogues to increase awareness should be encouraged, or telephone info-lines staffed by trained senior volunteers be established. Videos and pamphlets giving information on abuse could be shown in low-income housing units or residences for seniors.

A second important barrier relates to front-line para-professional and professional workers' awareness of services, their willingness to report elder abuse and their knowledge of the criminal justice system. Sadler and Kurrle (1993) from Australia note that the majority of respondents in their study were not aware of any cases of abuse, and that referrals to the police from community services were infrequent, and the police rarely referred to services other than solicitors. This reluctance to report may indicate a lack of knowledge about available services. Sengstock and Hwalek (1986) in the United States show that health and social service workers tend not to report cases to the police either. This study found that police used the agencies to assist them with cases rather than mutually participating in referrals. The agency workers claimed not to believe the police were likely to be of assistance to workers. Pillemer, Nicholson, Podnieks, Shillington & Frizzell, (1990) state in their study that one-third of the abused seniors surveyed claimed to be "not very aware" of public legal services. On the other hand, increased knowledge of legal options has been found to be a valuable tool for service providers who wish to enable abused seniors to bring about change in their situations. One avenue towards such increased knowledge is establishing an interagency protective-service system composed of social services, legal services, mental health, housing and health care. As documented by Filinson and Ingman (1993), caseworkers' regular consultation with an attorney from a legal-assistance agency in planning intervention strategies resulted in more successful interventions in elder abuse cases. As well, the limitations of the criminal justice system have been noted to be barriers in helping persons who have been abused and/or neglected (Sharpe, 1988). Limitations of scope or definition within the legislation may restrict its applicability. Furthermore, not all types of abuse and neglect—for example, contraventions of professional standards or transgressions of community standards—are able to be handled within the criminal justice system (see Stones, this volume). Other difficulties in carrying through interventions within the legal system have also been noted. An example of this can be mentioned from CLSC NDG/Mtl. West in Quebec in which health care professionals had little success when bringing abusers to the criminal justice system. Cases were thrown out of court on technicalities and at times seniors continued to be exploited. Whereas multi-disciplinary consultation with regard to legal intervention in elder abuse cases has been shown to be effective, problems surrounding legal interventions have not received a great deal of focussed attention to date.

The above studies indicate that a greater awareness and knowledge of services and resources related to abuse and mistreatment is vital to abused seniors and workers to ameliorate the utilization and the effectiveness of services. Gaps in services were also identified in research studies on abuse. Those inadequacies noted by Foekler et al. (1990) were: the need for more emergency shelters for abused seniors, day care and respite services; the need for more in- and out-patient and in-home mental health services; the need for more door-to-door assisted transportation services; and the need for more volunteers.

Volunteer advocates or "buddies" can often provide a personal source of help, encouraging people to confide their abusive situations and eventually to begin resolving them. Several Canadian programs such as Project CARE in Montreal (Reis & Nahmiash, 1994) have begun to train such advocates. In Calgary, Seniors Assisting Seniors uses volunteers to help abused seniors, and in particular, involves seniors themselves in the interventions to assist their peers with any type of problem including abuse and neglect (Health & Welfare, 1992). Seniors-to-Seniors hotlines and programs that link seniors with crime prevention agencies to combat abuse similarly exist in Alberta, Quebec and Ontario. The use of volunteers expands resources, makes better use of existing resources and provides non-professional confidantes for older abused seniors.

Podnieks et al. (1990) identify other gaps in Canadian services such as: respite care, homemaker services, caregiver support groups to relieve stress, and support services for those in troubled relationships and for abusers. Podnieks et al. (1990) also identify as useful services: individual counselling, self-help groups, emergency shelters, household help, medical help and English language assistance. In the authors' opinion, most of the above services do exist throughout Canada, with the exception of emergency shelters. The problem seems to be that the staff providing such services are often not trained to detect or deal with the problems of abuse and neglect. Also, when services do exist they are not in sufficient quantity to relieve the burdens of caregivers or elders receiving care. For example, a caregiver caring 24 hours per day for a dependant with Alzheimer's disease may need respite care every day of the week and may be receiving it only twice per week.

Co-ordination has been noted as an important issue in delivering services to older people who have been abused or neglected, and in the prevention of the abuse. Harshbarger (1993) has identified the need for co-ordination of law enforcement agencies in the United States. Filinson and Ingman (1993) highlight the need for case workers to co-ordinate the various systems involved in the delivery of services to abused seniors. Similarly Canadian researchers (Health & Welfare, 1993; McDonald et al., 1991) note the need for co-ordination and collaboration in the provision and implementation of services.

Difficulties have been described verbally to the authors regarding co-ordination of multi-disciplinary teams which represent a number of different sectors such as social work, law enforcement, mental health, public guardianship, crime prevention and human rights. Such teams may experience difficulties because of differences in styles of leadership, decision-making, philosophy, principles, values and approaches. There may be competitiveness or conflicts among professionals from different disciplines. Few studies have been done to evaluate the effectiveness of such team approaches in the area of abuse of older persons.

Sengstock and Hwalek (1986) state that health and social service providers must have precise knowledge of the criminal justice system and its utilization in order to devise appropriate interventions in mistreatment of older persons. Sharing of knowledge and information among different disciplines and sectors may be crucial to the success of interagency or interdisciplinary teams.

Finally, standards and norms for care need to be provided by agencies and national organizations (seeWatson, Patterson, Maciboric-Sohor, Grek & Greenslade, this volume). The Canadian Home Care Association and the Canadian Council on Health Facilities Accreditation are currently working on providing such national standards and norms for practitioners. Effective complaint mechanisms, including advocacy programs, such as those in Ontario and British Columbia will also have to be established to monitor whether these standards are being respected. Such complaint mechanisms, at present, may be relatively ineffective in monitoring services if they are under the administration of the organizations offering the services (Nahmiash & Reis, 1992).

## CONCLUSION AND RECOMMENDATIONS

To conclude this chapter, we would like to highlight the need for a broad-based community response to the problem of abuse and neglect of seniors. We cannot expect this problem to be treated by specialized teams or experts alone. Preventative programs and education of the public and service providers must be a necessary part of this process (see Podnieks & Baillie; and Ross & Hoff, this volume). Creative, appropriate, sufficient and accessible health and social services need to be provided. At the same time, as economic restraints make services more scarce, abuse and violence may also increase. Social service and health care practitioners need to be more aware of, and reflect upon, the ethical issues and dilemmas which were outlined in this chapter. They should reflect on the approaches and values underlying their practice interventions, and achieve a balance between competing ethical principles in each situation through using thoughtful judgement.

More knowledge about elderly people from ethnocultural and aboriginal communities is required to ensure culturally-sensitive approaches to service delivery in the area of abuse of older adults. We must pay attention to language differences and difficulties which may exist in using or accessing services related to abuse and neglect of seniors.

Practitioners must also have precise knowledge about the use of the criminal justice system and other resources which may be useful for abused seniors and/or abusers. They must identify gaps and barriers to services and lobby to ensure that such services become available, accessible and are well co-ordinated.

Finally, research studies must provide more information about the needs of abused and neglected older adults and their abusers. Such studies must evaluate the types of services and resources which would be most appropriate and which models are most effective.

To conclude, services must be available, accessible, affordable, known, and perceived as appropriate by those for whom they are intended. Those practitioners offering services must be well-informed about the criminal justice system and its use; they must provide co-ordinated delivery systems with standards and norms for services; and they must develop creative approaches, such as volunteer-based and senior-based services and projects in order to improve the quality of life of elderly Canadians who suffer abuse and neglect.

# 1-2

# COMMUNITY-BASED INTERVENTION STRATEGIES FOR CASES OF ABUSE AND NEGLECT OF SENIORS: A COMPARISON OF MODELS, PHILOSOPHIES AND PRACTICE ISSUES

*Pearl McKenzie, Linda Tod and Penny Yellen*

## INTRODUCTION

Professional and political recognition of elder abuse, and the concomitant pressure to end it, have inspired a variety of community-based programs and services for elderly persons (McDonald, Hornick, Robertson & Wallace, 1991). The developers of community models have been constrained, however, by the lack of comprehensive information in the literature of family violence and gerontology. Relatively little has been published about the extent, nature and outcomes of abuse and neglect of older adults (Fulmer, 1991). Much of what has been written concerns models tested in the United States; some information is also available on community models in Australia, Europe, and Canada.

There are many communities in Canada with locally developed intervention models: Centres locaux de services communautaires (CLSC), such as the NDG/Montreal West and René Cassin CLSCs in Quebec, Advocacy Centre for the Elderly in Toronto, Elder Abuse Resource Centre in Winnipeg, Kerby Centre in Calgary, and North Shore Community Services in North Vancouver, to name a few. This Chapter focuses on the existing Winnipeg and North Vancouver models and on a proposed new model for the province of British Columbia. In this Chapter, the first section looks at models found in the literature, first by type and then by country. The second section presents the three Canadian models. The third section of the Chapter, based on the authors' experience that any discussion of practice issues for abuse and neglect of older people leads to questions of legal implications, addresses the *Criminal Code* and civil law implications arising out of work in community-based programs. The fourth section considers the competency issues that complicate cases, especially when the needs of the adult are not addressed.

# ELDER ABUSE MODELS IN THE LITERATURE

## Types of Intervention Models

Virtually all of the models described in the literature on abuse and neglect of seniors fall into one of three categories: domestic violence/family therapy, advocacy and adult protection. The domestic violence/family therapy models are characterized by crisis intervention services, court orders for protection, emergency sheltering, support groups for the abused senior and the abuser, public education, and/or empowerment of abused seniors. Typical of such models is a reinforced role for law enforcement personnel including the police and the courts. Advocacy programs try to achieve both prevention and protection. Service providers are viewed as advocates helping the abused older person to assert his or her rights and to work toward specific goals. An important feature of these models is the advocate's independence from any service delivery system. Interventions are non-intrusive, and authority rests with the older person (Hudson, 1986; McDonald et al., 1991; Sengstock, Hwalek & Petrone 1989, Sengstock, Hwalek & Stahl, 1991; Wolf & Pillemer, 1989). In adult protection models, the action is protective, reporting is mandatory and limited authority in problem-resolution rests with the service providers. The abused senior loses the right to determine the action to be taken.

A second lens through which these programs may be viewed is their connection to public policy, especially policy formulated in provincial, state or federal codes of law. Here, the literature reveals a range in the level of awareness that the legislators of different countries have exhibited. For example, although many local authorities in Britain are now beginning to intervene (Ogg & Bennett, 1992), Holt (1993) found little evidence that the abuse and neglect of older adults is formally recognized in Britain. The literature, however, does not describe specific models for community-based programs on elder abuse in Britain. In Australia, Sadler and Kurrle (1993) noted that the problem is just beginning to be addressed by policy makers. In Canada and the United States, public policy is different in each province and state. A comprehensive review of the legislation is not included here other than in specific references to the various models being reviewed.

## Elder Abuse Models in an International Perspective

In 1980, the federal government in the United States established experimental model programs to treat and prevent abuse and neglect of seniors. The "Three Model Projects" resulted in three states testing different approaches to service provision: a service brokerage model, a service coordination model, and a mandatory reporting model. An analysis and evaluation of the Three Model Projects was provided by Wolf and Pillemer (1989) and by Spencer in this volume.

In attempting to respond to the needs of abused and neglected elderly persons, communities have created task forces of service providers and other interested individuals. Among the best organized of these task forces is the San Francisco Consortium for Elder Abuse Prevention which, beginning in 1981, developed a cooperative, multi-agency approach to abused seniors (Nerenberg & Garbuio, 1985). The "San Francisco Model" established goals and objectives for a service delivery program and advocacy but reached these goals with varying degrees of success (Nerenberg & Garbuio, 1985, 1987; Wolf & Pillemer, 1989).

Wolf and Pillemer (1994) reviewed four practice models that they felt were worthy of replication. They evaluated a multidisciplinary case consultation team, a senior advocate volunteer program, a support group for abused seniors, and a master's of social work degree specialization in adult protective services. They then discussed the models' low cost, flexibility, and level of success. Wolf and Pillemer (1994) conclude that these models emerge as creative treatment and prevention strategies and are worthy of replication. The greatest challenge identified was obtaining permanent funding.

In Europe, intervening in elder abuse cases is a new task for health and social service agencies. Only in France and the Scandinavian countries have researchers and policy makers in these fields begun to address the problem (Hydle, 1989). The only substantial study presented in the literature involves the development of elder protective services in Norway (Johns, Juklestad & Hydle, 1992). In 1988, the Norwegian Ministry of Social Welfare began financing a research project administered by the Department of Geriatric Medicine at Ullevaal Hospital, Oslo. The project, called "Protection for the Elderly," revolved around the central role of a mediator who was a social worker and could effectively relate to the needs of the abused older person and coordinate service plans (Johns et al., 1992). It was hoped that mediation and coordination would produce a flexible, client-oriented, inter-disciplinary model of service.

In Canada, McDonald et al. (1991) compiled a general review of Canadian programs and services that have recently responded to elder abuse. The Seniors' Secretariat (1992) also reviewed existing programs and reported only a few Canadian communities with a coordinated, interdisciplinary approach to the problem of abuse and neglect of seniors.

This brief international perspective clearly shows the divergent stages in the field of elder abuse. Some states in the United States have sophisticated programs but there is no consistency between states. The European countries are only starting to acknowledge the existence of elder abuse and therefore have little service provision in place. In Canada we are writing and talking about elder abuse and neglect, but we have very few service provision programs in place.

# ELDER ABUSE COMMUNITY MODELS IN CANADA

A variety of effective models used to investigate and intervene against abuse and neglect of seniors have evolved in Canada. The models included here reflect examples of different categories of programs in the literature on elder abuse, and are the models developed by the authors.

## Winnipeg's Model: Domestic Violence/Family Therapy

The Winnipeg model loosely fits into the domestic violence/family therapy approach. Staff members provide collaboration with other service agencies and counselling services to abused older persons. The model was developed at the Age and Opportunity Elder Abuse Resource Centre in Winnipeg, Manitoba. The Centre was designed to coordinate community services for elder abuse and neglect, to provide education for, and consultation with, agencies, individuals and post-secondary education facilities who serve older adults, and to provide counselling to the older adults who were abused. A multidisciplinary team comprised of nine health and social service professionals meet monthly to discuss cases, and to consult with service providers in the community. Thirty-five agencies work with the Centre and provide services to abused older adults. The Centre keeps a service inventory and documents referrals. This model of co-ordination has been adapted outside Winnipeg to meet the needs of other Manitoba communities.

An important aspect of the model is the involvement of older adults in the operation of the Centre. Older persons make up one-third of the Management Committee and they volunteer as peer partners, public awareness speakers and office assistants. One result of this involvement has been the granting of funds to a committee of older adults to provide training for these volunteer positions.

As both a provider of counselling to its clients and a collaborator with other community groups in the delivery of service, the Age and Opportunity Elder Abuse Resource Centre is a social service agency that functions from a framework of accepted standards of current social work practice. The counsellors in this Centre believe that issues related to abuse and neglect of older adults need to be viewed from a family violence perspective. That is, elder abuse in the family does not happen in isolation because someone has turned 60 years old but rather the abuse stems from long-standing conflictual family relationships, both spousal and parent-child. An abusive adult child often exhibits other dysfunctional behaviour and parents may continue to try to solve the child's problems rather than dealing with their own personal safety, health or financial issues. In cases of abuse taking place in institutional settings, we refer the person to the social worker or administrator of the facility, or to Manitoba Health, Long Term Care.

The manner in which a family has historically solved problems, dealt with crises, and developed coping mechanisms will affect the relationship between the abused older person and the abuser. Over one-third of the cases at the Centre are women who have experienced long-standing partner abuse. Before older adults are willing to consider options or change, they must first deal with incapacitating feelings of powerlessness and self-blame which results from the ongoing experience of abuse. The first step is to empower the abused older person. Options for change may not exist until the older adult becomes more self-accepting and recognizes and acknowledges that the abuser has committed a crime of fraud, assault or theft.

The Elder Abuse Resource Centre contracts with clients to give them counselling and support. Clients who are cognitively-impaired receive a psychogeriatric assessment so that areas of competence can be pinpointed. If the client's ability to make decisions is sufficiently limited, as defined by the *Manitoba Mental Health Act* (1987), the Public Trustee of Manitoba becomes involved. Some clients who are not found to be incapable as such may receive assistance to make decisions, especially those concerning safety.

The age of the client, his/her level of competency, the type of abuse that has occurred, and the type of action the client is prepared to take are factors that, when combined, indicate different forms of intervention. Centre staff bring clarity to the dynamics of abuse and neglect, and adapt its interventions and counselling services. For example, staff have found that providing group support for persons who have experienced spousal abuse is helpful for some of these clients. Therefore, more groups, in which individuals find support and share experiences, are being considered for parents abused by their adult children.

The Elder Abuse Resource Centre depends on government and/or private grants for funding. Reductions in grants have resulted in the curtailment of some of its services. The education and volunteer components were curtailed until a New Horizons grant enabled the training of volunteers to assist in public awareness, peer partnering and other services. More recently, the Coordinator position has been reduced and combined with another Management position at Age & Opportunity. The counselling, consultation and information and referral services have received more stable funding from the Government of Manitoba.

The Winnipeg model's strength has been in its multi-disciplinary and collaborative approach in assisting abused older persons who present many complicated problems, along with the counselling and group support it provides to clients. As stated earlier in the literature review, the greatest challenge is funding, and therefore the ability to maintain both its service and education components.

## North Shore's Model: Information and Advocacy

North Shore Community Services (NSCS) in North Vancouver, British Columbia has developed an advocacy model where the programs may best be described as a "one-stop" help centre for seniors requiring information and services. The Board and staff have built an intervention and support model that links the provision of information to support and advocacy. Seniors contact the centre for information, often financial or legal, and disclosures of abuse and neglect may emerge during the course of service provision. The service focus is not exclusively for seniors or for elder abuse and neglect, but to support all adults to live independently in their community.

The philosophy of this service is based, to some extent, on feminist ideology which links people's personal experiences with the larger context of society. It is also based on the legal model of advocacy which returns power and control to individuals by taking instruction from them. When compassionate care underlies the design of services there may be an attitude of "us", the service providers, knowing what is best for "them", the recipients of service. When a program is designed and evaluated by the people most affected by the delivery of the services, boundaries become more diffuse and issues are shared more broadly.

North Shore Community Services has had a Seniors' Advisory Committee since 1982 to guide the development of services and policy. Many members of this committee are also volunteers who offer practical support to older people experiencing financial and legal problems. This frequent contact with problems has contributed to a strong voice for social advocacy on issues affecting older people. Some volunteers are people who, in the past, used the information and legal services of the agency. They are passing on the knowledge gained through their own experiences to other people in need of help.

Funders play a significant role in the design of programs and services. Organizations that have assured funding benefit from that security in terms of continuity and long-term planning but may not see the necessity of evaluating how well they meet clients' needs. There is a delicate balance between supporting stable services and ensuring a response to the rapidly changing needs of the people using the programs. NSCS receives less than ten percent of its budget in ongoing funding. The remaining monies are raised through short-term project funding and donations. This constant search for financial and in-kind support puts a great deal of stress on the Board and staff. At the same time, it has also contributed to the evolution of a flexible agency that works directly with its community to address gaps in services.

The need for a legal counselling program was identified by an interagency committee. In 1982, NSCS received funding to provide paralegal services in poverty and family law. It was thought at that time that the clients would be mostly younger women. Staff of other organizations, who had been involved in initiating and promoting this legal service, began to refer people for information, and a considerable number of those people were seniors. Service delivery was structured to answer questions, to resolve problems by telephone, to offer clinics in seniors' centres, and to make visits to homes and institutions.

Other community law offices in British Columbia, who were not offering accessible services, did not see a similar demand for services from seniors. The staff person delivering legal information at NSCS turned to the director of the Advocacy Centre for the Elderly (ACE) in Toronto for guidance. ACE, which was much larger and staffed by lawyers as well as paralegals, became a model for the development and work of NSCS's legal programs.

The NSCS model of "hands-on" advocacy has found that early intervention and coordination of resources with other agencies is often enough to help people solve problems related to abuse and neglect of seniors. The people who need ongoing emotional counselling and support are referred to other services.

## British Columbia's Future Model: The Balance between Protection and Self-Determination

The British Columbia model is rooted in the experience of an agency, North Shore Community Services, and in the work of the British Columbia Coalition to Eliminate Abuse of Seniors, a group which obtained funding for projects to look at elder abuse and neglect on a province-wide basis. The Federal Government's Seniors Independence Program (SIP) has funded the development of Community Response Networks (CRNs) for seniors in some communities around British Columbia which has helped solidify the vision. At the same time, there has been a four-year community consultation on the laws governing adult guardianship, where the joint experience of North Shore Community Services and the British Columbia Coalition to Eliminate Abuse of Seniors helped guide the development of the provincial model. The experience gained from the SIP project is now being applied in responding to the needs of other adults to create an integrated model based on need instead of age.

Through the community consultation process, the standards for all emerging models of service provision have been established. These standards are based on the following fundamental principles from *How Can We Help?* (British Columbia Joint Working Committee, 1992):

1. All adults have a right to autonomy and self-determination and to the presumption that they are capable of living, and entitled to live, in any manner they wish.

2. When they need it, all adults are entitled to assistance, support or protection that returns power to them by means of the least restrictive, intrusive or stigmatizing form of intervention possible. This entitlement recognizes that there is no justification for abuse.

3. Adults are entitled to the legal presumption that they are capable of making decisions and they shall be supported in making informed decisions.

4. Court interventions occur as the last resort.

5. All procedures, protocols, and other processes associated with the provision of services shall be accessible to all adults.

A Joint Government/Community Policy Group has developed a strategic plan and framework to accompany the legislation. Regulations and other final details will be added as the CRNs are developed throughout British Columbia over the next three to five years. A small Provincial agency or office will be established to support the community development process. The *Adult Guardianship Act,* passed in July 1993 but not yet implemented, authorizes the Public Trustee to designate an agency in each community to respond to reports of adult abuse and neglect.

The framework defines a CRN as the local health, social service, and legal agencies, non-profit and government, pooling their resources to respond to reports of abuse and neglect of adults. Each community is to have its own, well-publicized, telephone number where reports of abuse and neglect, general inquiries, and requests for information can be responded to in a timely manner. It is planned that every geographic community in British Columbia will have a CRN.

Although there is much local autonomy in the design of the CRN, each community is expected to include all existing resources for health, justice and societal well-being in the design for their particular network. This will include the standard service agencies, and also advocates, churches, coroners, hospitals, legal services, licensed facilities, physicians, peer support counsellors, transition houses and victim assistance programs. The designated agency also has the power to investigate abuse and neglect that occurs in institutions so the effect will be more linkages of community-based services and programs with residents of facilities. Policies and procedures will spell out the cooperation, coordination and specific roles expected of each government and community agency.

The agencies in each CRN will designate members to a resource pool available to form a Multidisciplinary Team (MDT) of people who have knowledge that is pertinent to the person being assisted. Survivors of abuse and neglect will be encouraged, through self-advocacy organizations, to take an active role in the MDTs. The MDT will assist in the investigation and offer support and assistance plans as an integral part of that investigation.

In all cases of abuse and neglect, CRNs will begin each consultation with the adult by supporting the individual in making a choice between self-advocacy, naming an advocate from among friends or relatives, or, when an advocacy service is available, have someone assigned from the service. If, as abuse or neglect is being investigated, the adult's capability is called into question, the Adult Guardianship Act requires that an advocate, not necessarily a lawyer but a person from a prescribed list, (not as yet finalized in provincial regulations) be named and be available throughout subsequent proceedings. A lawyer to provide legal representation is also required for any court process. The courts will have the authority to make final decisions about capability and to order support and assistance plans. The designated agency in the CRN is responsible for its legal powers, including the right to obtain access to an adult or to remove an abuser by means of a court order. All criminal offenses must be reported to the police.

Capable adults have the right to live at risk but sometimes an individual will make what appears to be an irrational decision not to accept the services proposed. The MDT will then apply to the Office of the Public Guardian and Trustee to arrange for an assessment of the adult's capabilities. If the adult is found incapable, an application may be made to the court for another order authorizing the provision of services to the adult. If an adult is found capable, services will be offered. If the services are refused, the case is closed.

All cases will be monitored by a member of the CRN to ensure that every report elicits an appropriate response and will be tracked through the Central Agency for the purpose of data gathering and research. Trends within, and among, communities will be monitored. Such information will support applications for funding from the provincial government and from the new Regional Health Boards currently being established in British Columbia.

The British Columbia model tries to find a balance between protecting the abused adult and supporting the adult's right to self-determination. The manner in which the model evolves in the implementation period will be significant for its success in meeting the fundamental principles stated earlier. Its overall effectiveness in dealing with abuse and neglect of older people must await future evaluation.

## Comparison of the Three Models

The Winnipeg, North Shore and British Columbia models can be compared from the following perspectives: principles, legal responses, support for the person being abused, seniors' involvement and funding.

The principles underlying these models put individual rights as paramount. As the new Adult Guardianship system in British Columbia is implemented, the community will have to be vigilant to ensure that practice reflects the philosophy. The British Columbia model offers a government-mandated response to reports of abuse and neglect, whereas Winnipeg and North Shore models do not. All three models use the legal system for cases that come under the *Criminal Code*. These interventions are addressed in the next section.

Any system that provides services to seniors should consult with seniors in the design and delivery of those services to ensure that they are needed and accessible. Both the Winnipeg and North Shore models have older people involved in policy decisions and frontline service. The British Columbia model did not have much senior involvement in the development phase, therefore, it becomes imperative that such involvement is added at both the policy and community level.

The three models must do more than intervene to stop the abuse; they must provide a healing process for seniors who are abused to strengthen their ability to live free from abuse. Those wishing counselling must be given access to services sensitive to the specific needs of abused seniors. The Winnipeg model provides such a service as part of its mandate. The North Shore model refers counselling needs to other agencies but cannot ensure the appropriate response. The British Columbia model is silent on this issue, and it can only be hoped that each CRN sees development of such a service as a priority. In the Winnipeg model, abusers seeking help are referred to groups and other services in the community. Service providers are still developing responses to the needs of abused seniors, so developing specific services for older abusers is somewhere in the future.

Each of these models is dependent on funding which determines the extent of services. The Winnipeg model is now receiving Provincial funding for its counselling component but the rest of the service depends upon grants. The North Shore model is totally dependent on short-term grants. The British Columbia model has some allocation of funding for the designated agency but is mainly based on the realignment of existing resources. The ability of existing agency involvement in each community may well be curtailed because of lack of funding.

## CRIMINAL CODE AND LEGAL INTERVENTIONS

### Interpreting and Enforcing Criminal Code Provision

Intervenors with abusers or with people experiencing abuse need to distinguish between deliberate and inadvertent abuse and neglect in determining whether to offer services or to use the sanctions of the criminal justice system. Intentional abusers, who deliberately target and repeatedly exploit people, are difficult to confront. They isolate the persons they abuse from sources of help, and tend to respect only those people or systems that represent power. Unless subject to penalties, they lack motivation to change their behaviour.

A policy of the Ministry of the Attorney General in British Columbia (Revised Wife Assault Policy, 1986) and a 1983 directive by the Manitoba Attorney General direct their justice systems to recognize the criminality of assault of women in intimate relationships, and to take the necessary measures to ensure the protection of the women concerned when there are reasonable and probable grounds that an assault has taken place. Therefore, in British Columbia and Manitoba, the police officer, not the abused person, has the responsibility for recommending to Crown Counsel that a charge be laid. This policy recognizes that abusive family relationships have distinctive dynamics that are not present in other types of assault. The policy directive is based on a belief that an emphasis on response by the justice system will, in the long run, prevent further assaults by sending a clear message that our society does not tolerate this behaviour.

The policy of the Public Prosecutions Branch of Manitoba Justice is: "... to proceed with substantive charges which are grounded in a pattern of abuse against elderly victims, irrespective of the willingness of the victims to give evidence, or the level of assault. It will be expected that the police will consult with the prosecution." (Manitoba, Dept. of Justice Guideline No. 2:ELD:l)

The Family Violence Court in Manitoba, established in 1990 exclusively to handle spousal, child and elder abuse cases, is unique in North America. During these four years, there has been an increase in public awareness of elder abuse, a better understanding of the issues by law enforcement personnel and legal communities, and the implementation of a "zero tolerance" policy. More older adults understand the issue and feel that they can use the court system to assist them in making changes. This has resulted in a steady increase in the number of elder abuse cases coming through the court system.

Older adults who have been abused seldom think of invoking legal interventions. Criminal and civil law are not familiar ground to most Canadians, and the isolation of abused seniors can contribute to ignorance of their rights and of the help available to assure those rights. These adults often require time to consider legal options when they are suggested. Their loyalty to family, their shame that violence has occurred in their family, or their belief that they have been responsible in some way for provoking abusive behaviour, often make them reluctant to lay charges against a family member. When the police do lay charges, the abused senior may try to have the charges dropped or may fail to testify at the court proceedings.

Victim assistance programs can be powerfully instrumental in supporting abused seniors through criminal proceedings. "No contact" orders can be used to restrain the abusers and prevent them from intimidating witnesses. Also, older people can learn that a judge has a range of options in sentencing, including mandatory treatment and/or restitution, and that conviction does not always result in imprisonment. Educating seniors and service providers about legal rights, legal systems and the use of existing legislation is fundamental to the success of any intervention in the area of abuse and neglect of seniors.

Legal advocates and workers for women-based services speak of returning the power of choice to the persons who have been abused. It is difficult to do this work when the abuser is still in the home. Advocates believe that it is inappropriate to offer information and options when there is not safety, and that justice system interventions that initiate charges and remove the abuser do two significant things: 1) create a safe place and time for the abused person to seek help; and 2) send a clear message that violations of the criminal code are breaches of our societal values.

## Advocates

Knowing one's rights is one thing, acting on them is another. There is an increasing demand on already extended social and legal services. The person who can apply the most pressure is often the one who gets the attention. Unfortunately the person with the greatest need for assistance, because of disability or isolation, may be the least likely to get help.

Advocates frequently must facilitate delivery of service, so they need to be well-versed in the complex bureaucracy of entitlement and legal issues and remedies.

Effective advocates are problem-solvers working with their clients and with other service providers to overcome obstacles and coordinate activities.

In addition to individual advocacy, there is a need for people to come together to demand changes to a legal system that many older people identify as being, at best, unresponsive and, at worst, abusive. For example, in British Columbia, if an older person is exploited and loses his/her home to a relative, he/she may not be entitled to legal aid because legal representation is usually provided free only for those people charged with a crime or involved in a serious marital dispute. The person who took his/her house, on the other hand, if he or she had no money or minimal income, would receive free legal help and representation if charged with a criminal offense.

## Competency Issues

Seniors who are abused are often treated differently from people of other ages. The characteristic behaviours of a person who has been mistreated over a long period of time tend to involve depression, confusion, forgetfulness, and indecision, and these are often interpreted as incapability in the older adult. The result is that decision-making is transferred to someone else, sometimes even to the abuser. The issue of competency is commonly brought forth when doubts arise regarding an older adult's judgment and ability. The opportunist abuser needs only to be in the right place, at the right time, to assume control. In addition, there are many seniors who are forgetful or in the early stages of a cognitive impairment but who, when examined, are assessed to be competent. These people are often the ones who are easily influenced by others, and they often become abused financially. Assisted or associate decision-making, which supports the individual in making decisions and helps with routine tasks of independent living, is a constructive resource that is now offered in some provinces thanks to partial guardianship legislation.

British Columbia's new legislation, policies and regulations on adult guardianship will be attempting to move away from assessing capability in terms of mental competency and to look at the needs of the adult. There is recognition that people experience varying levels of physical and mental abilities during a lifetime and, with support and assistance from others, are able to manage without formal intervention. For instance, a senior who has difficulty remembering to pay bills on time or who can no longer write cheques is quite capable of making the larger decision to stay in his/her own home which includes paying the utilities. The problem that needs to be addressed is the need for help in some minor daily activities, and not the loss of ability or competence to do for him/herself.

## CONCLUSION

The Elder Abuse Resource Centre in Winnipeg and the North Shore Community Services program have demonstrated the effectiveness of connecting the older person's needs needs to the existing service system. However, no program will work efficiently or achieve results that are fully satisfactory within a system that has overlooked underlying issues. Until issues are recognized and addressed by a comprehensive network of support services and protocols, there will not be complete resolution of any individual case of abuse and neglect of seniors.

All existing systems will be affected by the future increase in the senior population and by the proportionate increase in numbers of abuse cases. Education, interdisciplinary intervention, and the input of seniors themselves will be necessary to meet the challenges in the area of abuse and neglect of older people.

# 1-3

# INTERVENTION IN LONG-TERM CARE INSTITUTIONS WITH RESPECT TO ELDER MISTREATMENT

*Marie Beaulieu and Lise Bélanger*

*Mocking the elderly is to destroy*
*the house in which we reside.*
Chinese proverb
(Montraynaud, Pierron & Suzzoni, 1989)

## INTRODUCTION

Why should there be concern over intervention practices with respect to elder mistreatment in long-term care institutions? This is a logical question to ask considering that most elders live in the community. The fact remains, however, that 7-8% of older people live in institutions. They enter institutions as a result of their inability to provide for, or have those close to them provide for, their biological, psychological and social needs. This situation fosters a physical, psychological and social vulnerability to mistreatment. These elderly people have been identified as experiencing the greatest difficulty in asserting their rights (Government of Quebec, 1989).

This chapter focuses on current knowledge of policies and programs governing institutional practices, and subsequently on intervention strategies developed by various social actors in institutions, with reference to two particular practice models. We the authors have elected in this chapter not to address abuse among fellow residents, which would entail consideration of abuse among peers and among persons with dementia and other cognitive deficiencies, but rather to focus our attention on abuse committed in institutions by persons in a position of responsibility *vis-a-vis* the elderly residents. The first part of the chapter comprises an analysis of scholarly publications. In part two, we have chosen to use two Canadian initiatives as the basis for our analysis. The first initiative is the policy governing intervention practices in private and public institutions recognized by the Government of Quebec, Health and Social Services Department. This policy is included in the new act governing health and social services (R.S.Q., 1991), commonly referred to as Bill 120. The second initiative is by the Association des centres d'accueil du Québec (ACAQ; Quebec Association of Nursing

Homes) (1991), which developed the concept of gerontological services, which are to be made available from the time that a person takes up residence in the institution. The ACAQ proposes a socializing model in which all interventions to help elderly people are geared to fostering their adjustment to their environment so that their biological, psychological and social health is maintained to the greatest extent possible. In our conclusion to the chapter, we suggest that the advances made so far be discussed, and we propose avenues to be pursued to ensure that institutions are healthy places of work for caregivers directly or indirectly involved, and the most pleasant and adequate surroundings possible to meet the needs of the elderly people residing there. In most cases, it is the last place in which these persons will live.

## EXISTING KNOWLEDGE AND THE MAIN CHALLENGES WITH RESPECT TO INTERVENTION

Scientific and practical concerns of mistreatment of elderly people in institutions are more recent and less developed than corresponding research with respect to those living in the community. The first scientific publication on this topic appeared in 1973, entitled "Old Folks and Dirty Work: The Social Conditions for Patient Abuse in a Nursing Home". It described and analyzed the behaviour of employees with respect to an elderly clientele (Stannard, 1973). To gain a fuller understanding of institutional practices, one can refer to the acquired knowledge of mistreatment in other settings. One could cite research on mistreatment in institutions such as prisons or psychiatric hospitals; in this chapter we refer to knowledge about mistreatment of seniors in the community. Most studies of elder abuse in the community seek to understand the phenomenon through a cause-effect analysis rather than taking a broader analytical approach as outlined below.

Various studies reveal that from 1 to 12% of elderly people are reportedly mistreated (Sergerie, 1991). The major variations in this percentage can be explained by methodological differences, such as the lack of consensus regarding what constitutes mistreatment, recourse to non-validated instruments, choices of unrepresentative samples, and lack of reliability. The conclusions of each of these studies lead us to further reflection and comprehensive research on such issues as the multitude of behaviours which could be considered as mistreatment, their impact on the lives of elderly people, the vulnerability of the latter and the characteristics of those doing the mistreatment. Although these studies fail to provide accurate information on the phenomenon, they are useful in that they raise numerous scientific and ethical questions.

In Canada, the two best-known studies were produced by Shell (1982) and by Podnieks, Pillemer, Nicholson, Shillington and Frizzel (1990). Caregivers and service clientele were surveyed during the course of other studies (Block, King & McGrath 1984; Stevenson, 1985; Grandmaison, 1988; Bristowe & Collins, 1989) to obtain a glimpse of the scope of the mistreatment, the vulnerability of elderly people, and the consequences of mistreatment in their lives. Having summarized the conclusions of the explanatory studies of elder mistreatment, we identified five perspectives which take account of the circumstances under which it occurs (Beaulieu, 1992).

The first perspective emphasizes individual and social characteristics of the older person. For example, a woman of advanced age with physical or intellectual limitations, who is dependent on the persons helping her and whose adopted behaviour reflects general indifference, is reported to be more vulnerable to mistreatment. This explanation does not put the blame on the elder, but illustrates the extent to which he/she may be a burden on the person offering help. The second perspective focuses on pathological characteristics of the caregiver who may, for example, be experiencing normal life crises or suffering from a psychosocial problem related to alcohol, drugs, mental illness, emotional or relational impairments. The third perspective analyses the past or present dynamics of the caregiver-older person relationship. Violence and neglect of the older person are seen as the consequences of an earlier stage in their relationship, arising from circumstances involving a reversal of previous roles, stress caused by caring for a dependent person, or feelings of shame or rejection toward a parent who is becoming less autonomous. A fourth perspective deals with socio-environmental factors such as poor financial status, inadequate accommodation, job dissatisfaction or joblessness, or a lack of social support. A fifth perspective looks at mistreatment as a reflection of the ageist values and behaviours which underlie the way in which our society operates. Indications of such ageism include our society's oblivion to, and denial of, violence against seniors, the lack of structure and support for persons who are natural caregivers, and the absence of clear and specific social policies for the elderly population. None of the five perspectives alone is sufficient to explain the phenomenon of senior abuse and neglect; it is necessary to take account of all five perspectives in seeking to understand any particular situation of elder mistreatment.

The extensive literature dealing specifically with the mistreatment of institutionalized elders has produced four established facts (De Beauvoir, 1970; Stannard, 1973; Bélanger et al., 1981; Stathopoulos, 1982; Kassell, 1982; Doty & Sullivan, 1983; Halamandaris, 1983; Solomon, 1983; Tarbox, 1983; Mercer, 1983; Kellaher, 1986; Couture & Beauvais, 1987; Bouvier, 1998; Schlesinger & Schlesinger, 1988; Podnieks, 1988; Roberge & Beauséjour, 1988; Moamai, 1988; Baril & Beaulieu, 1989; Cassell, 1989; Diessenbaker, 1989; Hamilton, 1989; Pillemer & Moore, 1989; Lemke & Moos, 1989). First, literature on the mistreatment of elders in institutions is far less developed than that on mistreatment of elders living in the community. It contains a brief analysis of the phenomenon and describes the context in which the mistreatment occurs. Mistreatment is defined in contrast to quality of care and services: if the quality of care and services decline, the risk of elder mistreatment increases.

Second, nursing personnel and other paid caregivers are identified as playing a pivotal role in the structure of institutions. On the one hand, these persons are seen as having the potential to mistreat elders; on the other hand, they are perceived as most able to intervene by virtue of their position in the organization, their ongoing presence with the older persons, and their training.

Third, the extensive literature on abuse and neglect of older persons in institutions reveals that organization and management methods are being questioned (Steinmetz, 1981; Falcioni, 1982; Shell, 1982; Beck & Phillips, 1983; O'Malley et al., 1983; Giordano & Giordano, 1984; Pillemer & Finkelhor, 1985; Health & Welfare Canada, 1986; Brillon, 1987; Pollick, 1987; Schlesinger & Schlesinger, 1988; Podnieks, 1988; Gouvernement du Québec, 1989; Podnieks et al., 1989 & 1990). Some organizations, especially private, self-financing institutions, have been suspected or even accused of putting profits ahead of quality care by making false statements, cutting services deemed essential and mismanaging other people's property (Lemke & Moos, 1989; Halamandaris, 1989). Moreover, the research cited above shows that staff may be poorly supported and trained, and may be tired and overstressed by jobs which require them to deal with physically or psychologically frail persons. This list of factors spawns mistreatment of all types in a setting where elderly people have little choice and control over their living conditions. If one takes a more panoramic view of institutions, it becomes evident that a) there is a lack of clear policies regarding the services to be offered to elderly people; b) legislation exists which fosters the creation of various types of institutions without regard to control over their quality of services; and c) little attention is paid to the older person's autonomy and the freedom of choice.

Fourth, general explanations of elder mistreatment in the community also apply to the problem of mistreatment of elders in institutions. In both settings we witness situations in which elders are physically or intellectually impaired, caregivers experience personal problems, and the relationship between an older person and a caregiver gives rise to various types of stress, creating an environment in which neither elders nor caregivers are able to flourish.

Research is limited in the area of predictive studies on the actual risks of mistreatment in institutions. Pillemer and Moore (1989) showed that mistreatment is not limited to isolated, publicized events. Instead, abusive actions are commonplace and frequent in the everyday life of institutions. The authors stress the importance of training staff with a view to achieving prevention. Causal explanations, however, are limited, as "[d]espite evidence indicating that deliberate mistreatment of patients exists in nursing homes, little is known about factors that increase the likelihood that such abuse will occur." (Pillemer & Bachman-Prehn, 1991, p. 74). Using a quantitative study containing data on auxiliary nursing staff, the authors discovered a correlation between staff burnout and cases of mistreatment; and between the levels of staff-resident conflicts and mistreatment. This study therefore suggests that the work atmosphere and the biological, psychological and social health of staff are areas to focus on for preventive intervention. The fact that there are few quantitative studies on mistreatment in institutions does not detract from the quality of what is known. In research, there are two major ways of gaining knowledge: the observation/analytical method and the experimental method. The literature leads us to conclude that knowledge regarding elder abuse in institutions is to be pursued in observation/analytical rather than in experimental fields.

Cassel (1989) maintains that legal, political, curative, or preventive strategies contribute little toward resolving the problem of elder mistreatment. He sums up the problem as a manifestation of an exercise of power. To prevent this misuse of power *vis-à-vis* elderly residents, institutions would do well to develop checks and controls for ensuring that staff members properly fulfill their responsibilities towards the older persons. "It seems to be in the nature of the human condition that, in the absence of checks and restraints, power is almost invariably abused... Obligations and responsibilities to sick persons remain the primary defense against the abuse of the frail." (Cassel, 1989, p. 162).

In a comprehensive study of management intervention practices in public institutions, Beaulieu (1992) observed that sensitivity to mistreatment is changing. Managers occupy managerial positions; in most cases, however, they continue to deal directly with elders and staff under them. They are therefore at the centre of all activities which take place in institutions. Managers in this study stated that, in the past few years, they had changed their understanding of mistreatment as limited to serious physical actions such as blows and injuries, to a more nuanced definition. They currently consider elder abuse to include more subtle forms of physical mistreatment, psychological mistreatment, material and financial mistreatment and, to some extent, violations of the person's rights. Of course, not all managers had reached this stage. Across the board, however, managers defined abuse as both actions and omissions, and they attributed responsibility for this abuse to either the person or the institution. In the first instance, (i.e. personal responsibility), managers distinguished between unintentional abuse committed, for example, through incidental loss of patience or through ignorance of the effects of certain behaviour on the older person; and intentional abuse, deliberately committed by persons who may be predisposed to mistreating older persons. Employees directly involved in service delivery are most often identified as those who mistreat the elderly residents.

In the case of mistreatment defined as an institutional responsibility, managers' comments suggest that they recognize that questions are raised by the fact that institutions constitute both a place of residence for elderly people and a work environment for caregivers. The policies and practices formulated both by the provincial government and the institution itself can result in mistreatment. For example, breakfast policies stipulate that the residents must rise at 5:30 am. because they have to eat breakfast during the night employees' shift, and therefore rise early enough that everything can be completed by 8 am. (Beaulieu, 1992). This raises a question as to their quality of life. Is it more important to have breakfast than to sleep in? If breakfast is more important, can other arrangements be made to avoid imposing such an early start to the day?

Beaulieu's study (1992) analyzed intervention procedures, such as prevention, detection and direct intervention. Prevention, the best-documented component, focuses mainly on training staff, the elderly residents and family members, and their roles in senior mistreatment. Reducing the potential for abuse will be achieved also through creating a healthy work atmosphere and providing resources to caregivers who are grappling with behavioural problems, whether these problems originate within the workplace or from the outside.

Detection is the phase in which managers have the greatest difficulty. Acts of mistreatment which are deemed to be less serious—for example, undue familiarity— may occur in public situations, but more serious abusive acts are hidden. In cases where such abuse is suspected or alleged, managers must conduct a police-like investigation, because evidence must be gathered. They focus on visual indicators, the elderly resident's rendition of the incident when possible (60-70% suffer from confusion), and denunciation by witnesses involved either directly or indirectly. This detection process is often initiated by the middle manager and pursued by the senior manager. In Quebec, there are no specific regulations on the reporting of abuse, although regulations do exist on the management of health care institutions. Regulations for reporting abuse and neglect vary from province to province (see Robertson, this volume).

When the process reaches the direct intervention stage, management starts disciplinary procedures. When mistreatment is deemed less serious, a verbal warning on the spot or during ensuing hours will be issued to the "guilty" party. If a more serious incident of mistreatment has occurred, the procedure spelled out in the collective agreement is applied (i.e. verbal notice, a written notice, a suspension or even dismissal). In fact, dismissals take the form of forced resignations. It must be remembered that not only the subjectively-determined seriousness of the abuse is taken into account when evaluating a case and choosing the adequate procedure; the caregiver's work record is also evaluated. An employee with an impeccable track record stands a better chance of being given only a warning than does an employee previously known for misconduct. As far as the abused older person is concerned, interventions have not been developed to any great degree. Managers may give occasional information and support to older persons, but it is the front-line workers who offer support on a daily basis. Rarely is there any long-term support and feedback on what action was taken with the perpetrator. One way to further develop intervention would be to organize more systematic support and follow-up for the abused senior, for example, in the form of managers' doing individual follow-up with older persons and possibly with their family members, and through providing follow-up intervention with the perpetrators.

Beaulieu's study (1992) also showed that strides have been made with respect to intervention in the area of elder abuse. Efforts are being made to transform what was a hazy, multi-faceted concept into new rules stipulating which practices are correct and which are not. These rules are supported by individual and group values which are drawn closely along the lines of the zero tolerance philosophy espoused during family violence awareness campaigns.

The literature on intervention practices with respect to mistreatment in institutions reveals that much intervention is along the lines of prevention, and that little research delves deeply into detection and direct intervention with the abused older person or the perpetrator. It can be noted that this lack of research applies also to abuse perpetrated by fellow residents. The prevention strategies proposed in current literature are (1) awareness-raising, (2) training programs, (3) the learning of new intervention techniques, (4) individual and group follow-up, and (5) the creation of locations and time so that caregivers can relax (see Education section, this volume). One example of a prevention program in a residence setting is CARIE (Coalition of Advocates for the Rights of the Infirm Elderly) which is a training program with three aims:

1.   to increase the staff awareness of abuse, neglect and potential abuse in long-term care facilities;

2.   to equip nurse aides with appropriate conflict intervention strategies; and

3.   to reduce abuse in long-term care facilities, thus improving the quality of life for residents (Hudson, 1992).

## INTERVENTION STRATEGIES

Generally speaking, intervention strategies encompass many facets: physical and human resources and a variety of practical and theoretical approaches and procedures. Developing appropriate, effective and coherent intervention is a complex task requiring flexibility and receptiveness on the part of staff members and the institutions.

We believe that intervention strategies must:

● consider the needs of all persons concerned and recognize the complexity of the problem of mistreatment. To this end, we believe that the intervention practices outlined in the Quebec Health and Social Services Act—the users committee, the ethics code and the review of users' complaints—constitute worthwhile methods of action and intervention;

● change attitudes, behaviours and prejudice concerning elderly people that associate old age all too often with sickness, dependency, handicaps and death. We suggest two avenues toward possible solutions—the first being the gerontological services conceptual model of the Association des centres d'accueil du Québec (ACAQ, 1991), which basically is taking a human approach to aging; and the second, the training needs of staff working in institutions;

● empower staff in the use of detection, evaluation and intervention protocols to promote and facilitate a holistic approach in responding to the needs of abused seniors.

We will take a closer look at these various intervention strategies to see how these measures contribute to living conditions which can afford elderly people greater respect in long-term care institutions.

## THE USERS' COMMITTEE (ACAQ, 1993)

The sections on Users' Committees, the code of ethics and the review of complaints are based largely on three ACAQ publications: *Le guide sur la création d'un comité des usagers dans un établissement de santé et des services sociaux* (A Guide to the Creation of a Users' Committee in a Health and Social Services Institution); *Le code d'éthique : une démarche et un outil de mobilisation* (The Code of Ethics: An Approach and an Instrument to Achieve Mobilization); *Guide sur l'examen des plaintes formulées par les usagers d'un établissement de santé et de services sociaux* (Guide to the Examination of Complaints Filed By Users of a Health and Social Services Institution).

Under the Health and Social Services Act, the Users' Committee is responsible for informing, promoting, evaluating, defending, accompanying and assisting the residents. The law prescribes that a Users' Committee must be created in any institution with twenty or more beds and that the Committee consists of no fewer than five members elected by all the residents.

It can be said that the implementation of a Users' Committee is an undertaking which has an inherent, though not unworkable, level of difficulty. The Users' Committee is not an immediate solution to dealing with abuse and neglect of older people in institutions, because its implementation calls for giving further attention to potentially problematic areas. In particular, the web of formal and informal networks within the institution, the organization of the institution's services, the needs of the residents, the ethnic diversity of the population, and individual interests that may conflict with organizational constraints will need to be addressed. All these components are such that members of the Users' Committee and authorities of the institution must meet and make decisions with the utmost respect for the roles of each party, to ensure the well-being of the elderly residents.

## THE CODE OF ETHICS (ACAQ, 1993)

The code of ethics is a legislated requirement for long-term care institutions aimed at instigating a positive reflection on the meaning and the extent of users' rights. This in turn prompts each institution to translate these rights into actions which reduce the gap between the rights which are spelled out and the actual situation with regard to the provision or the organization of services. The purpose of the code of ethics is two-fold: it contains information on the rights of users, and it creates awareness of the practices and conduct expected of persons working in the institution. The code of ethics applies to the user of institutional services, his/her representative, the family or close relatives, and all persons working in the institution. Furthermore, to be successful, it must be suited to, and subscribed to, by each of the members of the organization.

The success of this joint project depends greatly on the quality of the approach. The more it is imposed in a coercive, oppressive and expeditious manner, the more resistant and defensive reactions will undermine the best intentions to the detriment of the user. Therefore, a vital element in the approach toward developing a code of ethics is to involve residents, staff, family members and volunteers, and to take into consideration the responsibilities as well as the rights of all individuals, including residents. Such widespread involvement in the development of the code of ethics will facilitate its being understood and its implementation on a day-to-day basis, for the persons implicated are thus more likely to believe in the code and its effectiveness. Put succinctly, actions to involve the people concerned will speak louder than the code of ethics' words alone.

In organizations where this participation is ignored in developing the code of ethics, the following adverse effects can occur:

- non-involvement of staff with respect to the collaborative operation which the code of ethics ought to be; in this situation, personnel might resent the code because they feel it is imposed on them and they might easily question the good of the code if all it does is make the user the "master" of the place;

- disinterest in ethics and defensive reactions on the part of the staff, since those principles are perceived to benefit only the user and management, who are out to catch the personnel at fault;

- excessive tolerance by staff of acts, attitudes or disparaging or improper remarks on the part of residents, since management is perceived as "pro-client"; for example, sexual touching of attendants by users, may go unreported or may even be tolerated.

The point here is not to ask too much of users, who may be vulnerable. Their responsibilities must be commensurate with their physical, intellectual and psychological capacities, and put to them in ways that respect their capabilities. Because of the variety of possible situations, for example when helping a cognitively-impaired resident with his/her responsibility to make decisions about the care or services he/she needs, it is important to involve either a family member, a volunteer, a staff member, or a professional, and to work also with the resident's remaining capacity to assume responsibility for his/her own life. Time and time again, the resident is too quickly labelled "competent" or "incompetent" and his/her rights and responsibilities are readily dismissed.

Finally, a code of ethics imposed by an uncommitted management runs every risk of collapsing because of a lack of real consensus and participation by all members of the organization. Without this commitment, people simply will not accept such statements, and the organization will feel the negative effects for months or even years after. No matter how good the code of ethics is, it can never take the place of compassion, personal and group conscientiousness and professionalism on the part of those working with the user.

## REVIEWING COMPLAINTS (ACAQ, 1993)

The law makes it compulsory for a complaint examination procedure, which is accessible, simplified, flexible, objective, fair and diligent, to be put in place. "Accessibility" means ensuring that the procedure is known and understood by users and that the complaint admissibility criteria are given the broadest possible interpretation. This would suggest, for example, that complaints pertaining to all services offered by the institution be admissible, and that complaints may be submitted verbally as well as in a written form. The process should be "flexible" to facilitate the bringing forward of a user's complaint, not to discourage him/her or have him/her go through an endless maze of bureaucracy. The "objectivity" sought is the ability of persons who are the subject of the complaint to disregard their personal interests, and the ability of authorities examining the complaint to disregard their organizational or corporate interests. All forms of complaint then become good opportunities to improve services and do things differently for the benefit of residents and staff. "Fairness" refers to the respect of the user's rights and the natural meaning of justice. The purpose of a "diligent" complaint review process is to resolve a user's complaint promptly and effectively, which means that the institution or the person reviewing complaints is expected to find an appropriate solution within the required time specified by the law ( i.e. within 60 days).

A review of complaints and their validity from 1986 to 1990 in the Montreal area (Toupin, 1990) indicates the importance of a transparent, credible and effective complaint processing mechanism as the organization's preferred method of evaluating the choice or quality of services. An analysis of complaints reveals in particular that as far as communication is concerned, the dissatisfaction experienced by users and their families focuses on the lack of time spent on listening and on information; the lack of understanding and empathy by some professionals; rough, scornful attitudes, and rigid and narrow positions adopted by staff and work teams; and the lack of participation by the user and his/her family in the development and implementation of the service plan.

Dialogue between the provider of services and the user is essential. Moreover, a premium must be placed on dialogue, because any adjustments arising therefrom benefit users first and then the entire network.

## GERONTOLOGICAL SERVICES IN LONG-TERM CARE INSTITUTIONS

The concept of gerontological services advanced by the ACAQ (1991) over the past ten years is a socializing model which aims at satisfying biological, psychological and social needs of the elderly person in institutions. This concept also calls on all of the employee's resources, as he/she is no longer considered just a provider of services.

The concept of gerontological services is inspired largely by Bowker's framework (1982), which focusses on humanizing the approach to aging. The framework targets six major aspects of the socializing model, four major intervention dimensions with thirty-seven indicators to make it easier to measure intervention outcomes. The six aspects of the socializing model are: maintaining the person's biological system, humanizing interventions, responding adequately to individual needs, protecting the person's integrity, integrating the person into his/her environment, and maintaining the functioning of equipment. The four intervention dimensions emphasize social relationships (eight indicators), programming (eight indicators), policies and administration (eleven indicators) and the physical organization of the premises (ten indicators). This model is interesting in that it questions personal values, and therefore facilitates the questioning of practices, attitudes, behaviours and mentalities which are often the source of abusive situations involving seniors in institutions.

## STAFF TRAINING

Though relevant knowledge can be obtained at various educational levels and formats, the fundamental objectives remain the same: from a cognitive standpoint, the students must become familiar with the current body of knowledge; from an emotional standpoint, they must develop their personalities to their fullest by confronting head-on the physical, psychological and social realities of aging; and from a professional standpoint, they must learn techniques specific to gerontology. We the authors, feel it is becoming increasingly evident that it is important to create an awareness of the problems of seniors among college and university students preparing to work in the health and social services field; and to provide on-the-job training for persons working with seniors in these sectors (see Education section, this volume). In the area of gerontology, on-the-job training must focus not only on the technical and human enhancement of staff but also on improving teamwork (Zay, 1981). The committee report on the abuse of elderly people "*Vieillir...en toute liberté*"/"Growing old and remaining free" (Government of Quebec, 1989) recognized that on-the-job training is indispensable to ensure that staff develop skills which enable them to provide better services and to prevent and counter situations of abuse. This report also stresses that the basic training of all professionals, including medical doctors, must incorporate adequate knowledge regarding the aging process, the problems of abuse, intervention methods and the use of resource networks. Beaulieu's (1992) study found that on-the-job training on the mistreatment of seniors in institutions must respond to specific needs. The needs cited concerned the development of knowledge of various forms of abuse, intervention techniques for seniors or abusive employees and the use of existing intervention protocols. Moreover, the study goes on to say that the management of the institution must be convinced that training is not a luxury but an essential ingredient for success, and requires a follow-up program. In other words, a practical training program should not be limited to one or several discrete activities. On-the-job training should include a variety of topics such as the nature of abuse in institutions, different types of abuse, screening instruments and intervention programmes (crisis, short-term, and long-term treatment). For further insight into training programs for health professionals, see Ross and Hoff, this volume.

## DETECTION, EVALUATION AND INTERVENTION PROTOCOLS

The evaluation of an abusive or a high-risk situation calls on psychosocial expertise in addition to focussing specific attention on some physiological, emotional and environmental factors pertaining to elderly people. This evaluation process should also take into account the behaviours and attitudes of persons responsible for the provision of care and services to the potential abused senior. According to Quinn and Tomita (1986), an assessment or evaluation protocol is needed to identify and assess the possibility of elder abuse and neglect, and such a protocol contains usually four sections: assessment of the client's functioning; a physical examination of the client; interview of the potential abuser; and collateral contacts (p. 112). The intervention phase consists of a wide range of approaches, considering the many different situations facing the staff. Ideally, the method chosen will be determined by the client's need and by various factors which may affect the course of action selected. This boils down to time, available resources, the abused senior's cooperation and capacity, the seriousness of the situation or the abuser's pathology. When possible, it is important for direct intervention to include the abused senior, the abuser or both. In some cases, crisis intervention may prove most appropriate, and in other cases, short-term or long-term intervention is called for. Often more than one method of intervention may be used to ensure effectiveness. The professional develops an intervention and therapeutic consultation plan with the abused senior and, if possible, with the abusive person. A range of care and services can be offered at the same time to ensure the client's future security.

Three separate and complementary protocols in the areas of detection, evaluation and intervention are necessary to support comprehensive intervention for abused seniors. The detection protocol emphasizes risk factors, thereby making it easier to identify potentially abused seniors who may otherwise go unnoticed (Breckman & Adelman, 1988). The evaluation protocol is used in investigating suspected cases of abuse, and constitutes the basis of the identification phase in the intervention plan. The intervention plan offers the staff support by delineating the options from which they must select to correct the abuse and assure follow-up. In addition to facilitating staff intervention, these three protocols are a means of creating awareness and training for those concerned. For further elaboration on evaluation and intervention protocols, *Elder Abuse and Neglect* by Quinn and Tomita (1986) is a very useful document.

## CONCLUSION

After approximately ten years of practice in the area of elder mistreatment, the time has now come to take stock of the situation. Although the literature shows that our knowledge has advanced less in the area of mistreatment in institutions than for elder abuse in the community, a greater understanding of this social problem has been achieved, and a greater awareness has developed that a healthy workplace is important for both the caregivers and the elders. From a practical standpoint, a multidimensional framework is being created, thereby yielding new strategic areas in which changes can be made, affecting the social actors in the institutions. The attitudinal and practical changes seek to achieve the same ultimate objective—detection, evaluation and intervention to stop mistreatment.

Many studies cited in this chapter propose that instances of mistreatment be evaluated based on comments and actions by nursing and care staff. We believe that this philosophy should change, such that intervention practices that take account of all staff, are analyzed instead. A strategic approach elicits a broader and more systematic conception of institutions, in which each unit has a major influence on the resolution of problems encountered. A common thread links the users' committee, the code of ethics and the complaint review procedure—concerted action is stressed, and elders are in a good position not only because their rights are being recognized but also because they are being given the means to make some decisions. Current practices can be summarized by stating that the era of preventing elder mistreatment is under way, but that practices to counter this mistreatment in long-term care institutions have a considerable way to go.

Work to identify the problem has begun in several institutions. Elder mistreatment, though still a difficult issue to discuss, is becoming less taboo. Governments and institutions have pondered the problem and have discovered paths which may yet lead to solutions accompanied by legislative reform. Is it time to consider consolidating these new practices? Detection, evaluation and intervention plans and protocols have been developed. Would it not be desirable to adapt intervention service plans and protocols, test them out, validate them and use them? Legislative measures in Quebec, for example, are too recent to be able to determine their effectiveness, but hopefully there will be a mutual sharing among the provinces of measures that prove successful. Can new instruments and innovative approaches be developed which are suited to the situations of various types of institutions and the elders residing in them? Finally, who will promote these changes, ensure that they materialize, and evaluate them?

By adopting a futuristic perspective, can one contemplate the possibility that some institutions will agree to becoming experimental laboratories? One of the avenues worth exploring is the action-research area, involving respectful partnerships between (a) researchers seeking to gain a better understanding of the practices and needs of elderly abused seniors and those of the persons mistreating them; (b) persons who intervene with the abused senior or the perpetrator; and (c) caregivers wishing to improve their practice by becoming more efficient personally, professionally and collectively. Through such action-research, knowledge will become a by-product of practice, and will be directly retransmitted in a form which is accessible to the caregivers, elderly people, and the persons representing them.

# SECTION 2:
# POLICY

# INTRODUCTION:

## SOCIAL, LEGAL AND HEALTH CARE POLICY ISSUES RELATED TO THE ABUSE AND NEGLECT OF OLDER CANADIANS

*John B. Bond Jr.*

Depending on an individual's profession and perspective on social issues, the word "policy" stipulates a specific framework and reference system for the analysis and resolution of social and health problems. The three chapters in this section reflect different views on the breadth and context of policy issues related to abuse and neglect of elderly people.

Neysmith places abuse and neglect of seniors in the domain of current power imbalances within society. She suggests that abuse is likely not a new phenomenon, but a problem receiving new attention. After a brief review acknowledging the problems at theoretical and empirical levels, she applies a feminist perspective to intrafamilial and institutional abuse. In both situations, the gender of the abuser and the status of the participants are critical variables, as pressures related to caregiving increase. The limits of current legal remedies are discussed, and arguments against drawing parallels to the child abuse sphere are provided. She concludes with specific policy issues such as the role of shelters, and the wider issues of dependency, isolation and stress.

Robertson takes a more confined perspective of abuse and neglect, with a focus on legal approaches. Law is one example of public policy, defined by Pal as "a course of action or inaction chosen by public authorities to address a given problem or interrelated set of problems" (1992, p. 2). Paralleling Neysmith, Robertson points to the ineffectiveness of criminal law in addressing elder mistreatment. He then considers the potential remedies deriving from provincial legislative domains, including guardianship, powers of attorney, and institutional concerns. The final section focuses upon a critical examination of adult protection legislation as it varies among the provinces, with particular attention to the recent initiatives in British Columbia.

The last chapter in this section by Watson, Patterson, Maciboric-Sohor, Grek and Greenslade focuses the scope of abuse and neglect of seniors even further to the level of workers in the health care system. Societal parameters and legal remedies ultimately become translated into an interaction between an abused individual and practitioners who may be employed in general social service agencies dedicated to seniors, shelters for abused persons, hospitals and long-term care institutions, among others. After clarifying various needs for policies regarding elder abuse and neglect, the authors briefly describe the development of protocols related to abuse and neglect of seniors, citing examples of existing models. Specific issues in the development of policy are then examined, including detection and screening, the use of multidisciplinary teams, and the perspective of the abused person. Next, the role of health care professionals in the development of policies is examined, followed by a scrutiny of institutional abuse, paralleling many of the observations presented by Neysmith. The final section indicates the directions that are needed in policy and protocol development.

This brief overview of these three chapters cannot do justice to the vision, combined with detail, of these chapters. Without well-considered policy that is informed by the ideas and concepts of various disciplines, responses to abuse and neglect of older persons will remain a collection of disjointed and idiosyncratic approaches. While no singular policy can encompass all issues, these chapters will likely be provocative and informative in areas not yet considered by all readers.

# 2-1

# POWER IN RELATIONSHIPS OF TRUST:
# A FEMINIST ANALYSIS OF ELDER ABUSE

*Sheila M. Neysmith*

## INTRODUCTION

This chapter assumes that abuse of older persons is not a new phenomenon but rather that during the 1980s it became an issue worthy of public attention. One factor influencing its emergence is the aging of the Canadian population, with the implication this has for social policy. Another, of course, is our increased awareness of abuse experienced by vulnerable segments of the population. Calls to address the issue are resulting in a range of policy and program responses. Assessing the adequacy of these is dependent upon an understanding of what the problem is. This chapter uses the experience and knowledge gained from addressing woman abuse as a lens for assessing explanations of elder abuse and considering various policy initiatives and recommendations.[1]

Historians like Linda Gordon (1988) document the long history of woman and child abuse—and the struggle to address it. This struggle was riddled with contradictions, tensions and conflict. On the one hand, help was sought by abused persons and their families, but that did not mean that they got what they wanted under the terms and conditions desired. On the other hand, genuine concern by service providers became translated into professional issues and research agendas that took on a life of their own, only partially reflecting the priorities of those experiencing the problem. In other words, those who have the power to define social problems are usually not the same persons who are experiencing them (Hugman, 1991). There is no reason to believe that different dynamics characterize our concern with elder abuse today. An appreciation of the effects of such contradictions, however, is critical if we hope to develop policies and programs that address the underlying causes of elder abuse while meeting the needs of abused seniors.

Research is one, but only one, influence on prevailing definitions of and responses to elder abuse. The political economy of the moment also shapes our understanding of social phenomena and the range of possible responses. In the United States, the elder abuse discourse has been dominated by what might be called the family violence perspective while the United Kingdom approach, as a result of several public inquiries, has focused on abuse in institutions (Glendenning, 1993). Even though there has recently been more attention paid in the North American literature to abuse occurring in formal settings (Chichin,1991; Pillemer & Hudson, 1993; Tellis-Nayak & Tellis-Nayak, 1989), the predominant concern is abuse by informal caregivers, only some of which is sensitive to who these caregivers are. The explanation of abuse by formal care providers is seen as quite separate from that which occurs in kinship situations, and thus studies focus on one or the other.

In this respect our understanding of elder abuse shares many conceptual commonalities with our understanding of caregiving. In both, people's lives are split into public and private domains. Consequently, when abuse occurs within a familial setting, it is understood and addressed as family violence. When it occurs in an institutional setting, it is viewed as essentially different and thus requiring a different response. When caregiving is provided by family members, the quality of such care is assumed to be unproblematic. When care is provided in institutional settings or by home care workers quality control is of prime importance. Because of these parallels in how we construct knowledge in examining policy issues—that is, the separation of the private world of family life from the public world of community life—I will consider the theoretical frameworks underpinning discussions of elder abuse alongside those on caregiving which have been so influential in shaping policy on home care. Furthermore, the now extensive literature on caregiving documents the differential experiences of men and women (see Abel & Nelson, 1990 for the American experience; Baines, Evans & Neysmith, 1991 for studies using Canadian data; Ungerson, 1990 for an overview of research in Britain and Scandinavia). I argue in this chapter that, as does caregiving, abuse reflects the gendered nature of attitudes, behaviour and expectations in Canadian society. Thus, we would expect to find differences between the experiences of older men and women, despite the gender neutrality of the term "elder abuse".

## DEVELOPING A POLICY PERSPECTIVE

Not all old people are equally likely to experience abuse. The longer history of wife abuse research would suggest that a focus on the psychological, social or physical characteristics of either the abused person or the abuser is a precarious explanatory path to tread. It can too easily excuse the abuser and blame the person who has been abused. Although less well-documented than in the area of woman abuse, we probably will find little to distinguish abusers of elderly people from non-abusers. If we, however, focus on the conditions that permit abuse to occur, the burden of explanation shifts from the individual to the social institutions which shape the options available to individuals. Social policy can open up, or foreclose, these options.

Recent models of the welfare state have been centrally concerned with power resources associated with (1) state-market relations, (2) stratification, and (3) social citizenship (Esping-Andersen, 1989; Korpi, 1989). However, these models, and resultant policy debates that are informed by them, for example around employment and retirement, reflect a concept of labour which turn workers into de-gendered entities seemingly unattached to families and communities! Researchers and policy analysts sensitive to disparities arising from gender and race document the effects of such universal assumptions on women and other historically excluded groups (Pascall, 1986; Williams, 1989). However, to use a now familiar expression, you cannot just "add gender and stir" (Bunch, 1987). Policies are transformed when gender is considered. Gender is not just a variable modifying the effect of a policy on individuals but one of several social dimensions that permeate the structures of Canadian society and shape social relations. Thus, feminists have focused on whether social policy can alter gender relations by lowering power resources held by men and/or increasing those available to women. Social policies can then be assessed in terms of how effectively they do this (Orloff, 1993). For instance, families are significant providers of welfare, but the unpaid caring and domestic work of women is not reflected in pension entitlements. Thus, older persons with long years in the labour force are entitled to the Canada Pension Plan and employer pensions; those whose work was in the home must apply for federal and provincial income tested supplemental pension benefits. This positions older men and women quite differently in terms of resources available to them in negotiating their relationships with others—both inside and outside of the family. The role of the state, as operationalized through particular policies, or lack thereof, needs to be examined to see how it shapes these relations and thus the choices made by, and options available to, individuals.

Power is exercised and experienced through social relations. In such a model, power is not reified by lodging it in institutional structures, such as the health care system, nor is it seen as possessed by certain individuals, and thus susceptible to redistribution (Young, 1990). Rather, it flows through social relations and is made visible in actions. Behaviour, so to speak, is the visible part of the iceberg. Acts need to be placed within the social context of people's lives in order to give them meaning. Social policy can mediate power relations among people. Relevant to this chapter are those situations where our knowledge of woman abuse suggests that power differentials exist amongst elderly persons and between them and individuals and institutions providing care. Thus, individual behaviour will be examined within the context of power differentials operating within the social relations that exist in these situations.

The above understanding of power suggests that the public world of policy-making must recognize the existence of a private world of relationships that affect the responses of victims and abusers. The family is not a monolith but rather is made up of individuals with varying degrees of power (Eichler, 1988). Violence can result as family members of all ages contest for scarce material and emotional resources. However, these struggles among individuals are shaped by the political economy of the moment (Gordon, 1988). Thus, the emphasis in this chapter is on an analysis of the social location of elder abuse. Specifically, it is argued that abuse occurs where inequities are condoned. We are most likely to find it occurring then along the major fault lines in the social fabric of Canadian society that differentially affect people throughout their lives. For the purpose of this chapter, I will consider those inequities related to gender and age.

## EXAMINING THE INTERFACE OF RESEARCH AND THEORY

In their reviews of elder abuse research, writers such as McDonald, Hornick, Roberson & Wallace, (1991), Pillemer and Finkelhor (1988), and Podnieks, Pillemer, Nicholson, Shillington and Frizzell, (1989) have repeatedly pointed out its mixed quality. On the one hand, there is considerable concern over the small samples used in many studies, variable nomenclature, and reliance on reports from service providers. On the other hand, national prevalence and incidence studies rely on self-identification and reporting procedures respectively. Both are riddled with validity questions. Being mindful of these reservations, one does find some consistency across studies in the use of the broad categories of material, verbal, physical abuse and neglect as a schema for classifying abuse. Pillemer and Finkelhor (1988), although not including material/financial abuse in their random sample survey of greater Boston, estimated a total abuse rate of 63 per 1000. The Canadian prevalence study by Podnieks et al., (1989) did include financial abuse in their national telephone survey. They estimated a rate of 40 per 1000, or 4 per cent, when all categories are combined. This does not necessarily mean that Canadians are less abusive than their neighbours. Minor differences in the wording of questions and interview procedures could account for this degree of variation. The point I want to discuss is the differential contributions of the four categories to the total.

In the Canadian study, financial abuse was mentioned most frequently, with 25 per 1000 (2.5% of the sample) respondents reporting this form of maltreatment. Equal percentages of men and women were victimized. Perpetrators were not primarily family members, 40 per cent were friends, neighbours, acquaintances; only 29 per cent were sons or daughters. Chronic verbal aggression was the second most frequent abuse mentioned with 14 per 1000 (1.4%). Equal percentages of men and women also reported this form of abuse. All but one of these respondants were married. Perpetrators were primarily spouses. Reported physical abuse was only 5 per 1000 (0.5%). Again, most of these people were married, the majority of perpetrators were spouses, and equal percentages of men and women reported such violence. Neglect was the smallest category reported in this study. The authors express some reservations about their findings on neglect because the concept is more difficult to define. It is characterized by the lack of a needed resource and thus is conceptually different from the active stance implicit in the other forms of maltreatment. Finally, hidden somewhere in these figures is sexual abuse (Podnieks et al., 1989; Vinton, 1991).

I have summarized these findings because they underscore the difficulties we face in developing policies based on survey information. First, these data seem to indicate that elder abuse is perpetrated primarily by those who know the abused person, but for over half, that is those classified as cases of financial abuse, perpetrators are not primarily immediate family members. Second, if financial abuse is not included, of all perpetrators 58 per cent were spouses, 24 per cent were children. However, spousal and intergenerational abuse can have very different etiologies even though both are categorized as family violence.

In all these situations, the behaviour occured within an existant relationship (Sprey & Matthews, 1989). Also important to consider are the situational conditions that permit abuse. Living in the same space where there is extended contact between the parties is one of these conditions. People on their own may suffer from self and societal neglect, random violence, even extortion by friends, strangers and family members but the probability of intimate violence (a phrase coined to capture the fact that these actions are perpetrated by those usually considered to be intimate others; see Gelles & Straus, 1988; Crawford & Gartner, 1992) is less. In North America, elderly persons tend not to live with their children. Thus, the rate of intergenerational abuse may be low because some of the preconditions fostering it are absent. For example, if it were more common for elderly relatives to live with younger family members, patterns of abuse might be different.

The above-mentioned surveys (Pillemer & Finkelhor, 1988; Podnieks et al., 1989) confirm that elderly persons do respond when questioned about abuse. The more difficult issue is how to interpret these findings and translate them into effective policies. Our knowledge of violence against women would suggest that elder abuse is severely underreported. We are probably only scratching the surface in documenting elder abuse and thus statistics based on self-identification and estimates made by professionals need to be interpreted with reservation (Ogg & Munn-Giddings, 1993). Even carefully calculated estimates of prevalence or incidence may not accurately reflect the situation, and do not translate automatically into an understanding of the conditions that promote elder abuse. For instance, in these surveys slightly more men than women report experiencing abuse. What does this finding mean? Do men respond more readily when questions are posed? Do women have a higher tolerance threshold before considering behaviour abusive? The literature on woman abuse (for overviews see Stordeur & Stille, 1989; Yllo & Bograd, 1988) suggests that women probably do. Abuse has to be named and legitimated before you can speak of it. In a similar manner, Moon and Williams' (1993) comparative study of abuse identification scenarios found considerable variation among cultural groups in naming violence. Not surprisingly, this was also correlated with help-seeking behaviour. This line of questioning might lead one to ask why financial abuse is reported most frequently in the Canadian national prevalence study. Is it the least stigmatizing abuse to acknowledge?

## DECONSTRUCTING ABUSE AS A FAMILY AFFAIR

Family violence refers to a range of behaviors between different family members including incest, wife battering, marital rape and child physical abuse (*I would add elder abuse*). In families where the wife is battered by her husband, there is often child abuse as well. Although empirical data illuminating possible links between these various forms of abuse is sparse, researchers, clinicians, and lay people alike hold assumptions about how they are interrelated (Bowker, Arbitell & McFerron, 1988, p. 158).

About 45 per cent of abusers are spouses (McDonald et al., 1991) but spousal abuse, like family violence and elder abuse, is a gender-neutral term. The statistic of concern to practitioners and policy makers is that half of spousal perpetrators are reported to be women. This seems to contradict an understanding of violence which sees it stemming from gender-based power inequities. In interpreting these data, several factors unique to elder abuse warrant consideration. First, in most marriages men are older and die younger than their partners. Since older women tend to live alone or with men at least as frail as they, the number of potential male abusers, if you will, is bound to be relatively low. Second, reviews of research on spousal violence in younger cohorts suggest caution in relying on self-report data based on checklists of acts without assessing motives, meanings and consequences (see Dobash, Dobash, Wilson & Daily, 1992 for a detailed assessment of commonly used behavioural indicators in comparison with other measures of violence between men and women in the United States, Canada and Britain). For instance, verbal aggression by women is responded to by physical aggression by men; physical violence is seldom initiated by women (Saunders, 1988) but they do sometimes respond violently. This dynamic has even resulted in the emergence of "the battered wife syndrome" as a legal defence. I share with others a concern that categorizing this behaviour as a syndrome can quickly pathologize a political issue. However, it leads one to ask if the dynamic of a relationship changes when a formerly abusive spouse becomes incapacitated? Third, there is the issue of ascertaining the type of behaviour defined as abusive. Pillemer and Finkelor (1988) in a follow-up study to their survey of elder abuse, report that the extent of force used and the effects on the victim are quite unequal; specifically, only one man (6%) of those who reported being abused stated that he suffered injuries as the result of maltreatment whereas 8 (57%) of the women sustained injuries. This parallels findings from follow-up studies of wife abuse where reliance on behavioural categories in self-report surveys suggested a symmetry in spousal abuse patterns which did not actually exist (Dobash & Dobash, 1992).

Interpreting research data is an ongoing challenge for policy makers. Although there are, and will continue to be, competing explanations of elder abuse, the category of family violence can be as obfuscating when men and women are over the age of sixty-five as it is when they are younger. Families are made up of individuals with differential power resources. Most perpetrators are men; most victims are women and children. Battered women do age (Vinton, 1991). We, therefore, can assume that some elderly women caring for their husbands are survivors. One recipe for abuse might read something like the following: Combine individual biography with gendered expectations about providing care, mix in a good handful of cognitive limitations, add a scant teaspoon from the nearly empty package labelled social support, place these within a shell of isolation, and bake for 24 hours a day, 365 days a year for several years. Chang and White-Means (1991), using data on stress from a large U.S. study, confirm findings from other studies which show female caregivers, across the board, reporting higher levels of stress than males. This does not mean that abuse will occur. Perhaps the critical question to ask is what mitigates abuse in such cases? What supports need to be put in place and/or stresses relieved?

With this in mind, the feminist discourse on caregiving, with its emphasis on the differential effects of gender and class, may help to situate the abuse debate in a way useful to policy development. In gerontology, much of the caregiving research focuses on persons with dementia (for a recent example see Hinrichsen & Niederehe, 1994). Understandably in such demanding situations, relationship dynamics can change. Studies of spousal caregivers (Miller, 1990; Stoller, 1992) reveal different patterns for men and women. In her review of research in the area, Stoller (1992) concludes, however, that contradictory findings may be more apparent than real. Yes, among spousal caregivers, husbands constitute 45 per cent; but only 28 per cent of all caregivers are men (Stone, Cafferata & Sangle, 1987). Similarly in reports of spousal abuse, most women are excluded because they do not live with male partners.

It is primarily women who provide care to elderly spouses, immediate relatives, and friends (Gallagher & Gerstal, 1993). In their final years they care for themselves (Webber, Fox & Burnette, 1994), assisted by younger kin, volunteers, paid home help or institutional personnel (Dwyer & Coward, 1992). Across all these categories of formal and informal carers, women are the dominant providers of hands-on services, and this labour is a constant throughout women's lives (Baines, et al., 1991). This is not so for men. The gendered stereotyping of this labour is well recognized (Guberman, Maheu, & Maille 1992). It is not surprising then that elderly men count certain activities as caregiving while women do not think to mention them because they have always assumed responsibility for such tasks (Stoller, 1992). Similarly, knowledge about gender differences in experiences, emotions and behaviours needs to inform our attempts to understand elder abuse. For instance, it may not be surprising if abusive behaviour is also not worth mentioning when it has been a feature of a woman's familial relationships over a lifetime.

Kin-based abuse is more likely to occur in situations where one person wields power over another whether spouse, parent, child or other individual placed in a dependent position (Lee, 1992). As argued in this chapter, and as understood by the Family Violence Prevention Division of Health Canada, abuse frequently occurs in relationships of trust—in situations where one party depends upon the other for providing essential resources, whether these are provided within the context of informal or formal arrangements. However, trust between individuals in positions of unequal power is always precarious. Thus, the recommendation by Wolf and Pillemer (1989) that the dilemma can be resolved by adopting a family violence perspective needs to be carefully considered. This perspective can privatize the problem even as it highlights the fact that families can be arenas for violence. Elder abuse, like child and woman abuse, is not simply a family affair, a phenomenon peculiar to families or spawned by structures and relationships inherent to families. It occurs within familial relationships because these are sites of power, and locations that permit it to happen. It does not result from dysfunctional families as such. Thus, the number of elderly males who are abused does not invalidate a feminist analysis of violence so much as it underlines that differentials in power allow abuse, while lack of sanctions protect the abuser. This dynamic is somewhat more visible when abuse is examined in the public realm of formal care where assumptions about familial relationships are less likely to cloud the issue.

# DEFINING THE STRUCTURE OF INSTITUTIONAL ABUSE

Explanations of abuse in institutional settings such as nursing homes are seldom juxtaposed to explanations of violence within the social institution called the family. Treating abuse in institutions as a separate phenomenon not only obscures common issues of power and dependency, but can result in explanations that actually confuse the issue. For example, in a recent review of the literature in this area, one author (Gnaedinger, 1989, p. 5) notes that abusers in institutions are female, and then makes the following comment:

> It must be noted here, however, that any sample made up of front line health care workers in geriatric institutions will be predominantly female, and therefore any abuse inflicted by or observed by them will almost by definition be abuse by females. In short, a biased sample will produce biased results.

This commentary needs to be extended. One surmises that Gnaedinger (1989) is making the point that men cannot abuse in this situation because they are not there. This important observation, however, is glossed over by dealing with it as an issue of biased sampling. First, it is relevant that the respondents were women. It is primarily women who work in these low-paid, high-stress jobs (Crown, MacAdam & Sadowsky, 1992). Second, the finding needs to be considered within a setting where all staff, including paraprofessionals, hold considerable power in terms of help provided or withheld to residents. The persons involved also have an ongoing relationship which calls for some degree of trust. Gender is relevant but so is the institutional status of the players. This type of abuse shares with others the characteristics of a power differential between two actors, in this case resident and aide.

Pillemer and Moore (1989) in their study of abuse by staff in nursing homes note not only the willingness of staff to disclose abuse but also to stress the importance of focusing on the quality of interaction between staff and patients if it is to be stopped. Structural features such as institutional size or whether a facility is under private, public or voluntary auspice seem to have relatively little to do with the quality of life within an institution as experienced on a daily basis by patients and staff. Rather, patients place emphasis on the quality of the interpersonal relations between themselves and staff, and the resultant amenities of care. It is precisely these relationships, however, that are put under strain if working conditions deteriorate. The situation is exacerbated when limited staff have to handle abuse by patients.

Depending on how these findings are interpreted, responses will vary. One approach would be to provide training to staff so that aggressive behaviour by patients with Alzheimer's disease, for example, is understood and thus not misinterpreted. Unfortunately, no matter how well-intentioned, principles of good practice are difficult to carry out in a setting where economic constraints are dealt with by cutting the number of aides on a unit, where the average functional capacity of residents is much lower than it was a decade ago, and where wages are such that women who do this type of work are under constant financial stress (Chichin, 1991; Crown, MacAdam & Sadowsky, 1992; Diamond, 1990; Donovan, Kurzman & Rotman, 1993). The conflicting pressures on paraprofessionals and residents is vividly captured by Tellis-Nayek & Tellis-Nayek (1989: 311) in their research on nursing aides who were visible minority women.

Regulations specifying residents' rights can have only a limited impact in nursing homes because power in the form of authority and services rests in the hands of administration and staff. Also, since studies of abuse among staff in nursing homes suggest that maltreatment is, at least in part, a response to working conditions rather than an outcome of patient/staff relations per se (Pillemer & Moore, 1989), ensuring residents' rights addresses only one dimension of the dynamic. Indeed, it is the ability of aides, supervisors and managers in some settings to overcome social and economic hurdles that is so remarkable, and worthy of study. Specifying how these settings promote empowerment of residents and staff would be an important contribution to our understanding of how to counter conditions that promote elder abuse in institutions (see Beaulieu & Bélanger, this volume).

## THE LIMITS OF LEGAL PROTECTION

After an extensive discussion of the legal aspects of abuse in the Canadian context, McDonald et al. (1991) conclude that legal approaches are of limited utility. This is substantiated in Bond, Penner and Yellen's (1992) review of legislative approaches to elder abuse in Canada and the United States. Where reporting procedures are in place, they seem to be most effective when physicians, health professionals and social workers are mandated to do so. The question is "So what happens after?" This has been the conundrum in most evaluations of how the Criminal Justice System deals with domestic abuse. MacLeod and Picard (1989), in their review of research on wife assault, conclude that existing research repeatedly shows that most women who are battered do not want criminal justice involvement in their lives, and have little faith in its ability to stop the violence. Although active intervention by the authorities is welcomed, there is the assumption in law that the parties in conflict are strangers rather than actors in an ongoing relationship. In these situations, the effectiveness of legal tools is limited.[2]

The history of the response of the Criminal Justice System to domestic violence offers important insights for policy development in elder abuse. For instance, attempts to have domestic violence given the same credibility as public violence were actually hampered by the tradition of responding to domestic violence through family courts and the use of therapeutic professionals (Dobash & Dobash, 1992, p. 160):

> By the time of the discovery of the problems of battered women in the early seventies family courts and psychiatric and social work approaches had reduced these criminal assaults to problems of individual or social pathology. The Criminal Justice System was not considered the appropriate institution for dealing with violence against women within the home ...

Evaluations of legal remedies to domestic violence in the United States conclude that the whole process was quite complicated by the existence of crisis intervention and mediation which were supposed to be steps to solve the issue. For instance, training police resulted in a decrease in arrests. The officers did not themselves attempt to mediate but 80% claimed they routinely referred women to agencies that did. In observing the police, however, only 4% actually made the referrals and rarely were shelters mentioned to the women experiencing abuse. Furthermore, evaluations of the Neighbourhood Justice Centers Program in the United States reveal a poor rate of success in mediation. "Agreements between disputants in intimate relationships were found four times more likely to break down than agreements between parties with more tenuous relationships" (Dobash & Dobash, 1992, p. 164). Not surprisingly, there is a higher percentage of dissatisfied respondents in these cases than in others. A mediation model assumes two equals meeting to resolve differences with a neutral third party and works best, as the authors conclude, when the dispute is not deeply rooted or tremendously complex, but requires only a brief intervention. Nothing could be further from the reality of abusive family situations.

I mention the above evaluations because once we move beyond documenting elder abuse and developing protocols for screening and assessments, the question of appropriate programs of intervention will increasingly move to centre stage. In an understandable urge to do something about the situation, these same models may be uncritically adopted and transferred to elder abuse programs without benefitting from the knowledge gained through the experience of the battered women's movement.

A critical factor in securing a response to the issue of wife battering was public pressure by women's groups. At this point in time, this condition does not seem to be in place for effectively addressing the problem of elder abuse. Policies for addressing the abuse of women resulted from the combined efforts of activists in the Women's Movement and the willingness of some professionals and agencies to redefine laws and practices. On the one hand, eliminating abuse involves altering not just legislation but the structures, perceptions and cultural practices that are deeply imbedded in our system of justice— no easy feat. On the other hand, those arguing against the use of the legal system to deal with family violence do not consider the power and repression that can occur within families. A persistent theme in the Women's Movement is the centrality of power inequities. Violence against women in the home is based on power, and any form of intervention must be able to confront and redress power imbalances. Since power also plays a significant role in settling disputes, whether these occur inside or outside the courts, there are obviously problems associated with settlements where there is an assumption that the parties are equal and/or independent.

Keeping the above analysis in mind, Power of Attorney and Guardianship laws will have limited ability to avert elder abuse. At the time of writing, Ontario has just introduced new legislation (Bill 108—The Substitute Decisions Act, 1992) that tries to balance individual rights with the need for protection by allowing individuals to give power of attorney for personal care, authorizing family members or friends to make treatment decisions should the person become incapable. It also recognizes the authority of "living wills" and provides for partial guardianship. A companion piece of legislation is Bill 74—The Advocacy Act, 1992. These measures can be called on by abused people and their advocates but their impact will be limited. This is because our legal system is primarily concerned with ensuring the rights and freedom of individuals. In addition, there is the legal assumption that the adversaries are not connected and that the well-being of one party is not tied into that of the other. With elder abuse, however, the perpetrator is known to the abused senior and is probably involved in a long-term formal or informal relationship with her/him. Legal mechanisms are less likely to be invoked in such situations, and when they are, power differentials embedded in the relationship can blunt their effectiveness.

Despite the limited impact that legislation and aggressive legal responses have had on controlling violence, it has been very effective in putting abuse on the policy agenda, allowing for discussion of those factors that condone violence (Walker, 1990). The limitations of legislation and legal responses force all parties to recognize the power imbalances that exist in families and in institutions, and to debate policy directions that can change those social conditions that foster abuse.

## SOME QUESTIONS RAISED BY THE CHILD ABUSE ANALOGY

With the increasing use of protocols for screening elder abuse, there is mounting concern that we are modelling these programs after those in child abuse. Such models are inappropriate in that they ignore documented aspects of elder abuse, namely, the prevalence of financial abuse and that the persons involved are adults. Furthermore, there is need to question the assumptions underlying child abuse policies and programs. In cases of child abuse, the State exercises its control through ensuring that a responsible adult, usually the mother, protects the interests of the child. The presumption is a state of dependency where the authority of a trusted adult has been abused. Among adults there is an assumption of independence. One of the conceptual problems here is the artificial duality imposed when persons are classified into the either/or categories of independent or dependent beings (Fraser & Gordon, 1994). Not only does this make it difficult to think in terms of interdependence, or mutuality, but it fails to recognize that states of dependency are frequently socially created by our economic and social policies (Walker, 1980).

There is also a concern that elder abuse is becoming medicalized, as child abuse has been. I would suggest rather that, in both cases, physicians and other health care professionals are uniquely positioned to see it but poorly equipped to deal alone with it. It is probably fair to say that responses to elder abuse, as with child abuse, have been dominated by professional interventions. This is in marked contrast to woman abuse where interventions were developed by feminist activists. Elderly persons, and their advocates, have been minor players in defining the discourse on elder abuse. When groups of seniors and activists participate more in policy development, I suspect their priorities will differ from those of us who are primarily researchers or service providers. This comment rests on the repeated reference by seniors' groups to the issue of neglect which routinely drops off the research and policy agenda because it is so difficult to specify. Likewise, it has been seniors' groups who advocate that trained seniors, not health care professionals, be used as intermediators in suspected cases of abuse. It is also seniors' groups that emphasize the goal of improving the overall quality of the abused person's life by providing greater access to housing so that she has some options (Canadian Association on Gerontology, 1993). In evaluating these recommendations, policy makers would do well to keep in mind that it was women activists, not professional women, who redefined woman abuse and initiated some of the most effective models of intervention.

## CONCLUSIONS AND RECOMMENDATIONS FOR CHANGE

Elder abuse is frequently isolated from other types of abuse. An emphasis on family violence can move it out of the larger debate around the causes and consequences of violence in Canadian society. In this chapter, I have argued that these phenomena not be separated. The discussion is informed by a feminist analysis of the power differentials that are embedded in both violent and caring relationships, co-habitants throughout the lives of many women.

A range of exploitation can occur when people are in vulnerable positions, but a preoccupation with types and degrees of elder abuse can distract us from examining those social conditions that promote abusive behaviour and that need to be addressed in policy responses. It is to be expected that our definitions of elder abuse will continue to change as our understanding of it develops. Categories that are useful today may not be so tomorrow; some may even impede much needed policy changes. For example, until recently the concept of wife rape was a legal oxymoron that left married women open to intimate violence. Similarly, it took the revelations of institutional survivors for us to finally digest that sexual abuse is not strictly a family matter, and that it has little to do with male sexuality but has much to do with abuse of power by those in positions of authority. Thus, I suspect that the incidence of abuse reported by elderly people and, in particular, by elderly women will increase as public awareness and redefinitions of it take hold.

When it comes to developing programs to address elder abuse, we seem to be stuck on mechanisms for reporting. What happens next? In a recent report by Health and Welfare Canada (1992) information and referral were the two largest categories of services offered to abused seniors. As do the authors of this survey, I also wonder to whom the referrals are directed, and for what services.

In contemplating future policy directions, the role of shelters in addressing violence against older women should not be ignored. As a response to the needs of battered women these spaces not only provided safety, they became arenas for women to discuss the personal abuse they were experiencing and place it within the larger context of violence in Canadian society. In other words, abused women were encouraged not to split the personal from the political. With the help of peers and counsellors, women were able to evaluate the competing claims being made on them and develop alternatives. Shelters were also the sites where activists worked and strategized to bring about change (Walker, 1990). Although recommended by some authors, like Brillon (1987), an analysis of the function of shelters has not been picked up in the elder abuse literature. Similarly, examples of shelters for older women are scarce. With a few notable exceptions, such as the Maison Jeanne Simard in Montreal, which was specially designated for older women, shelters have been little used as a programme response to elder abuse. Partially this reflects the preoccupation of relatively young shelter workers with the needs of younger women. It may also reflect an assumption that shelters are not viable alternatives for elderly persons. However, the shelter movement in Finland (reported in Wolf & Pillemer, 1989; Hydle, 1989) has made use of beds in nursing homes, while in the United States, group homes have been used as shelters for abused older women.

I am not advocating that shelters are the only solution, but rather outlining why they were so central to addressing the needs of battered women. They are more than a safe haven. The setting allows for input from others who are not part of the abusive situation. Even when an older woman chooses to remain where she is, the increased presence of outsiders can redress power imbalances that flourish in conditions of isolation. Shelters also became nodes for developing support networks that extended into the community. Unfortunately, at the time of writing, examples of such support networks for older women are rare but the Older Women's Long-Term Survival Project in Calgary and the Older Women's Network in Toronto come to mind.

The wife abuse literature suggests other policy avenues. For instance, one of the limitations of police intervention in domestic violence cases was the lack of follow-up in the ensuing days and weeks, whether or not an arrest was made. Immediate follow-up was considered by abused women to be part of an empathetic approach—what professionally we call social support. Heavy case loads meant that it usually did not occur. In addition, abused women have articulated the need for information about their options after the incident. Such information is useful only if it can be provided in language that is understandable and conveyed in terms that are specific to her situation. In situations of elder abuse perhaps using seniors trained to do this work would facilitate crossing the communication barrier.

Finally, this analysis suggests that as we move from documenting elder abuse into developing strategies to control and prevent it, issues of dependency, isolation and stress will need to be clearly defined and addressed. If power imbalances within situations of dependency and stressful working conditions are seen as pre-conditions for abuse in institutions, the same can be said of home care—exacerbated by the factor of isolation. Pressures mounting in home care services need to be monitored. Potentially, home care can be instrumental in alleviating the isolation and stress experienced by certain groups of old persons and their kin carers. But we also need to examine home care policies from the perspective of home care workers. Home care is intended as a program of support, a supplier of concrete resources and services that are delivered within the context of meaningful relationships; relationships that are meant to be empowering to the elderly client; relationships that do not create dependency. There is cause for concern, given that the working conditions of homemakers, the lynchpins in home care services, are under strain. As provincial governments increasingly rely on home care as the primary source of formal help to elderly persons, the size of the home care population and its functional profile is rapidly changing. Shrinking resources result in hospitals discharging patients sooner and in poorer health, into domestic settings where the capacity to provide the type of care needed is highly questionable and the hours available from home care workers are being reduced. In addition, the elderly person and the home care worker frequently come from different cultural and linguistic backgrounds. The situation can become a pressure cooker where elderly persons and their care providers experience, at the personal level, the gender, class and racial inequities that riddle the larger society (Neysmith & Aronson, 1993).

A critical analysis of our understanding of elder abuse is not the end of the story. Research and theory can contribute to transforming the situation of abused elderly people but only within a political climate committed to eliminating the causes of abuse. In the area of violence against women, British policy makers embraced a psychological discourse, but then recommended material provisions. The United States more readily adopted a feminist discourse but were painfully slow to legislate resources for shelters and financial support (Dobash & Dobash, 1992). In Canada, the recent release of yet another report documenting the violence experienced by various groups of women makes recommendations for many of the very resources that have recently been cut. This does not bode well. However, it does underline the importance of not isolating elder abuse from broader discussions of abuse and violence. Social policy needs to address those social conditions that arise out of inequities related not only to age but also gender, class and race. When these intersect in the lives of individuals, social dependency is created which sustains abusive power relations.

## Endnotes

[1] Naming a phenomenon is critical in that it denotes the focus for attention. In the broad area of woman abuse there is considerable variation in nomenclature: Violence against women, wife abuse, wife battering, wife assault, intimate violence, and family violence are some of the more commonly used descriptors. In this chapter I will use the word abuse recognizing that this choice has limitations as well as strengths. On the positive side, the term is broad enough to cover verbal assaults and neglect. Unfortunately, the term focuses attention on the specific act, and the immediate players, that is, perpetrator and victim. While the term suggests that the perpetrator is contravening moral as well as legal and social standards of behaviour, attention is distracted from other social forces that permit or sanction such behaviour. The term violence is often used precisely because it signals a connection between the acts of individuals and the condoning of violence in an array of social arenas.

[2] The author is particularly grateful to Janet Mosher, Faculty of Law, University of Toronto for sharing with her a draft copy of a paper entitled "The Criminal Justice System Response to Wife Abuse" wherein the Canadian and international experience of an aggressive legal response to wife battering is assessed. Many of the references used in this section come from *A Curriculum Package on Wife Abuse for Law Faculties*, developed by her.

# 2-2

# LEGAL APPROACHES TO ELDER ABUSE AND NEGLECT IN CANADA

*Gerald B. Robertson*

## INTRODUCTION

The aim of this chapter is to provide a critical assessment of the various legal responses which have been used in Canada in addressing the problem of elder abuse and neglect. A number of legal models will be outlined, and their strengths and weaknesses examined.

It is important to emphasize at the outset that there are several potential problems involved in developing an appropriate legal response to elder mistreatment. Three in particular should be noted. First, as elder mistreatment continues to receive professional and media attention, policymakers and legislators come under increasing pressure to "do something"—and to be seen to be doing something—in response to the problem. Hence, there is a strong temptation to seek a "quick solution", which so often turns out to be simplistic and inappropriate (McDonald, Hornick, Robertson & Wallace, 1991). As one author points out:

> Once a problem such as elder abuse is recognized by policymakers and legislators, the tendency is to find a quick solution. The elements of the elder abuse problem, however, are varied, delicate, and complex. [Anonymous, 1983, p. 377]

A second problem (in many respects a product of the first) is the tendency of legislators to take legal models from other areas and apply them in the context of elder mistreatment, often without much thought being given to whether the legal transplant is appropriate or likely to be effective. This is most evident in the case of the child welfare model. As is discussed below, this model has had a significant influence on the adult protection legislation which has been used in many parts of North America as the principal legal response to elder mistreatment.

Third, one must be conscious of the danger of viewing a legal response as a panacea for the problem of elder abuse and neglect. The law undoubtedly has a role to play—perhaps even an important one—in addressing the problem, but it is only part of the solution. Without adequate funding, proper support services and programs in the community, any legal response, no matter how appropriate it may seem in theory, is almost certain to fail (McDonald et al., 1991).

## GENERAL LEGAL SAFEGUARDS

### Criminal Law

There are numerous provisions of the *Criminal Code*, R.S.C. 1985, which at first sight appear to afford elderly Canadians considerable protection from mistreatment (McDonald et al., 1991). For example, in the context of physical abuse, there are provisions dealing with offences such as assault, assault causing bodily harm, aggravated assault, unlawfully causing bodily harm, and sexual assault. Likewise with financial abuse, Parts IX and X of the *Criminal Code* provide for offences such as theft, fraud, extortion, breach of trust, and misuse of a power of attorney.

With respect to neglect, section 215 of the *Criminal Code* imposes a duty to provide necessities of life to persons under one's charge if they are unable, by reason of detention, age, illness, insanity or other cause, to withdraw from that charge, and are unable to provide themselves with the necessities of life. A parallel provision is also contained in provincial legislation in many parts of Canada (Gordon & Verdun-Jones, 1992; Robertson, 1994; Steel, 1988).

However, the real problem is not the absence of criminal laws dealing with elder abuse and neglect, but rather the ineffectiveness of these laws in practice. This is true of domestic violence in general, and elder mistreatment is no exception. All too often "practice falls sadly short of theory" (Law Reform Commission of Canada, 1984, p. 37). One of the principal reasons for this is the abused person's unwillingness or inability to complain to the police or to testify in court. Gordon and Verdun-Jones note that:

> A victim may be reluctant to report abuse because of the fear of the consequences for both the victim and the caregiver. The elderly person may have a fear of being removed from home and being placed permanently in an institution, or may experience loneliness if a caregiver is removed. Indeed, tolerating an abusive environment may be more acceptable to the elderly person than the perceived consequences of intervention. [Gordon & Verdun-Jones, 1992, p. 4]

In addition, there may be a reluctance on the part of authorities (such as police and Crown prosecutors) to prosecute, and difficulty in obtaining the necessary evidence to establish guilt beyond reasonable doubt. All these factors result in the criminal law being, in most cases, an ineffective remedy against elder mistreatment (Gordon & Verdun-Jones, 1992; Hornick, McDonald & Robertson, 1992; McDonald et al., 1991; Metcalf, 1986; Sharpe, 1988).

### Powers of Attorney

Recent studies have shown material abuse to be the most common type of elder mistreatment in Canada (Gordon & Verdun-Jones, 1992; McDonald et al., 1991; Podnieks, Pillemer, Nicholson, Shillington & Frizzel, 1990). Particular concern has been voiced by some commentators about the potential for abuse created by enduring powers of attorney. Unlike ordinary powers of attorney, an enduring power does not terminate on the mental incapacity of the donor, and hence it is ideally suited as a mechanism for planning for incapacity. An enduring power of attorney enables individuals, while still mentally competent, to appoint someone to look after their financial affairs after they become incapable of doing so themselves (Alberta Law Reform Institute, 1990a; 1990b; Gordon & Verdun-Jones, 1992; Robertson, 1994). All Canadian provinces (though not the two territories) now have legislation which provides for enduring powers of attorney, the first provinces to introduce such legislation being British Columbia and Ontario in 1979 and the last being Alberta in 1991 (Gordon & Verdun-Jones, 1992; Robertson, 1994).

Because it enables the attorney to exercise authority after the donor is mentally incompetent, the enduring power of attorney represents considerable potential for abuse and exploitation (Alberta Law Reform Institute, 1990a; 1990b). Some commentators have suggested that greater safeguards should be incorporated into the legislation (Gordon, 1992; Gordon & Verdun-Jones, 1992). In the words of Gordon & Verdun-Jones:

> The need for safeguards in the form of some measure of external involvement is reinforced by growing evidence of confusion surrounding the implications of donating an enduring power, marginal practices at the time of donation, the granting of powers to nursing home administrators and other persons in a conflict of interest situation, and various other abuses of enduring powers. [Gordon & Verdun-Jones, 1992, p. 122]

Despite these concerns, Canadian legislation contains relatively few safeguards with respect to enduring powers of attorney. The most stringent conditions are found in Alberta, where the *Powers of Attorney Act*, (1991) provides that an enduring power of attorney must incorporate a series of statutory explanatory notes and must be signed in the presence of a lawyer, who is required to certify that the donor appeared to understand the nature and effect of the document and acknowledged signing it voluntarily (Robertson, 1994). Strict safeguards (including provision for mandatory registration at a central registry) are also contained in the new legislation in British Columbia, which was enacted in 1993 but which has yet to be proclaimed in force: *Representation Agreement Act*, 1993.

## Guardianship

All Canadian provinces and territories have legislation which provides for the appointment of a guardian on behalf of individuals who are mentally incapable of managing their own financial affairs or personal care (Gordon & Verdun-Jones, 1992; Hughes, 1988; Robertson, 1994). Usually this involves an application to the court to have the individual declared mentally incompetent (or, in some provinces, incapable of making reasonable judgments with respect to person or property), with the court then appointing a guardian with the power to make decisions with respect to that individual's person or property or both.

Until recently the guardianship legislation in most provinces was viewed by many commentators as being in need of fundamental reform (Gordon & Verdun-Jones, 1992; Hughes, 1988; Robertson, 1994). Indeed the Supreme Court of Canada has described the legislation as "pitifully unclear with respect to some basic issues": *Re Eve* (1986). One of the principal defects in the law of adult guardianship is its "all or nothing" approach. This means that an individual is perceived as either totally competent or totally incompetent, and if the latter, as requiring a guardian with complete control over decision-making on the individual's behalf. This inflexibility of guardianship legislation makes it especially inappropriate as a response to the problem of elder mistreatment (McDonald et al., 1991).

In recent years, however, several provinces have significantly amended their legislation, including making provision for partial guardianship. This concept recognizes that an individual may need the assistance of a guardian in some areas but not in others. It also embraces the fundamental principles of the "least restrictive alternative" and guardianship "as a last resort" (Gordon & Verdun-Jones, 1992; Robertson, 1994). These changes enable the court to tailor the guardianship order to the specific needs of the individual, while allowing that person to retain as much decision-making autonomy as possible. Alberta, Quebec and Saskatchewan have all moved in this direction, and similar laws have been passed and are awaiting proclamation in Ontario and British

Columbia (Robertson, 1994). The latter two provinces are especially noteworthy for viewing guardianship legislation as one part of a larger, global legal response to the needs of vulnerable adults, encompassing issues such as guardianship, elder mistreatment, enduring powers of attorney, advance health care directives (living wills), and advocacy.

## Abuse and Neglect in Institutions

In recent years there has been increasing pressure from advocacy groups for greater safeguards against abuse and neglect in nursing homes and other institutional care facilities (Gordon & Verdun-Jones, 1992; Hornick et al., 1992; McDonald et al., 1991). One type of legal response to these concerns can be seen in Ontario, where in 1987 the provincial government introduced substantial changes to the *Nursing Homes Act*. Two aspects of this legislation are particularly significant. One is the requirement of mandatory reporting. Section 25 of the Act provides that:

> A person other than a resident who has reasonable grounds to suspect that a resident has suffered or may suffer harm as a result of unlawful conduct, improper or incompetent treatment or care or neglect shall forthwith report the suspicion and the information upon which it is based to the Director.

The other important feature of the legislation is the residents' "Bill of Rights", a concept which is quite common in the United States (Caldwell & Kapp, 1981; Opperman, 1981; Phillips, 1980). Though not without its critics (Rozovsky, 1980; Rozovsky & Rozovsky, 1987), the Ontario Bill of Rights (1990) lists numerous rights to which nursing home residents are entitled, such as the right to be treated with courtesy and respect and to be free from mental and physical abuse, and the right to proper shelter and nourishment.

## ADULT PROTECTION LEGISLATION

### Overview

Many states in the United States have responded to the problem of elder abuse and neglect by enacting special adult protection legislation, which has been heavily influenced by the child welfare model (McDonald et al., 1991). In Canada, the four Atlantic provinces have also adopted this approach (Gordon & Verdun-Jones, 1992; McDonald et al., 1991; Poirier, 1988; Robertson, 1994); starting with Newfoundland in 1973 (*Neglected Adults Welfare Act*, S.N. 1973), New Brunswick followed in 1980 (*Family Services Act*, S.N.B. 1980), then Nova Scotia in 1985 (*Adult Protection Act*, S.N.S. 1985), and most recently Prince Edward Island in 1988 (*Adult Protection Act*, S.P.E.I. 1988).

The underlying aim of adult welfare legislation is summarized in section 2 of the Nova Scotia Act as follows:

> The purpose of this Act is to provide a means whereby adults who lack the ability to care and fend adequately for themselves can be protected from abuse and neglect by providing them with access to services which will enhance their ability to care and fend for themselves or which will protect them from abuse or neglect.

The close connection which the legislation has with the existing child welfare laws can be seen from the statute's definition of "adult". This is defined in such a way as to mean someone who is not a "child" for the purposes of the child welfare statute, thus ensuring continuity between the two pieces of legislation. Hence, in Nova Scotia and

Newfoundland, "adult" means a person aged sixteen years or older, whereas the prescribed age is nineteen in New Brunswick and eighteen in Prince Edward Island (Gordon & Verdun-Jones, 1992; Robertson, 1994).

Though the exact statutory language varies in the four provinces, the underlying themes and concepts are, in large measure, the same. There are, however, some important substantive differences, one of which relates to the scope of the legislation. In Newfoundland, the statute applies only to "neglected" adults, and makes no provision for cases of abuse rather than neglect. Both cases are covered by the legislation in the other three provinces. In Nova Scotia, for example, section 3 of the *Adult Protection Act* defines an "adult in need of protection" as an adult who, in the premises where he or she resides,

1.  is a victim of physical, sexual abuse, mental cruelty, or a combination thereof, is incapable of protecting himself therefrom by reason of physical disability or mental infirmity, and refuses, delays or is unable to make provision for his protection therefrom, or

2.  is not receiving adequate care and attention, is incapable of caring adequately for himself by reason of physical disability or mental infirmity, and refuses, delays or is unable to make provision for his adequate care and attention.

Another major difference relates to mandatory reporting. Both Nova Scotia and Newfoundland impose a *duty* to report suspected cases of elder mistreatment (in Newfoundland, because of the limited scope of the legislation, this applies only to suspected cases of neglect). Under mandatory reporting, every person who has information (whether or not it is confidential or privileged) indicating that an adult is in need of protection must report that information to the relevant authorities. As is discussed above, Ontario also has mandatory reporting with respect to suspected abuse of nursing home residents. In addition, Ontario's new *Advocacy Act*, S.O. 1992, which is expected to be proclaimed in force in early 1995, contains a mandatory reporting requirement. Section 32(11) of the Act provides that information about an individual obtained in the course of an advocate's duties must be disclosed by the advocate to the Public Guardian and Trustee if the advocate has reasonable grounds to believe that the individual is a vulnerable person who is incapable of instructing an advocate, and that there is a risk of serious harm to the health or safety of the individual.

Neither New Brunswick nor Prince Edward Island has a mandatory reporting requirement—in those provinces, reporting is done on a voluntary basis (Gordon & Verdun-Jones, 1992; Robertson, 1994). The new legislation in British Columbia, which is discussed in more detail below, provides for voluntary reporting: *Adult Guardianship Act*, S.B.C. 1993.

The powers contained in the adult protection legislation in the Atlantic provinces are extensive. The adult protection authorities are given wide powers of investigation, including (in certain circumstances) the power to enter the adult's home and the power to have the adult examined by a physician. If the authorities have reasonable grounds to believe that the adult may be in need of protection, an application can be made to the court for an order declaring the person to be an adult in need of protection. The court then has a number of options at its disposal, such as authorizing the Minister to provide the adult with services, including placement in a facility approved by the Minister. The court can also order any person who is a source of danger to leave the premises where the adult resides, and can prohibit or limit that person's contact with the adult.

The parallel between the adult protection legislation and the child welfare model is also apparent from the way in which courts have interpreted the legislation. Courts have tended to adopt an approach which is similar to child protection hearings (Robertson,

1994). The court must first be satisfied that the person is an adult in need of protection. Once this has been established, the court then decides what type of remedy to grant, having regard to what it considers to be in the adult's best interests.

## Criticisms of Adult Protection Legislation

Numerous criticisms have been made of adult protection legislation in Canada and the United States, especially with respect to the utilization of the child welfare model as its underlying paradigm (Faulkner, 1982; Gordon & Verdun-Jones, 1992; Katz, 1980; Lee, 1986; McDonald et al., 1991; McLaughlin, 1979; Anonymous, 1983). Mandatory reporting has been a particular target of this criticism, with many commentators questioning its appropriateness and effectiveness (Gordon & Tomita, 1990; Gordon & Verdun-Jones, 1992; McDonald et al., 1991). Studies indicate that a mandatory reporting requirement does not result in a significant increase in reporting, since most reports are done on a voluntary basis (Faulkner, 1982; Katz, 1980; Lee, 1986). It has also been suggested that if the support services which deal with the reported cases are inadequate (as they often are), "mandatory reporting (even if effective) is at best nothing more than 'case finding', and at worst is simply legislating for the sake of appearances" (McDonald et al., 1991, p. 57). In addition, mandatory reporting may have a negative impact, particularly on how society views elderly people, thus encouraging "ageism" in society (Faulkner, 1982; Krauskopf & Burnett, 1983; Lee, 1986). As McDonald et al. point out:

> Mandatory reporting is based on the premise that the victims of elder abuse are unable to seek help for themselves. Many critics question that premise, and emphasize that one should not assume that older people will not seek assistance if it is available... [E]ven if victims are reluctant to report elder abuse, it does not necessarily follow that others should be required to do so. [McDonald et al., 1991, pp. 57-8]

## The Canadian Charter of Rights and Freedoms

The *Canadian Charter of Rights and Freedoms* (1982) is part of the Constitution of Canada, and affords constitutional protection to certain fundamental rights. For example, section 7 of the *Charter* guarantees the right to life, liberty, and security of the person, and the right not to be deprived thereof except in accordance with the principles of fundamental justice. The rights contained in the *Charter* are, according to section 1, subject only to "such reasonable limits prescribed by law as can be demonstrably justified in a free and democratic society". If a court finds legislation to be an unjustifiable infringement of any of the rights guaranteed by the *Charter*, it may strike down the legislation as unconstitutional, in which case the legislation will be of no force and effect (Hogg, 1992).

It has been suggested that Canadian adult protection legislation may be contrary to the *Charter* (Bissett-Johnson, 1986; Gordon & Verdun-Jones, 1992; Hughes, 1988; McDonald et al., 1991). Citing, in particular, the lack of due process provisions and the vagueness of the statutory terminology, these commentators argue that the legislation infringes some of the basic rights guaranteed by the *Charter* and that this infringement cannot be demonstrably justified as a reasonable limitation. The issue has been considered by the courts of Nova Scotia on a number of occasions, but as yet no clear answer has emerged (Gordon & Verdun-Jones, 1992; Robertson, 1994). In one case, the Act was held not to infringe the *Charter*. *Nova Scotia (Minister of Community Services) v. Carter* (1988). However, in a more recent decision the court held that the Act is "so unbalanced and uncompromising" that it offends the *Charter*. *Nova Scotia (Minister of Community Services) v. Burke*: (1989).

## The New Legislation in British Columbia

A significant new initiative has taken place in British Columbia with the enactment of the *Adult Guardianship Act*, S.B.C. 1993. Based on a discussion paper by a committee comprising both government and community representation (Joint Working Committee, 1992), this legislation was passed in July 1993 but its proclamation into force has been delayed to allow affected agencies to prepare for the new law. The Act (together with the companion *Representation Agreement Act*, S.B.C. 1993, the *Public Guardian and Trustee Act*, S.B.C. 1993, and the *Health Care (Consent) and Care Facility (Admission) Act*, S.B.C. 1993, constitutes a complete revamping of British Columbia law relating to the protection of vulnerable adults. Part 3 of the *Adult Guardianship Act* deals with support and assistance for abused and neglected adults. It is significant that British Columbia has chosen to introduce these provisions as part of an omnibus legislative response to the needs of vulnerable adults, rather than by way of more limited legislation which focuses only on elder abuse and neglect, as in the Atlantic provinces.

One of the most striking features of the *Adult Guardianship Act,* (1993) is its wide definition of "abuse". Section 1 defines "abuse" as:

the deliberate mistreatment of an adult that causes the adult

1. physical, mental or emotional harm, or

2. damage to or loss of assets,

and includes intimidation, humiliation, physical assault, sexual assault, overmedication, withholding needed medication, censoring mail, invasion or denial of privacy or denial of access to visitors.

By comparison, the Act's definition of "self-neglect" is much more circumscribed, being qualified by a requirement that the neglect cause or be "reasonably likely to cause within a short period of time, serious physical or mental harm or substantial damage to or loss of assets" (*Adult Guardianship Act*, 1993, s. 1).

The Act does not impose a duty to report suspected cases of elder abuse or neglect, but instead provides for a system of voluntary reporting. As with the legislation in the Atlantic provinces, the *Adult Guardianship Act* (1993) confers extensive powers of investigation on designated agencies, including the power to apply to the court for an order authorizing the provision of support and assistance if the adult is incapable of deciding whether to accept the services being offered by the agency.

Unlike the corresponding legislation in Newfoundland and Nova Scotia (and, to a lesser extent, Prince Edward Island), the British Columbia legislation has a much higher level of due process protection. For example, under section 54 of the Act, the adult, his or her nearest relative, representative and guardian, and the Public Trustee, must all be notified of any court application, and they are entitled to appear and make representations. Likewise, the application for court-authorized support and assistance must be accompanied by a support and assistance plan prepared by the agency, and it is up to the agency to prove to the court that the adult needs, and would benefit from, the services proposed in the plan. In addition, section 56 provides that the court must choose the most effective, but the least restrictive and intrusive, way of providing support and assistance.

In summary, the new legislation in British Columbia is a significant step in the direction of striking the appropriate balance between, on the one hand, the need to protect vulnerable adults from abuse and neglect, and, on the other hand, the need to respect the right of these individuals to make their own autonomous decisions. The new legislation reflects the following fundamental principles identified by the British Columbia Joint Working Committee in its discussion paper:

- an adult is entitled to live in any manner he [or she] wishes, so long as it can be determined that it is the adult's own decision, and does not cause harm to others;

- society as a whole has a responsibility to offer support to adults who are experiencing abuse, neglect or self-neglect;

- society has an obligation to protect adults who have been found not capable of making decisions about abuse, neglect and self-neglect;

- any intervention undertaken shall be the least intrusive or restrictive in nature, in order to restore power to the adult or effectively remedy the situation in the most timely manner possible, and shall be subject to review and revision as the adult's situation changes;

- there is no justification for abuse. The Criminal Code of Canada will be applied, where appropriate and consistent with the manner in which other Criminal Code matters are handled. [Joint Working Committee, 1992, p. 30]

## CONCLUSION

This chapter has outlined the principal legal models which have been used in Canada as a response to elder abuse and neglect. It is evident that these have a number of serious deficiencies. The model which relies primarily on existing legal safeguards, such as the criminal law, suffers from the problem that these laws are all too often ineffective in practice. The special adult protection legislation used in the Atlantic provinces is open to many criticisms, especially in relation to the requirement of mandatory reporting and the lack of due process protection, and may well be vulnerable to challenge under the *Canadian Charter of Rights and Freedoms*.

What does the future hold as far as possible legal developments are concerned? It seems likely that the recent initiatives in British Columbia will be a precursor of what will happen in other parts of Canada. The criticisms of the special adult protection legislation, both in Canada and the United States, have been so extensive and so severe that its credibility is damaged, perhaps irreparably. Legislators and policymakers probably now realize that the "quick solution" offered by that model is illusory, and that the problem of elder mistreatment demands a more considered response. Once the problem is seen in a more holistic context, as only one part of the challenge of meeting the needs of vulnerable individuals in society, it becomes clear that the appropriate legal response must likewise be more global in its approach. British Columbia may well have shown the path which other provinces, in time, will follow.

# 2-3

# POLICIES REGARDING ABUSE AND NEGLECT
# OF OLDER CANADIANS IN HEALTH CARE SETTINGS

*A. Elizabeth Watson, Christopher Patterson,*
*Sharon Maciboric-Sohor, Adrian Grek and Loreley Greenslade*

## INTRODUCTION

Elder abuse and neglect has become a growing concern for policy makers, practitioners and researchers. Administrators and practitioners in health care facilities have come to recognize that elder abuse and neglect is an important issue in the health care of older adults. In reaction to cases of abuse, some institutions have developed policies and protocols to deal with abuse, including prevention, detection and intervention.

These institutional policies complement macro-level policies that have been developed by professional associations or municipal and provincial governments. Provincial governments have issued white papers on elder abuse and neglect. Governmental agencies in both federal and provincial jurisdictions have a stake in the problem of elder abuse, rendering difficult the development of uniform policies.

This chapter focuses on policies related to elder abuse and neglect in health care facilities such as hospitals, nursing homes and guest homes. Policies will be examined which guide health care and social service professionals who encounter abuse and neglect of seniors perpetrated by friends and family members. Policies which pertain to abuse which occurs within institutions will also be considered. The purpose of this chapter is to outline the need for institutional policies, to propose guidelines for the development of policies in institutions, and to address issues related to implementation, such as problems with detection and competency assessment.

## THE DEVELOPMENT OF POLICIES AND PROTOCOLS

Only a few health care facilities and institutions have developed formal policies for dealing with possible cases of elder abuse and neglect (Glendenning & Decalmer, 1993). For example, the Baycrest Centre for Geriatric Care in North York, Ontario, has developed policies to deal with abuse of patients perpetrated by family members and by staff, as well as abuse of staff members by patients (Baycrest Centre for Geriatric Care, 1994). Some institutions broadened existing policies to cope with residents who have been abused to include older persons. Typically, the initial drive to develop these policies was external to the institution. As different professional groups that work in the health care of elderly people became aware of the problem of elder abuse and neglect, they developed policies to guide their members (Fulmer, 1984; Ontario Association of

Professional Social Workers [OAPSW], 1992; Ross, Ross & Ross-Carson, 1985). Professional guidelines have sometimes become incorporated into institutional policies.

## The Need for Policies on Elder Abuse and Neglect

Any group, agency or institution that provides services to elderly people should be encouraged to develop a policy with respect to elder abuse and neglect that is compatible with their goals and/or mission statement (Mental Health Division, Health Services Directorate, 1993). By definition, protocols are procedures or guidelines supporting the policy that ensure a consistent response to incidents of abuse and neglect.

Such policies and protocols serve three important functions within health care institutions. First, such policies sensitize health care workers to elder abuse and neglect, and promote education in the area. Through education, professionals recognize the complexity of elder abuse and neglect cases. Education draws attention to risk factors which may contribute to elder abuse and neglect cases, the wide variety of social and psychological situations of abused older persons, and the symptoms and manifestations of abuse (see the Kozak, Elmslie & Verdon chapter in this volume for a discussion of risk factors). Protocols should include assessment guidelines to alert workers to aspects of the social, psychological and physical situations of both the abused person and caregiver which may place them at risk for abuse.

The second function of these policies and protocols in health care institutions is to develop a consistent response to cases of elder abuse and neglect. This is particularly important because the most common response to any situation in which there is uncertainty about the required action is no action at all (Social Planning and Research Council of British Columbia, 1989). Although each case must be assessed individually, both health care professional and client should ensure that there is consistency in the steps taken during assessment and intervention. For the health care worker, guidelines should outline steps in psychosocial and health assessment for a thorough examination of risk factors and symptoms, then point to intervention strategies that may be effective in light of these factors. Protocols establish a framework for intervention, and clarify the roles and responsibilities of various workers (Mental Health Division, Health Services Directorate, 1993). From the perspective of persons who have been abused, fears about the consequences of discovery of abuse can be alleviated if they are fully informed on the steps which occur in the assessment and intervention process (Canadian Association of Social Work Administrators in Health Facilities [CASWAHF], 1989). Once abused seniors are made aware of the assessment procedures and the options available for intervention, they can make informed decisions to accept or decline the services offered.

The third function of elder abuse and neglect protocols in health care institutions is to facilitate accurate data collection on this issue. Data collection is important for researchers, practitioners, and administrators. From a research perspective, data collection can provide information on prevalence rates, risk factors, and the effectiveness of various intervention strategies. Collecting and sharing accurate data on the physical and mental health of abused seniors and their caregivers is crucial for practitioners in a multidisciplinary team to ensure effective intervention. Thorough initial assessment should eliminate the necessity for repeated assessments by workers in the various disciplines. Each worker involved in the case could gather the information pertinent to his/her field, without overlapping the data collected by other professionals. For instance, physicians and nurses assess the physical consequences of suspected abuse, while social workers explore the psychological and social conditions which may be the antecedents and/or results of the alleged abuse. Multidisciplinary-team members can discuss aspects of individual cases during team conferences, to reduce both gaps and overlaps in intervention provision. Effectiveness of these interventions can be better evaluated when accurate data are collected (Mental Health Division, Health Services Directorate, 1993). For administrators, data collection provides information on the extent of the problem in their facilities. This helps in the allocation of resources to provide services, and in justifying additional funds to establish programs for abused seniors and their families.

## Formulating Policies and Protocols

The Manitoba Seniors Directorate Guide for the Development of Protocols outlined five steps in the development of policy on elder abuse for institutions: assessing the need for protocols; development of working groups; developing protocols; approval and implementation of protocols; and review process.

### 1. Assessing the need for protocols

This should include a statement of the problem and whether protocols exist in similar service delivery organizations. Review of the goals and current policies of the organization can be helpful, as is conceptualizing policy to meet the mandate of the institution. This involves recognizing both strengths and limitations of the facility in its ability to deal with elder abuse and neglect cases. A facility which has limited resources to investigate or treat cases may be restricted to developing protocols which guide referral of suspected abuse and neglect cases to other agencies.

### 2. Developing a working group

In the development of a working group, professionals from both service and administrative levels should be involved, as well as health and social service professionals from a variety of disciplines. Multidisciplinary teams are often better-positioned to develop that address the complex needs of seniors who have been abused and neglected. Involving professionals from different disciplines in the planning stages promotes understanding of the important roles of the various groups in the detection and intervention process, and fostering trust and respect among those involved in the working group (Hamlet, 1992). Other community agencies could contribute by educating health care professionals on the needs of abused seniors, and on protocols which have been successful in their own agencies (Mental Health Division, Health Services Directorate, 1993).

### 3. Development of protocols

In the social work and nursing literature, protocols have been developed for case-finding in institutions (see Podnieks, 1986; Ross, et al., 1985). Protocols developed for social workers in health care facilities (CASWAHF, 1989) include guidelines for emergency measures, assessment, intervention, and discharge planning. They emphasize counselling abused seniors on assessment and intervention procedures, and involve professionals within the health care facility and community agencies. Instructions for interviewing abused seniors and their caregivers are offered. These include obtaining demographic and health status information, assessing attitudes toward the abuser and the abused senior, and background on the abuse situation.

Quinn and Tomita (1986) developed a protocol for suspected elder abuse in community settings which can also be used in institutional settings. The protocol combines traditional psychosocial approaches, crisis intervention and psychiatric diagnostic techniques, and it involves three phases. The first diagnostic phase includes accepting the referral, case-finding, and initial contact with the allegedly abused senior. During this phase, emphasis is placed on reducing the senior's distress and alleviating fear. During the second diagnostic phase, the allegedly abused senior and the caregiver are interviewed, using scripts and questions which are provided. After psychiatric and physical evaluations are conducted, a tentative diagnosis of the likelihood that abuse has actually occurred is made. During the final phase, intervention is offered, depending on the competency and the consent of the abused senior.

Similar guidelines have been developed in Britain by representatives of social service agencies, the British Association of Social Workers, the British Geriatrics Society, the Police Federation of England and Wales, and the Carers' National Association, as well as caregivers and older adults. These guidelines were designed to help health and social services professionals detect and intervene in elder abuse and neglect cases (Glendenning & Decalmer, 1993). Guidelines focus on education about risk factors, including health, psychological and family characteristics of the abuser and the abused senior. Checklists of physical, social and emotional indicators are provided. Case management for intervention is handled by social workers, who follow a series of steps in data collection, coordination with other professionals, and counselling. These guidelines are intended to be an outline for health care and social service workers in the development of policies and protocols for individual institutions and agencies.

When developing such protocols, several issues must be considered. The protocols must meet the needs or mandate of the institution, while respecting the confidentiality of the abused senior and the abuser. Policy must accurately reflect the resources available to deal with the problem of elder abuse. The policy and protocols developed by an institution that provides health, social and homecare services would encompass a wider range of assessment and intervention options than those developed by a facility with limited resources. Clear guidelines for intervention must be provided, and resources must be in place to carry out the interventions.

## 4. Approval and implementation of protocols

After developing the protocol, approval from the governing board or management may be necessary for formal adoption. An implementation plan can also be detailed by the working group. During initial implementation of the protocol, education of health care and social service professionals is crucial (Hamlet, 1992) to make workers aware of the mechanics of the protocol, and to emphasize the importance of adhering to the guidelines so that elder abuse and neglect cases are met with consistent responses. On-going dialogue is important to share new developments in elder abuse research, and to discuss modifications to existing protocols.

## 5. Review Process

This should include revisions and refinements after familiarization of the organization to the problem of elder abuse and neglect. In most organizations with Quality Assurance Programs, this type of protocol can be reviewed regularly (Glendenning & Decalmer, 1993). This review should also involve health care and social service professionals from a variety of disciplines. Guidelines which are found to be especially effective, as well as those which have been ineffective, should be discussed by all members of the working group. Any difficulties which may have developed in the multidisciplinary teams should be addressed to ensure smooth implementation of the protocols (Mental Health Division, Health Services Directorate, 1993).

# ISSUES IN POLICY AND PROTOCOL DEVELOPMENT

Assessing and intervening in elder abuse and neglect cases requires a high degree of sensitivity among health care and social service professionals. Many abused seniors and their families are afraid or confused, and reluctant to admit to or discuss their abuse (Langley, 1981). Practice issues which are important in elder abuse detection and intervention must be considered when formulating effective and sensitive policy and protocol.

In this section, we examine three issues with regard to policy and protocol development on the topic of abuse and neglect of seniors. The first is the problem of detection and screening for abuse, including the ethics of mandatory reporting. Secondly, we discuss the importance of multidisciplinary teams in policy development and practice. Thirdly, we examine the need to take the perspective and preferences of the abused seniors into consideration when developing protocols and intervention plans. Service providers face many difficulties when assessing abuse and deciding which intervention strategy may be most effective. Many of these problems are outlined in the McDonald, Pittaway and Nahmiash chapter in this volume.

## Detection and Screening

Most of the protocols and policies developed for use by health care and social service professionals include guidelines on confirming cases of elder abuse and neglect, or screening for abuse within the general client population. Typically, detection and screening protocols involve checklists for risk factors for the senior or the caregiver, or lists of physical, social or psychological symptoms of abuse (CASWAHF, 1989; Glendenning & Decalmer, 1993). When preparing such protocols, several issues must be given careful consideration.

Detection and screening for elder abuse and neglect is plagued by three major problems. First, consistency in detection and screening necessitates the use of formal detection tools. Although many such tools have been developed in the past decade, few of these have been shown to be effective in detecting or confirming elder abuse and neglect (see Kozma & Stones, this volume, for a discussion on the problems of detection and screening).

The Canadian Task Force on Periodic Health Examination (1993) examined the evidence on the detection, assessment and management of abuse or mistreatment of older individuals, with a view to prevention. The Task Force concluded that there is insufficient evidence to support or exclude case finding in the Periodic Health Examination (Canadian Task Force, 1993). Although these recommendations may appear counter-intuitive, a review of the evidence concluded that detection is notoriously difficult, and no combination of risk factors has been shown to be sufficiently sensitive or specific to be useful in case finding. A number of elder abuse identification measures have been developed, but many of the items rely on professional judgement rather than objective data, and most have not been empirically tested (Kozma & Stones, this volume; Sengstock & Hwalek, 1987).

The second problem facing policy makers with respect to detection and screening for elder abuse and neglect is the issue of service provision. Callahan (1988) has argued that case-finding and detection of elder abuse and neglect is ineffective without sufficient services and personnel to deal with the cases. Health care and social service professionals may resent detection and screening procedures which increase their workload. Before implementing screening and detection procedures, resources must be in place to deal with the outcomes of such assessment.

The third issue of importance to health care and social service professionals is that of reporting and intervening in abusive situations. Even where there is mandatory reporting for elder abuse, as in the case of many states in the United States, and in the Canadian provinces of Newfoundland, Nova Scotia and Prince Edward Island, health care and social service professionals are often unaware of the legislation, or fail to recognize the problem. It has been estimated that only one in 14 of elder mistreatment cases is reported to a public agency (American Medical Association, 1992). An ethical analysis of mandatory reporting reveals conflict between maintaining confidentiality, potential good and potential harm (Gilbert, 1986; Robertson, this volume; McDonald, Pittaway & Nahmiash, this volume). The possibility of producing harm by an overzealous search for elder abuse and mistreatment must not be overlooked. For example spontaneous fractures occur in elderly people and may simulate injuries incurred by physical abuse (Kane & Goodwin, 1991). The consequences of falsely accusing a caretaker are considerable, and many such incidents have been reported.

From a service perspective, health care and social service professionals may feel a moral obligation to intervene in situations to alleviate or prevent abuse of their older clients. However, such intentions are sometimes thwarted by abused seniors who refuse the services offered. Policies and protocols must clearly outline the role of the health care providers in such cases, within their professional mandates. Guidelines for dealing with abused seniors who refuse services should be offered; recognition of the right of self-determination should be encouraged and "rescuing" of older adults discouraged (Decalmer, 1993; McDonald, Pittaway & Nahmiash, this volume; Mental Health Division, Health Services Directorate, 1993).

## The Importance of a Multidisciplinary Approach to Elder Abuse and Neglect

In elder abuse cases, researchers and policy makers frequently advocate the coordination of health care and social service professionals in the detection and intervention process (Decalmer & Marriott, 1993; Hamlet, 1992; Mental Health Division, Health Services Directorate, 1993; Podnieks, 1988). The Council on Scientific Affairs of the American Medical Association (AMA, 1987) strongly recommends that case management and intervention in abuse cases should involve a team of professionals from multiple health care and social service disciplines. They suggest that a team consist of a primary care physician, a nurse, a social worker, a psychiatrist, a psychologist, a lawyer, a police officer and a case data coordinator. Although little research has been conducted on the effectiveness of these teams, most researchers and practitioners believe that the sharing of knowledge and experience enhances the quality and quantity of intervention strategies that are available to abused seniors and their families (Mental Health Division, Health Services Directorate, 1993).

## AWARENESS OF THE PERSPECTIVE OF THE ABUSED PERSON

### Cultural and Ethnic Differences

Canada is an ethnically-diverse country. However, little research has examined the implications of this diversity for the detection, intervention and prevention of elder abuse and neglect. Differences in the attitudes and beliefs of various groups of older adults, such as new immigrant seniors, aboriginal seniors, and second- or third-generation seniors, influence the definition of abuse and neglect used, and the types of interventions accepted (see McDonald, Pittaway & Nahmiash, this volume). Not enough is known about the ethnology of abuse, but the prevalence and definition of elder abuse may differ from culture to culture, as may the nature of help-seeking behaviour. Moon and

Williams (1993) showed, for example, that elderly Korean-American women were significantly less likely to evaluate scenarios as reflective of elder abuse than were their white and black contemporaries. A choice made from the perspective of one culture with regard to elder abuse intervention may not be considered wise from the point of view of another culture. This issue is becoming more important in the area of abuse and neglect of older Canadians in health-care settings because of the increasing number of seniors from ethnically-diverse backgrounds seeking health care in these settings.

## Competency of the Abused Senior

Elderly people are presumed to be competent adults, capable of making informed decisions about their lives. However, when an abused senior rejects an offer of professional help, a clinical observer may wonder whether the older person is making a competent decision. The question arises because it seems a puzzling and poor choice to remain in a degrading and even dangerous situation, and because incompetence is a possibility commonly raised in clinical encounters with elderly people (Paveza et al. 1992; Coyne, Reichman & Berbig, 1993). The issue of competency is an important one faced by health care professionals (see McDonald, Pittaway & Nahmiash, this volume). At present in Canada, only a licensed physician can issue a certificate of incompetence to manage affairs. The role of the other health care and social service professionals is to furnish the physician with the information required to make such a decision. Policies and protocols developed for health care institutions should include policy statements about the implications of competency based on assessment and intervention strategies, and guidelines on the assessment of competency by members of a multidisciplinary team.

Extreme caution is required before labelling an individual mentally incompetent because the label is laden with value and fraught with sinister implications once pronounced. As a result, such labelling is difficult to call back, and it brooks neither qualification nor contradiction. The clinical determination that a person is incompetent to make decisions should be based upon efforts to understand the context of the situation, and the process by which the person makes such decisions.

Drane (1984) suggested a sliding scale for the assessment of competency to make a decision. According to this view, the less significant the decision, the lower the threshold for a finding of competence. So, for example, choosing to go on living with verbal abuse could be a competent choice, while electing to remain physically abused would not. This is a pragmatic approach as the assessment is with reference to risk to the individual, rather than to a standard of competence per se.

It can be helpful to compare a choice being made by a person in the present with those he or she tended to make in the past, and to gather information about the personal values and beliefs which formerly guided his or her decision-making. Elliott (1991) writes about the "authenticity" of a person's choice in a particular situation or context: if a person's choice is consistent with previous decisions, then it is more likely to be authentic. An authentic choice is not necessarily a competent one, but clinical decisions will be wiser if they are based on an understanding of the preferences that have characterized the person's life so far.

Two necessary features for being competent to perform an activity are that one understands what the activity is and knows when he/she is performing it (Culver & Gert, 1982). To make a competent decision, the person must be able to know that a decision is required, understand the relevant information, weigh the information, the situation, and its consequences, reach a conclusion, and communicate the decision to others (Alexander, 1988; Appelbaum & Grisso, 1988).

Some authorities recommend the use of standardized questionnaires in the evaluation of competence. However, instruments do not yet exist for the assessment of competence to choose a home, or to make decisions if one is facing abuse. The validity and reliability of standardized measures of competency have not been satisfactorily established, and the matter is not helped by the publication of unvalidated modifications of existing tests or scoring systems (Weisstub, 1990).

The ultimate purpose of the evaluation is not to decide the competency level of the person, but to try to bring about appropriate protection and assistance for him/her. The kinds of services that the person needs are determined not only by what he/she cannot do, but by what he/she can do. To the extent that the individual's autonomy can be preserved, this should be done. A detailed evaluation of the day-to-day functioning of the person, in his/her own environment, will help to clarify what protective services are necessary.

If the clinician cannot be satisfied that the person is competent to choose a course that is appropriate to the situation, then there is no resort other than a legal, compulsory solution. In some jurisdictions, this may involve application to the court for appointment of a guardian; in others, or in urgent cases, it may even require committal to a psychiatric hospital for the protection of the person. Even though the person will not voluntarily accept it, the solution proposed should be suited as much as possible to his/her needs, as identified during the evaluation.

# THE ROLE OF HEALTH CARE AND SOCIAL SERVICE PROFESSIONALS IN THE DEVELOPMENT OF POLICY AND PROTOCOLS

## Elder Abuse Cases Detected by Health Care and Social Service Professionals

Health care and social service professionals play a crucial role in the detection and treatment of elder abuse and neglect cases among seniors living in the community (Lucas, 1991; Ross & Hoff, this volume). Abused seniors are often isolated by their families in an attempt to conceal the evidence of abuse. Although health and social service professionals may detect abuse and neglect, family physicians and home care nurses are particularly well positioned to detect abuse among this group, because they are often in regular contact with the older adults. Some researchers (Lucas, 1991; Pratt, Koval & Lloyd, 1983) suggest that, because of the nature of their work, physicians and other health care workers may be more likely than other professionals to encounter elder abuse and neglect in their daily practice. However, physicians and nurses may only detect abuse after it has progressed to the point when symptoms become visible (Bookin & Dunkle, 1985). These health care practitioners, if educated on the risk factors and indicators of elder abuse, may detect abuse during routine visits and provide access to both medical and social services to alleviate the abusive situation. The range of risk factors, and the physical, economic, social and psychological consequences of abuse, are vast and complex (see Kozak, Elmslie & Verdon, this volume, for a discussion of risk factors). To date, educational programmes in health care and social service disciplines have not provided adequate emphasis on the recognition and detection of elder abuse and neglect (Ross & Hoff, this volume).

A variety of health care and social service professionals encounter abused and neglected older persons in their practice. Because of their role in health care provision, each is in a unique position to detect and treat elder abuse and neglect. Each should therefore be involved not only in practice but also in policy development around this issue.

Most institutional policies and protocols focus on the roles and functions of their employees. However, health care and social service professionals involved in the care of people in institutions are not always employees of the institution. Most physicians follow patients before, during and after institutionalization. Referrals to the emergency department for suspected abused seniors are from a variety of practitioners, including public health and home care nurses, private practice social workers, and other health care professionals.

## Physicians

The primary care physician is usually in regular contact with older patients who have multiple chronic illnesses. Ideally, the physician follows these patients through hospitalization and/or institutionalization. With such sustained contact, the physician gains an understanding of the family history and environment of the older adult, such as chronic family stressors which may point to risk of abusive behaviour. Cultural variations in health care and family practices are also taken into consideration. Because of this knowledge, physicians may be in a strong position to detect shifts in health and family functioning which may point to the occurrence of abuse.

Once the possibility of elder abuse is detected, the physician acts as a resource person to social and health services (Lucas, 1991). With appropriate implementation of services to ease the situation of the abused senior and his/her family, the physician can contribute to long-term planning. There is also an opportunity to investigate suspicious injuries and excess or inappropriate use of medications.

Occasionally, ethical problems arise in the detection and treatment of elder abuse cases by physicians. In provinces with mandatory reporting requirements, physicians must juggle these statutes against the confidentiality of medical information (Decalmer, 1993). Conflict of interest situations may arise if both the abused senior and the abuser are patients of the same physician (Noone, Decalmer & Glendenning, 1993). Such issues must be addressed in the policies and protocols of health care institutions.

## Nurses

Public health and home care nurses are often first to pick up the more subtle clues surrounding abuse and neglect as they are often better informed than physicians on this issue (Anderson, 1989). The lack of basic clothing or sanitary supplies, and the observation of the reactions of the elderly person to the family can often give clues to the nature of their relationship. In many physicians' offices or clinics, the practice nurse is the confidant of the older patient. Given the opportunity, this relationship can be quite fruitful with respect to discovering suspected cases of elder abuse.

## Social Workers

In most health care institutions, there are social workers with expertise about elder abuse which may support that of other members of the health care team. Social workers are also aware of the community resources that can deal with the financial and legal aspects of the problem.

## INSTITUTIONAL ABUSE

Institutional abuse and neglect refers to mistreatment perpetrated by staff, other patients, or visitors in nursing homes and other care facilities (American Medical Association, 1992). Institutional abuse of seniors is being recognized among practitioners and policy makers as a problem that warrants separate consideration from abuse which occurs in the community. There are differences in risk factors, in the relationship between abusers and abused seniors, and in policy implications.

Older individuals in long-term care institutions are a particularly vulnerable group who may not complain about abuse because of fear of retaliation by staff, ignorance of their rights as residents, or lack of cognitive ability. Typically very frail and dependent, and often suffering from cognitive impairment, the residents of these long-term care institutions may lack the ability and resources to report, or to take other action against the abuse (American Medical Association, 1992). Staff members may lack adequate training or experience, or may be overburdened because of insufficient staffing or poor supervision. This not only increases the potential for abuse, but also decreases the likelihood that abuse will be detected and treated if it does occur (American Medical Association, 1992).

Broadly speaking, institutional abuse and neglect falls into physical and psychological categories. Sengstock and Hwalek (1990) categorize physical abuse, physical neglect, psychological abuse, psychological neglect, material abuse, and violation of personal rights as aspects of elder abuse that can occur in long-term care institutions.

In one of the few rigorous studies conducted in nursing homes, Pillemer and Moore (1989) interviewed a random sample of staff from 31 nursing homes in New Hampshire (577 nurses and nurses' aides). Physical abuse had been witnessed by 36% of staff in the preceding year; psychological abuse was observed by 81% of the staff. In another survey, carried out among dental practitioners in Canada (Galan & Mayer, 1992), it was revealed that several dentists recognized elder abuse, 37.2% of the abuse having occurred in nursing homes, 49.6% of the abuse having occurred in private homes. These studies indicate that institutional abuse occurs with alarming frequency, and point to the urgent need for policies to detect and treat, as well as prevent, such abuse.

Both structural and personal factors have been implicated in the occurrence of elder abuse within long-term care institutions. Structural factors believed to play a part in abuse in institutions include low pay, and poor working conditions, including long working hours and understaffing (see Neysmith, this volume). The profit motive in proprietary nursing homes has been implicated in causation of institutional abuse (McDonald, Hornick, Robertson & Wallace, 1991).

Personal factors which may contribute to elder abuse include stress experienced by care workers, and aggression by residents toward the workers. Stress among staff is undoubtedly a major factor contributing to abuse. In another study of New Hampshire nursing homes, Pillemer and Moore (1990) reported that 32% of staff admitted that their job was very stressful, 44% stated it to be moderately stressful. One in ten respondents reported that they themselves had committed one or more physical abuse actions in the previous year. Forty percent of staff reported that they had committed at least one act of psychological abuse in the previous year.

Patient aggression was also a factor in elder abuse cases in institutions. A survey of nurses and nurses' aides in 32 long-term care facilities in New Hampshire showed a high frequency of patient aggression toward staff. Almost all of these health care professionals had been insulted or sworn at during the preceding year, and 41% had been pushed, grabbed, pinched or shoved ten or more times by residents. Residents had hit or thrown something at 70% of the staff during the preceding year (Pillemer & Moore, 1990).

## Implications for Policy

Policy and protocols should address both the structural and the personal factors which contribute to abuse of seniors in long-term care institutions. Among ways of addressing the structural factors, protocols should stipulate regular staff training, adequate levels of staffing, clear procedures for investigating alleged cases of elder abuse, and the provision of services to reflect the cultural composition of the residents (Glendenning & Decalmer, 1993). Protocols developed in California include the implementation of random inspections of the care facilities, the development of a patient-satisfaction index to ensure the maintenance of patients' rights, and stiffer penalties for violating guidelines and statutes for the provision of care (Cowell, 1989).

To address the personal risk factors that may contribute to elder abuse in long-term care institutions, policies related to on-going education programs have been advocated. Hudson (1992) describes an 8 module curriculum which requires 6-8 hours to complete. Each module contains a list of objectives, resources and methods, a sample quiz, recommendations to assist trainers in program implementation, presentation notes, a case discussion or an exercise in selected modules. It also includes suggestions for role playing and handouts. A training program was also offered by Pillemer and Moore (1989) to 32 nursing homes that participated in the survey of elder abuse. Given the realities of institutional funding faced by provincial health ministries across Canada, it would seem that the educational approach offers a more practical option to the problem of elder abuse in long-term care institutions, than structural change involving enhanced funding for care.

## SUMMARY AND RECOMMENDATIONS

In this chapter, we have examined the development and implementation of elder abuse and neglect policies and protocols for health care institutions. Such mezzo-level policies should be developed in any institution that provides services to elderly clients.

Policies and protocols serve three important functions within health care facilities: (1) to promote and enhance education of health care and social service professionals on the causes and consequences of elder abuse and neglect; (2) to provide a framework for consistent responses to abusive situations to make service providers and abused seniors more comfortable with the detection and intervention process; (3) to provide means of collecting accurate data on the prevalence and causes of abuse, and on the effectiveness of interventions implemented to deal with this abuse.

The steps outlined to develop such policies and protocols emphasize the need to examine the mandate of the institution, and its ability to deal effectively with abuse cases. Education of the workers in these facilities is extremely important, not only in the initial stages of protocol implementation, but also as an on-going dialogue with workers for additions and modifications to the protocols.

When developing these policies and protocols, it is also important to acknowledge problems with detection and screening. Although poor screening and detection tools hamper accurate assessment, health care and social service professionals must be trained to recognize risk factors and symptoms which indicate possible abuse. Education should focus not only on the recognition of risk factors, but also on any regulations for mandatory reporting and case management once elder abuse is detected. Professionals must be aware of available resources, for cases to be dealt with effectively.

Although expensive, multidisciplinary teams provide the opportunity to share knowledge and case information, as well as share the responsibility for intervention. Options for case resolution are broadened through a multi-disciplinary approach, which allows care plans to be tailored to meet individual needs rather than being limited by the services that one professional group offers. Regular case conferences with representatives from the different disciplines ensure effective case management, facilitate an individual care plan, and address problems faced by the case manager when implementing protocols and coordinating with other workers.

Institutional abuse presents a unique problem in health care facilities. Job stress, overwork and understaffing, low pay, negative attitudes toward older adults, and abuse by residents all contribute to abusive behaviour toward seniors by health care and social service professionals. Faced with reductions in funding, institutions can do little to alleviate the structural factors contributing to abuse. Small improvements in the lives of residents and workers, such as resident and staff councils to voice concerns about infringements of personal rights among both groups, may help to alleviate the stress associated with poor working and living conditions, and help bring about solutions to problems. Alteration of personal factors which contribute to institutional abuse can be approached through education on stress management, modification of negative attitudes, and the responsibilities and expectations of both staff and residents. Frequent, random monitoring may improve detection of elder abuse in health care institutions.

**In summary, we put forth the following recommendations:**

## POLICY DEVELOPMENT

- Each health care institution or service delivery organization serving elderly people should develop policies and protocols related to abuse and neglect of seniors which are compatible with its mission statement and goals. These policies and protocols should include specific data required to refine the protocol and to establish outcomes of specified interventions. Ideally, policies should be developed before cases arise, rather than as "emergency measures" policies once cases are encountered.

## SCREENING AND DETECTION

- The development of effective screening and detection tools to discover cases of elder abuse is a priority. Screening and detection protocols should be implemented in all health care institutions.

## DATA COLLECTION

- In all instances of suspected elder abuse, circumstances of the initial contact should be recorded, as well as the type of intervention offered, whether it was accepted or refused, and the outcome. Many cases of alleged abuse found in institutions require a competency assessment, and the result should be noted. Staff in health care institutions should be encouraged to report incidents of abuse (verbal or physical) by residents to assess interventions. Data collection has important implications for practice, research and administration related to elder abuse in health care settings.

## MULTIDISCIPLINARY TEAM INVOLVEMENT

- Because of the complexity of elder abuse and neglect cases, multidisciplinary teams may offer the best solution to effective assessment and intervention. Practitioners from health and social service professions should be involved in both the development and implementation of policies and protocols.

## AWARENESS OF THE NEEDS OF OLDER CLIENTS

- Policies and protocols must take into consideration the ethnic and cultural composition of the clients and health care and social service practitioners, and its implications for detection and intervention. The protocols should also be sensitive to issues of older persons' rights to self-determination, and of their competency for decision-making on personal issues.

## EMPHASIS ON EDUCATION

- Education of health care and social service practitioners is important in all stages of policy implementation on elder abuse and neglect in health care settings. Education is needed to sensitize workers to elder abuse, to improve recognition of risk factors, to familiarize them with the policies and how to handle abuse cases consistently, and to promote awareness of the perspectives and value of workers in other disciplines to participate in the multidisciplinary team. Education must be relevant and applicable to the work situation, and should be integrated with previous knowledge (see Ross & Hoff, this volume).

## REVIEW OF PROTOCOLS

- Policy and protocol should be frequently reviewed through quality assurance programs to ensure that the policy is meeting the needs and goals of the institution and abused seniors. Analysis of the data collected during assessment and intervention, and discussion within the multidisciplinary team, can suggest ways in which the protocols can be modified to meet the needs of abused seniors more effectively.

# SECTION 3:
# EDUCATION

# INTRODUCTION:

## EDUCATION ISSUES RELATED TO THE ABUSE AND NEGLECT OF OLDER CANADIANS

*Elizabeth Podnieks*

Within the field of aging there is a commitment to developing strategies through which human service providers can increase their knowledge and enhance their skills in working with older adults on the issue of elder abuse and neglect. The need to develop resource materials, information packages, training programs and professional curricula on this topic is a matter of urgency. Health care and social service professionals of all disciplines should have elder abuse as an ongoing subject for updating through continuing education programs for practitioners, educators, and administrators. The training of clergy, counsellors, policemen, legislators, bankers, and lawyers should be a major component in any effort to assist abused older people and their families. Public education should inform lay persons of the scope of elder abuse and its prevention and treatment.

The chapters in this section strive to demonstrate how elder abuse training and education can collaboratively bring community professionals together to educate themselves about this common problem and facilitate the development of cooperative solutions. The first chapter by Podnieks and Baillie discusses informal approaches to learning for older adults in order to prevent elder abuse. There is an emphasis on peer support and self-help. Everyone can be involved in raising awareness of elder abuse, and such concepts as positive imaging should extend across the educational system. Human beings have a history of interactions across the generations and the value of these intergenerational relationships and linkages has been identified. The need for greater recognition and understanding of the value of exchanges across generations is emphasized. The print and broadcast media are encouraged to inform the public of the issues of elder abuse, and also increase their programming about the aging process by including older adults on their production boards. Caregivers, both formal and informal, have expressed their need for training programs, in-service education, and adequate orientation courses, and they want the accompanying benefits of support groups.

The second chapter by Ross and Hoff is on curriculum development for professional education regarding elder abuse. Despite the potential and good will of individuals, the topic of violence against older adults presents a greater than average challenge to most educators and clinicians charged with teaching and role-modelling on this community-practice issue. Besides the usual complexities of psycho-social care, the topic of abuse and neglect is linked to values and structures that touch lifeways and social interaction considered sacrosanct by many. It is these very values and structures that are dangerous to some groups, especially older adults. Consequently, the purpose of this chapter is to provide a guide to curriculum development that assists faculty and others concerned with the prevention of societal violence and the care of abused older people to approach the topic in a manner that is: (1) comprehensive in scope, (2) attentive to survivors' needs, (3) inclusive of new insights uncovered in everyday life and community practice settings, and (4) humane, caring and skilled in professional service delivery on behalf of older adults. The chapter concludes with methods of dealing with personal and professional issues that have contributed to professionals' historic inattention to the needs of abused older people.

These chapters lead the way towards understanding the critical significance of education in addressing the social issue of elder abuse and neglect. Indeed, it is through educational efforts such as described in these two chapters that a broadly-based, collaborative approach to dealing with elder abuse and neglect can be achieved.

# 3-1

# EDUCATION AS THE KEY TO THE PREVENTION OF ELDER ABUSE AND NEGLECT

*Elizabeth Podnieks and Elaine Baillie*

## INTRODUCTION

Focus on elder abuse and neglect is a recent phenomenon in Canada (McDonald, Hornick, Robertson & Wallace,1991; Podnieks, Pillemer, Nicholson, Shillington & Rizzall, 1990). Therefore, efforts to improve public awareness and to educate people about the complex issues involved in this area are also new. Education is not only about acquiring information, it is about changing attitudes, behaviours and values. As such, education is one of the most significant primary prevention interventions in elder abuse and neglect (Gallagher, 1993; Podnieks et al., 1990). It is important that human service and health care professionals (Novak, 1993; Breckman & Adelman, 1988; Fulmer & O'Malley, 1987) as well as family members (Hudson, 1988) have the opportunity to learn about the issues related to elder abuse and its prevention. This chapter describes how, through education, people can effect positive change in the social problem of elder abuse and neglect.

This chapter will focus on formal and informal approaches to raising awareness of elder abuse with respect to several groups of people who can have an impact on this social problem. We will present material on educating professionals, caregivers, older adults, members of the general public and children about issues related to elder abuse and neglect. We will discuss examples of community collaborative methods for all these groups to become involved in the prevention of elder abuse and neglect because we believe that education is the cornerstone to the prevention of this social problem. It is important for all social service and health care professionals to be aware of issues related to abuse and neglect of older adults in the community (see Ross & Hoff, this volume) and in institutions (see Beaulieu & Bélanger, this volume). It is also important for caregivers to know of the warning signs of potential abuse and neglect. Given that older adults are lifelong learners who are able to change themselves, and become agents of change in others (Grams, 1992), it is important to present information that educates them about issues related to elder abuse. Seniors' input must be sought in any plan to intervene in, or prevent, elder abuse and neglect. It is inappropriate to have only professionals with expertise in psychology, medicine, nursing, law and social work and other disciplines deciding what is best for seniors with respect to elder abuse and neglect (see Neysmith, this volume). We also believe that members of the general public must be provided with information about abuse and neglect of seniors because they can also contribute to its prevention. Finally, it is also important for children to know about the issue of elder abuse and neglect in the interest of developing a comprehensive prevention approach to this social problem.

## EDUCATING PROFESSIONALS

Health care and social service professionals are important contributors of care for elderly people who have been abused or neglected. These formal caregivers make a significant contribution to the prevention of further abuse of the elderly people with whom they work. Unfortunately, health care and social service professionals also have been known to contribute to the abuse of older people. For example, Solomon (1983, p. 410) notes that "[h]ealth professionals are a major source of victimization and abuse of the elderly, much of which is secondary societal stereotypes and attitudes held by health workers. Another major source is ignorance." Solomon cites research that shows, however, that attitudes can change and knowledge can be increased through education and training. Sensitizing professionals to their own attitudes on aging, for example, can help decrease negative stereotypes about growing older, and may contribute to the prevention of elder abuse and neglect.

Shell (1982) recommends increasing professional awareness of elder abuse through training sessions and seminars on different forms of abuse and their dynamics. Since then, numerous strides have been made. Increasingly, aspects of elder abuse have been on the agenda of most educational and scientific meetings, conferences and workshops in gerontology and in disciplines related to seniors' health care and social services such as medicine, social work, nursing and dentistry, as well as well as those offered by seniors' organizations. Also, a growing number of articles in professional and scholarly journals for health and social service providers include information on how to detect elder abuse and how to access resources. Such educational materials also contribute to the development of protocols for the assessment of elder mistreatment (see Kozak, Elmslie & Verdon, this volume).

Edinberg (1986) also recommends that health care and social service professionals learn more about the aging process and about cues for detecting potential abuse and neglect situations. Recent work by British gerontologist Michael Davies (1993), while directed toward nurses, includes useful information for all health care providers on this topic. Davies concentrates on the need for training and guidance, particularly in interviewing and assessment skills. He also stresses the importance of a multidisciplinary approach to education on the issue of elder abuse. This approach would include representatives from social work, medicine, nursing and law, and could be both hospital- and community-based (see Watson, Patterson, Maciboric-Sohor, Grek & Greenslade; and McDonald, Pittaway & Nahmiash, this volume). Several professions working collaboratively could produce comprehensive educational packages to inform those providing care for older adults about the potential risks of abuse. Increased awareness of the signs and symptoms of mistreatment will contribute to initiating actions to reduce or prevent an abusive situation for seniors at risk.

In a proactive attempt to prevent elder abuse, with attention directed particularly towards ageist attitudes and behaviours, the Deer Lodge Centre, a long-term care facility in Winnipeg, has initiated several innovative teaching methods as part of their staff orientation and continuing education programs. "The Aging Game," for example, involves a variety of activities simulating some difficult aspects of aging such as sensory deficits, loss of physical independence and financial loss. The aim is to sensitize players to the process of aging and to the effects of inappropriate treatment of elderly people. Playing The Aging Game gives staff a brief personal picture of some aspects of aging. For many, it elicits feelings of anger at being patronized or ignored, and feelings of frustration, anxiety, sadness and withdrawal. Players have commented that the game allowed them to experience inappropriate treatment of older people firsthand; feeling, for example, they were automatically considered frail, incompetent, confused and childlike. The Deer Lodge Centre also has an elder abuse committee that supplements this experiential educational approach by organizing ongoing sessions on abusive behaviour, focussing on staff/resident and resident/staff aggressions.

Health care and social service professionals need more undergraduate and continuing education in gerontology (see Ross & Hoff, this volume). Elder abuse must be an ongoing topic in continuing education programs for practitioners, educators and students. The training of counsellors, policemen, lawyers, legislators and the clergy, among others, is a major component in any educational undertaking to assist abuse seniors and their families.

A survey of professionals from a variety of disciplines (Pennsylvania Elder Abuse Project, 1988, discussed in Fiegener, Fiegener & Mezaros, 1989) indicated they want to learn skills to detect elder abuse and make appropriate responses, referrals and interventions. This project suggests that training should also focus on increasing awareness of the roles various agencies play within the elder abuse network. This may help decrease possible duplication of services. In the same survey, over fifty percent of respondents indicated they had not encountered any cases of elder abuse during the past year. Some of them may have witnessed abuse but may not have known how to identify it. The better we train health care and social service professionals to detect elder abuse, the greater our potential for understanding the nature and prevalence of such abuse.

The education and training of professionals about all aspects of abuse and neglect of seniors is a critical step in the prevention of this abuse. Health care and social service practitioners who come into contact with elderly persons must be aware of their own reactions to aging and to the possibility of abuse and neglect of seniors. The combination of education and experience on the topic of elder abuse and neglect will contribute to skills being developed to readily detect potentially abused seniors, and will lead to ways to alleviate and prevent this abuse.

## EDUCATING CAREGIVERS

*"What is as important as knowledge?" asked the mind.*

*"Caring," answered the heart.*

(Flavia)

Caring for elders at home or in long-term care facilities has consequences for the caregiver that can lead to elder mistreatment (Zarit & Toseland, 1989). It has been suggested that caregiver stress is a risk factor for elder abuse and neglect (McDonald et al., 1991; Benton & Marshall, 1991). In a study of 119 dependent elderly persons and their caregivers, Steinmetz (1988) found that caregivers who perceived caregiving as stressful and burdensome had significantly higher levels of elder abuse and neglect. Caregivers may become abusive because of the overwhelming responsibility of providing care and emotional support to an older adult. Although this idea is not supported by some research surveys (Hudson & Johnson, 1986), there is enough empirical data (Pillemer & Moore, 1989) to lend validity to the inclusion of caregiver stress as a risk factor for elder abuse.

Researchers Kahana and Young (1990) argue the need to examine the complexity of caregiving situations and consider the various situations that are possible with potential negative consequences for both the caregiver and the care recipient. They discuss the diversity of caring and emphasize its dynamic and changing nature. The degree of stress experienced by the caregiver can change from day to day. It is difficult to predict if caregiver stress will lead to abuse and neglect because what is stressful for one caregiver may not be stressful for another (Nolan, 1993).

Training can assist caregivers in managing difficult patient-care situations, in reducing stress and in handling anger, aggression and conflict. Various psycho-educational programs have been developed to reduce the stress experienced by caregivers, and to serve as a primary prevention of potential elder abuse (Smith, Smith & Toseland, 1991). These programs aim to help caregivers improve their coping skills, involve other family members in the care of the older person, understand and respond to the psychosocial needs of care receivers, use formal and informal resources, and ventilate distressful feelings. These programs may also offer counselling to caregivers regarding long-term care placement, and strategies to improve the quality of the caregiver/care-receiver relationship (Smith, et al., 1991).

Lindgren (1993) identifies three caregiving stages as important for developing primary prevention strategies for interventions with caregivers regarding elder abuse and neglect. In this model Lindgren suggests that the process of learning, adapting to role demands and restructuring the caregiver's life evolves around three phases. First is the encounter phase, in which the caregiver needs to adjust to the major life changes and losses that occur as a direct result of caring for an elderly person in need. Second is the underlining phase. This is the long-term, heavy-duty caregiving where coping with everyday stress is the norm, and supportive intervention is needed to prevent the caregiver's physical and mental exhaustion. Third is the exit phase when the caregiver seeks help to reduce her/his burden, either through placement of the elderly person in an institution or by soliciting increased help in the home. It may be helpful to consider these stages in planning programs and counselling sessions to address the physical and psychological needs of caregivers.

Any educational program aimed at caregivers in the home setting should be highly accessible in order to optimize opportunities to participate. Caregivers' attendance at discussion groups on elder abuse and neglect, for example, may depend on the availability of respite care. Timing classes to fit caregivers' schedules would be ideal. Furthermore, many caregivers may have been long out of formal educational situations and may be reluctant to participate in an educational program. It is important in such circumstances to use educational styles that, along with building knowledge and skills, also build caregivers' confidence in their abilities to learn and to provide care (Bane, 1991).

Research shows that women are primary caregivers for elderly people (Horowitz, 1985; Neysmith, this volume). However, the proportion of caregiving by husbands, sons and other male relatives is growing (Stoller, 1990). Therefore, the need for caregiving courses directed to male caregivers, and their special needs, is only now being recognized. Given that Bristowe and Collins (1989), in their British Columbia study, found that male caregivers were significantly more likely to be involved in abusive situations than were their female counterparts, it is important to determine gender differences in terms of the needs of caregivers.

Caregiving courses are currently available across Canada, although not in many rural areas. Efforts are being made to assist caregivers of seniors in remote areas in Canada. These include: radio and TV programs addressing problems related to elder abuse and neglect and how to deal with them; and correspondence courses which may include videos and tapes (e.g. Ryerson University's Open College in Toronto).

Caregiving courses in Canada are typically offered through health and social service agencies, seniors' organizations, community colleges and family service agencies. Caregiving information is also available from Health Canada and provincial ministries for seniors. Church groups, medical faculties, Telemedicine and help lines are other helpful resources. Many local banks, daily newspapers, insurance agencies and an increasing number of companies also provide information about caring for elderly people. People in remote areas may access information through libraries or the visiting nurses association. In northern Canada, the Royal Canadian Mounted Police, who may be a significant contact with family caregivers, should be aware of signs of elder abuse and neglect.

Support groups help in raising awareness of significant issues involved in elder abuse and neglect. Community support groups have become a regular intervention offered to caregivers, be they family members, nurses or health-care aides. A support group can help caregivers maintain their sense of purpose and self-esteem, which in turn may improve their caregiving, decreasing the likelihood of abuse or neglect. Telephone counselling is another supportive intervention for caregivers, and may be easier to institute, and more appropriate, in rural areas than some other interventions (Kinney & Stephens, 1989).

The use of guided imagery to better understand abused older persons can be a powerful exercise for caregivers, professionals and seniors. It can be used in a group setting or with as few as two participants. Breckman and Adelman (1988) describe the process: one participant closes his or her eyes and listens, while the other slowly reads, "Imagine a person you love very much. How do they look when they are smiling? Now imagine this person slapping your face. How do you feel? What are you going to do? Whom are you going to tell? Open your eyes." Participants then discuss their thoughts and feelings. They are offered questions as a guide to discussion. For caregivers, such exercises provide a deeper insight into the emotions and feelings of an abused senior. Abused seniors themselves can be led through a process of change from a life with mistreatment to a life free of mistreatment. According to Breckman and Adelman (1988), there are three essential changes abused people must pass through: reluctance to recognize their abuse, recognition of the fact that they have a problem, and "rebuilding," in which they reshape their identities and seek alternatives to the abusive situation.

For caregivers of elderly people in long-term care facilities and in the community, it is important that educational programs address the issue of abuse brought about by mechanical and chemical restraints used to control behaviour. Educational programs need to provide caregivers with suggestions for less restrictive, less harmful but safe alternatives to mechanical and chemical restraints. Grace Hospital in Scarborough, Ontario has initiated some creative ways of ensuring patient safety without the use of physical, chemical or environmental restraints; for example, beds at floor level. More research is needed on the process of implementing policies of least-restraint. Formats for restraint reduction must be developed and documentation of restraint use must improve (Folmar & Wilson, 1989).

In summary, caregiving has been reported as a pivotal factor in elder mistreatment (McDonald et al., 1991). Education and training of formal and informal caregivers to increase their awareness of elder abuse and to offer support in their diverse caregiving situations is a significant strategy to reduce the potential incidence of abuse of older people. Additionally, educational courses may be useful as part of discharge planning when elderly persons with caregiving needs are released into the care of unprepared or stressed family members. Training programs can be useful adjuncts to caregiver support groups and the relief from stress they can provide may prevent abuse or unnecessary institutionalization (Scogin, Beall, Bynum, Stephens, Grote, Baumhover & Bolland, 1989).

## EDUCATING OLDER ADULTS

The importance of educating older adults about risk factors for elder abuse and neglect and informing them of available resources cannot be overstated. Every educational and training program directed toward elder abuse prevention should be elderly-centered. For example, older people should be asked about their experiences and perceptions of what constitutes abuse. This information should be used in developing educational and training programs to deal with elder abuse. The perceptions of older adults are particularly important as they may influence their help-seeking actions in an abusive situation (Moon & Williams, 1993).

Health care and social service professionals and trained volunteers can help establish support groups for abused seniors, their families and abusers. Support groups for abused seniors might focus on their needs for companionship, affection, encouragement, guidance and help. Such groups can serve as an adjunct to other forms of treatment (Reuveni, 1985). Abused older persons frequently develop overwhelming feelings of fear, isolation and anger. They often can benefit from counselling to regain their independence and strengthen their self-esteem which will enable them to prevent another cycle of abuse. In a national survey (Podnieks et al., 1990), 18 per cent of abused seniors reported that support groups would have been helpful to them.

There are numerous reasons why an abused elderly person would benefit from joining a group comprised of other seniors who have been abused. Many persons, as evidenced by research on other forms of family violence (Wilcox, 1983), become empowered within a supportive group environment composed of those with experience of similar problems. Mutual feedback from others provides problem-solving ideas applicable to their own lives. Support groups are also feasible and affordable. It is not surprising that community support groups have become one of the most frequent interventions offered to caregivers. The "healing circle" is an example of a support group among First Nations people. Group members share their feelings about being abused within their families and receive solace and compassion by meeting others with the same problem. This process helps the older person deal with specific issues related to the abuse, and it also helps to put the abuse in a social context rather than keeping it within an individual context.

In a way similar to a support group, peer counselling brings people together on a one-to-one basis. The abused senior may feel comfortable with a person of his/her own age who is a caring listener and who may or may not have been in a similar situation. Peer counselling often evolves out of support groups which exist in seniors' organizations and social service agencies across the country. An excellent example is the Bernard Betel Centre for Creative Living in Toronto, Ontario.

The American Association of Retired Persons (AARP) has developed an innovative training program that can assist older adults and health care and social service providers to achieve primary prevention of elder abuse. The idea is to train seniors and others in the identification and recognition of signs and symptoms of elder abuse before an incident occurs, rather than after intervention and treatment have taken place. The training program, called "Toward the Prevention of Abuse" (AARP, 1990), takes place in a group setting where participants become both learners and teachers. A facilitator guides the participants through the training in which information about elder abuse is organized into learning units which, after adequate study, attendees teach one another.

The course was initially developed for older persons as a Senior-to-Senior program. However, it can also be a useful tool in the community work of health care and social service providers working with elderly people. The aim of this teaching method is to facilitate learning through group support. One goal of the program is to increase participants' knowledge of the causes and manifestations of elder abuse and neglect. Another goal is to focus on intervention and prevention strategies for elder abuse and neglect. A further goal is to alert each participant to the possibility of his or her own potential vulnerability to abuse or neglect. The modules covered in this training course are shown in Table 1.

## TABLE 1: Toward the Prevention of Elder Abuse *

**Unit A** **General Substantive Introduction**
✔ Elder abuse is a relatively new social problem. People must become aware of it and find ways to prevent it

**Unit B** **Manifestation of Mistreatment**
✔ Definition of active and passive neglect, psychological abuse, material or financial abuse, physical abuse

**Unit C** **Causes of Mistreatment—Clues to Understanding**
✔ Overburdened caregiver
✔ Complexity of individual and family behaviours
✔ Dependent relationships—perpetrator on victim, victim on perpetrator
✔ Isolation
✔ Alcohol or drug abuse of the perpetrator or the victim (or both)

**Unit D** **Vulnerability and Culpability in Domestic**
✔ Mistreatment of the Elderly
✔ Unprepared caregiver
✔ Long-standing interpersonal conflicts
✔ Criminal intentions
✔ Psychopathic or sociopathic behaviours
✔ Unavailable community resources
✔ Changes in circumstances (loss of a job)
✔ History of family violence

**Unit E** **Intervention in Domestic Mistreatment of the Elderly**
✔ Provide support to victim
✔ Older competent adults have right to refuse any or all intervention
✔ Services available to family
✔ Treatment for abuser or criminal charges

**Unit F** **Prevention of Passive (Unintentional) Neglect**
✔ Incapacitation planning by older adult
✔ Identify person of trust to make legal or financial transactions if the need arises
✔ Discuss power of attorney, advocacy

**Unit G** **Prevention of Active Neglect, Abuse and Exploitation**
✔ Reduce isolation
✔ Family members keep in close contact and remain informed about the physical, emotional and financial status of their elderly
✔ Caregivers can acknowledge their own limitations and either seek help or surrender their responsibilities to others who are more appropriate for the task, e.g. professionals
✔ Communities must consider methods of preventing mistreatment, e.g. neighborhood watch
✔ Training programs on home care of frail elderly, on the signs of mistreatment, and on how to provide assistance, referral or intervention

* American Association of Retired Persons (1990) Washington DC. Adapted with permission.

In summary, older adults are excellent advocates for finding solutions to the problems that confront them around the issue of elder abuse and neglect. This does not mean they must act alone when faced with this issue. Health care and social service practitioners can be involved in the education, training and counselling of older adults in order to increase public and professional awareness of elder abuse (Douglass, 1989). However, the formal and informal educational programs for older adults on this issue will, undoubtedly, be more effective if they are developed in partnership with older people themselves.

## EDUCATING THE PUBLIC

Public education is an important aspect of preventing elder abuse and neglect. The general public must become aware of the types of elder abuse, how to recognize the signs and indications, and where to turn for help. Public education campaigns should be geared toward abused seniors and to those in a position to recognize when abuse may be occurring, such as family members, neighbours, friends and public service providers (e.g. postal workers, bank tellers, utility meter readers). Much of the impetus behind the recent increase in awareness of elder abuse and neglect stems from the efforts of community groups, often started by volunteers. Many of these groups develop pamphlets, hold conferences, lobby the media and initiate creative strategies aimed at preventing elder abuse and neglect.

One creative strategy was used in El Paso, Texas, where the Department of Human Services sponsored a poster contest for school children (Texas Department of Human Services). The "Bag Elder Abuse" contest had children decorating 3,000 donated grocery bags with their own picture-messages of the problem of elder abuse, and the local elder abuse hotline number. The children came up with such slogans as "Don't scold the old." The winner was chosen by a committee of older citizens. It portrayed an elderly person walking hand-in-hand with a child and had the message "We need each other" on it. The bags that did not qualify as winners were returned to the grocery store that donated them and were used to bag groceries. The region received considerable publicity for this effort. The day the store used the decorated bags, a local television station interviewed shoppers for their thoughts on the problem of elder abuse. This strategy created considerable public awareness of the social problem of elder abuse and neglect in the community and the state. It also contributed an intergenerational activity which had the potential to prevent abuse and neglect of older people.

In Canada, many excellent public educational tools and materials have been developed to address the issue of elder abuse and neglect. One comprehensive manual was developed by the Seniors' Education Centre, University of Regina. This manual contains, in English and French versions, instruction on how to run a workshop, information about the role of the facilitator, directions for group activities, and supporting overhead transparencies. This manual, with its clearly-presented and organized material, can provide considerable assistance to health and social service agencies and to community groups wanting to carry out educational activities towards greater public awareness of elder abuse and neglect.

Federal and provincial funding of the efforts of community groups working to prevent elder abuse and neglect has increased in recent years. For example, since 1989, seven federal departments have collaborated in a family violence prevention initiative, in which approximately 20% of the $136 million funding is to be spent on elder abuse. As well, abuse task forces have been developing and implementing educational programs for those who work with older adults. For example, the Sudbury Elder Abuse Committee aims to educate the public on what elder abuse is, why it occurs, who is at risk and where help is available. Another example is a pamphlet, *Seniors' Awareness: Elder Abuse: Financial, Physical, Emotional, Criminal*, produced by Cam Jackson, Ontario MPP for Burlington South, for the Halton Regional Police Force Victims Services Unit. It has been widely distributed in Ontario. There still exists, however, a lack of awareness of the resources available to caregivers, family members and abused and neglected seniors themselves. Many communities do have hotlines, distress centres, public health services, visiting nursing services, legal aid clinics, police services, social support agencies and suicide prevention centres which provide public education about elder abuse and neglect.

One largely-untapped community resource for raising public awareness about elder abuse and neglect is religious institutions. Educational programs aimed at faith leaders in churches, synagogues, temples and mosques, among others, could provide impetus for them to alert their members to the issue of seniors' abuse and neglect. Religious leaders could exert great influence on their followers, drawing the attention of congregations to this largely unrecognized problem, calling on them to become more aware of what is happening in their communities. Unfortunately, there is a myth that elder abuse does not occur in religious homes, and religious communities have been slow to respond to the issue of elder mistreatment. Abused older people may seek help from religious leaders and find their needs unmet. Few religious leaders have been trained to work with abused older people and their advice may be limited to theological issues (Pagelow, 1988). In addition, the mistreatment of older people has not been adequately addressed because of the overburdening of faith leaders by the weight of other social problems they face in their religious communities (Friedrich, 1988). It is essential that this group of professionals be knowledgeable about the problem of mistreatment of older people and positive in their approach to its solution.

Religious leaders need training to educate them about elder abuse issues, to identify service roles and to build skills in prevention, intervention and treatment (Friedrich, 1988). Pastoral workers and theology students also should be exposed to educational concepts regarding this problem. In an age of ecumenism and interfaith movements, religious leaders must become a conduit for the well-being and safety of older adults. Conferences, seminars, workshops and counselling are ways by which religious leaders and members of their communities can become more sensitive and informed about elder abuse issues.

The Church Council for Justice and Corrections, an Ottawa-based ecumenical organization mandated to develop public education resources and strategies to help churches address social problems related to the fields of criminal justice, has recently taken a promising initiative with regard to the churches and family violence. In a three-year pilot project begun in 1991, they have worked ecumenically within communities across Canada to sensitize congregations to family violence in their community, and to empower them to act against it. A report on the project is expected early in 1995.

The media, too, can be a powerful tool in raising public awareness about elder abuse and neglect. Yet they often highlight only the most sensational acts of physical violence against older adults. However, the media can be a very positive influence by sending reporters to conferences and encouraging responsible reporting of the abuse of older adults. For example, through newspaper articles, talk show programs and public service announcements and campaigns such as the "Speak out against Violence" launched in 1994 by the Canadian Association of Broadcasters, the media can be influential in calling attention to the issue, and in disseminating information about what to do and where to go in cases of mistreatment. Reporters need to become better informed on the issues, and responsible reporting needs to be encouraged rather than the customary sensational approach to abuse and neglect of seniors. Positive imaging and a greater role for older individuals in the media will also help reduce stereotyping and raise awareness of the substantial issues facing older adults. Through these means, the issues of elder abuse and neglect may eventually become as highly profiled as child abuse or spousal abuse. This would result in greater resource allocation toward solving the problem and contribute positively to its prevention. Finally, in addition to informing current media people on the issue of abuse and neglect of seniors, it is also important to reach journalism and other media students to inform them of the problem of elder mistreatment so they will provide their readers and listeners with sensitive stories and guidelines for action.

There is also a growing urgency for educational initiatives and choices in the media to be developed for, and with, older people (Comer-Calder, 1992). A valuable tool is the Learning Channel on television. This channel offers a rich mix of programs and could be a powerful primary prevention tool, informing both older adults and the general viewing audience on a wide range of topics related to elder abuse and neglect. Multicultural media must also be encouraged to report on events addressing the prevention of elder abuse, such as lectures, discussions and interviews with people knowledgeable about the issue, including elderly people themselves. The media can also be very important in bringing information on issues of elder abuse and neglect to rural elderly people.

The Family Violence Prevention Division of Health Canada has assumed a leadership role in developing and implementing an action plan on media violence (National Clearinghouse on Family Violence Annual Report, 1992-93). Two major issues are addressed: media violence and its effect on children; and the portrayal of women, including older women, and violence against women in the media. Initiatives in this action plan include: production of a short animated piece to promote discussion about the issue of media violence; a television series examining the portrayal of women, including older women, in the media; and a multimedia literacy guide for use in elementary schools to foster critical viewing skills in young children. Although they do not focus on elder abuse as such, by addressing attitudes which underlie our society's tolerance and use of violence in general, these initiatives will help to prevent elder abuse and neglect.

In 1988, the National Film Board produced two excellent documentaries "Mr. Nobody" and "A House Divided", on the various forms of elder abuse, with detailed discussion guides. These are helpful resources for public forums or educational programs sponsored by seniors' groups, religious groups and schools.

Family violence in any form is a community problem. It is not just a burden shared by abused older people and perpetrators; it is not just a problem to be handled by a social agency. The community and the public at large must ensure the security of older adults by raising general awareness and understanding of elder abuse and by providing adequate resources, education and training to empower seniors to seek and accept help when they are caught in a web of abuse or neglect (McDonald et al., 1991).

## EDUCATING CHILDREN

Attitudes and stereotypes are formed early in life and influence behaviour continuously throughout one's lifetime (Maddox, 1988). A major premise in many theories of causality in domestic violence is that violence is a normative behaviour pattern learned within the context of the family. According to social learning theory, children learn from observation and participation within the family that violence is an acceptable response to stress, and they learn a variety of scripts for future violent behaviour (Anetzberger, 1987). Gelles, Steinmetz and Straus (1980) argue that this establishes a cyclical pattern in which each generation learns violent adaptive behaviour from the preceding generation, practises it and passes it on to succeeding generations. These researchers found that exposure to violence as a child is correlated with general approval of violence as an adult.

The importance of influencing positively children's attitudes on aging and older adults cannot be overstated. Sensitizing children to old age and providing opportunities for intergenerational relationships may be critical factors in the prevention of elder abuse and neglect. By including lessons on aging in elementary school curricula, children may develop an increased respect for seniors, may be less inclined to mistreat elderly people, and may even attempt to prevent others from doing so. The hypothesis is that children who understand older persons will have more positive attitudes toward them and will be concerned about their well-being. Curriculum content on aging can be incorporated into relevant class studies such as health, social studies, family-life education and personal safety. The school is a vehicle through which children may learn nonviolent approaches to problem-solving while also learning about the wealth of talent and experience of senior citizens.

Education with an intergenerational focus can also be instrumental in encouraging children to question some stereotypical information which serves to promote conflict between younger and older people. For example, in today's climate of recession and diminishing government funding of social and health programs it has been argued that old and young are being pitted against one another in the political arena, in a competition for government resources (Kingson, Hirshorn & Harootyan, 1987). Elderly people are sometimes portrayed as receiving more than their share of resources. The resultant hostility created between generations may become a risk factor for elder abuse and neglect. It is extremely important, therefore, that this concept of intergenerational conflict not be transferred to children who may then feel resentment toward older adults and not be concerned about their mistreatment.

To address the need for communication and cooperation across generations, many intergenerational programs have been developed in Canada. Teachers, program coordinators and seniors' organizations all describe the value of bringing young and old together to create an enriched learning environment for both (Allred & Dobson, 1987; Dellman-Jenkins, Lambert & Fruit, 1986). Such positive interactions may defuse potentially abusive situations. Intergenerational programs are taking place in the schools, in long-term care facilities and in the community. For example, a creative intergenerational program has been organized by the Council of Positive Aging (COPA) in schools in Thunder Bay, Ontario in which seniors and students prepare topics for public debate. This positive experience has lead the COPA to support a Brief jointly-submitted by the Educational Centre for Aging and Health, McMaster University in Hamilton, Ontario and the Northern Educational Centre for Aging and Health, Lakehead University, Thunder Bay, Ontario to the recent Ontario Royal Commission on Learning, calling for more intergenerational programs in elementary and secondary school curricula.

Primary prevention programs that emphasize the value of children's learning early in life to respect older adults have been developed throughout Canada. Two such programs have been produced in Ontario. "Old Friends," developed by The Ontario Network for the Prevention of Elder Abuse and funded by Health Canada's Seniors' Independence Program, is an interactive story kit for children aged four to eight. While elder abuse is not addressed directly, the book fosters positive imaging of old age and is replete with the wisdom of older people. Another segment of this intergenerational program is the development of a drama kit for youth aged 11 to 14. The kit will comprise two or three plays on elder abuse and will depict cases of elder abuse that young people can recognize and intervene in; for example, a scenario in which a young person realizes that his or her grandparent is being mistreated. The drama kit can be used in schools, nursing homes, summer camps, conferences or seniors' events. Young people can work with older adults in the production and presentation of the plays. At times seniors and young people may reverse their roles so a younger person can walk in the shoes of an older person who in turn can be reminded of what it feels like to be young and always in a hurry. The drama kit will include a video that can supplement the plays or stand on its own.

Another initiative involving youth in the primary prevention of elder abuse is a project currently being developed by T.M.D. Promotions Ltd. of Burlington, Ontario. T.M.D. Promotions produces youth-related educational materials and is now collaborating with The Ontario Network for the Prevention of Elder Abuse to target elder abuse. T.M.D. Promotions is already involved with the Crime Prevention Committee of the International Association of Chiefs of Police and has produced materials on "The ABC of Police," "The ABC of Seniors" and other themes. It is timely that elder abuse should be addressed now. This multimedia project combines interactive CD-ROM, original songs, teacher and student worksheets and lesson ideas, and offers a unique resource for introducing and/or reinforcing knowledge and awareness of elder abuse. The format enhances a variety of skills and disciplines such as language, social studies and interpersonal communications. "The ABC of Elder Abuse" will provide an environment in which students will gain knowledge of the risk factors linked to elder abuse, and how they can become intervenors. This project has been funded by Health Canada's Seniors' Independence Program. It will serve to strengthen relationships between seniors and youth in the prevention of abuse and neglect of elderly people (T.M.D. Promotions Ltd., 1994).

Educating children about elder abuse and neglect must be recognized as a necessary primary prevention strategy. Through educational programs on the topic of abuse and neglect of seniors, young people can be encouraged to work toward the prevention of this social problem. Such programs and experiences for children will foster positive attitudes and a concern for the safety and well-being of older people, at the same time as contributing to increased intergenerational interaction.

## CONCLUSION AND RECOMMENDATIONS

This chapter has emphasized the need for education directed toward the prevention of elder abuse and neglect. From early childhood through old age, the need for education about, and sensitization to, the issue of elder abuse and neglect is an important component leading to the prevention of this social problem. As indicated in this chapter, a great deal has been accomplished in terms of education for professionals, caregivers, older adults, the general public and children on the topic of elder abuse and neglect. However, there remains much to be done to prevent the abuse and neglect of older adults in Canada. In closing, a list of general recommendations and specific needs about education is presented below in the interests of making an impact on the prevention of elder abuse and neglect.

## General Recommendations

1. improve efforts to educate all members of the general public about the social problem;

2. increase awareness of the resources currently available to caregivers and elderly people;

3. provide comprehensive educational programs for those responsible for elder care, and for others in a position to detect elder abuse and neglect; and

4. develop an ongoing evaluation of the effectiveness of educational programs concerned with the prevention of elder abuse and neglect.

## Specific Needs:

- develop more theory-based educational materials

- present in-service education for all levels of staff in long-term care facilities

- introduce educational programming on elder abuse and neglect in school and university curricula

- encourage media coverage that promotes positive imaging of elderly people and provides responsible coverage of the issues surrounding elder abuse and neglect.

Increased public and professional understanding of the problem of elder abuse will result in the development of more preventive educational programs that will lead to a reduction in—and eventually, we hope, the elimination of—the abuse and neglect of elderly people. The material in this chapter is a contribution to this important goal.

# 3-2

# EDUCATION OF HEALTH PROFESSIONALS: INTERDISCIPLINARY CURRICULUM GUIDELINES RELATED TO ABUSE AND NEGLECT OF OLDER CANADIANS

*Margaret M. Ross and Lee Ann Hoff*

## INTRODUCTION

The purpose of this chapter is to provide guidelines for educators of health professionals regarding the abuse and mistreatment of older Canadians. Underlying assumptions regarding curricula development include the need for relevance and accountability to critical sectors of society. However, despite increasing acknowledgement of the reality of elder abuse, for the most part issues related to abuse of older adults are addressed only incidentally, rather than systematically. Both practice and research literature provide evidence that health care workers face difficulties with problem-solving and decision-making regarding situations of actual or potential elder abuse (Philips & Rempusheski, 1985; Ross, 1988). There is little consensus about what actually constitutes abuse of elderly persons. Incidence and prevalence data are imprecise, theoretical explanations embryonic and service delivery models few in number and, generally, devoid of evaluation (McDonald, Hornick, Robertson & Wallace, 1991). Even the well-informed practitioner has limited direction and support in the struggle to assess and intervene in situations where the physical, emotional or material well-being of older adults is at stake.

It is crucial that all who work in health care develop a heightened awareness of older adults as possible victims of abuse. Equally important is an understanding of the social and political inequities experienced by older persons and an appreciation of the values that perpetuate power differentials within personal and professional relationships. These concerns demand a commitment by educators to the systematic preparation of students regarding prevention and detection and the development of effective intervention on behalf of older Canadians at risk.

This chapter addresses these issues in four aspects of professional education: 1. Theoretical and Contextual Issues, 2. Elements of Curriculum Development, 3. Core Content, 4. Implementation Issues and Methods, Although focussed on health professionals, the chapter is also relevant to policy analysts and human services administrators. Without progressive policies and administrative structures supporting curricular guidelines, health professionals will confront additional obstacles in their work with older Canadians, despite their education-based competency.

## THEORETICAL AND CONTEXTUAL ISSUES

The approach taken in this chapter places the abuse of older adults within the context of social acts of violence with far-reaching effects on personal and public health, for which perpetrators are morally accountable (MacLeod, 1989; Health and Welfares Canada, 1991; Yllo & Bograd, 1988). Such violence is learned in a milieu permeated with social inequities based on age, ethnicity, gender, and images of physical and emotional force as the dominant method of conflict resolution. Accordingly, we avoid the term "family violence" because it obscures the socio-cultural roots of abuse that extend beyond the family to deeply embedded cultural values and traditional social structures which particularly disempower women and older persons (Hoff & Ross, 1993; Hoff, 1995). Family violence is also inadequate for addressing abuse in and out of institutions by therapists and other professionals.

In an era of increasing longevity coinciding with global fiscal crises, public expectations are moving towards increased "family" responsibility for caregiving. It is important to make explicit the fact that women perform most of this unpaid work. If support resources are lacking, this public policy issue places both givers and receivers of care at risk. Finally, this chapter assumes that service and educational approaches emphasizing the principles of Primary Health Care are well-suited to situating professional practice in the realities and complexities of the older person's experience. Such principles include the maximum participation of older adults in identifying their needs and making decisions about the types of services that will best meet these needs; and accessibility to responsive, user-friendly and cost-effective services. Needed also are educational approaches that go beyond traditional models and improve prospects for enabling older adults to increase control over their situations and thus improve the quality of their lives. In addition, it is crucial that the use of technology (including the use of medication) for both institutional and community-dwelling older adults and inter-disciplinary and inter-sectoral collaboration among health care providers be improved. The challenge for educators lies in developing curricula that are relevant to the social and political realities of older adults and include approaches to ensure the systematic sensitization of learners to these realities.

### Why Health Care Curricula?

Health care professionals are in an ideal position to contribute to prevention, detection and effective intervention in situations of potential or actual abuse against older adults. Because of their numbers, the variety of their practice locations and the nature of their practice, health care workers are in close contact with a large segment of the elderly population at risk for violent episodes. They work in emergency rooms, outpatient clinics, private practice offices, acute and chronic-care institutions, community health clinics and public health departments. Most importantly, they also work in people's homes. Health care workers are often the first line of contact with the health care system and are, therefore, in a position to mobilize resources and initiate intervention. The scope of professional practice, including front-line intervention, education and research, is congruent with primary, secondary and tertiary levels of prevention (Podnieks, 1985).

At the primary (health promotion) level of prevention, health care workers are in a strategic position to engage in educational programs that heighten public and professional awareness of abuse of older Canadians. They can participate in establishing policies and procedures that protect the rights of such individuals within community and institutional facilities. They can also engage in research aimed at determining the antecedents and consequences of inter-personal conflict and violence, testing the validity and reliability of assessment tools and evaluating clinical interventions for their efficacy in solving problems associated with the prevention of violence against older adults. At the secondary (treatment) level of prevention, health care workers are in a unique position to establish screening programs for elderly individuals at risk, participate in the medical treatment of injuries resulting from violent episodes and coordinate community services in an effort to provide continuity of care. At the tertiary (rehabilitation) level of prevention, they can facilitate the healing and rehabilitative process with ongoing counselling to individuals and families. They can also provide support to groups of survivors and individual older adults who strive to achieve their optimum level of safety, health and well-being. Reasons for health professionals' failure in preventive and responsive care for older abused people lie, in part, in their inadequate preparation for these tasks. This means that health workers so affected must be provided with continuing education opportunities to compensate for deficits in their initial training.

## Current Educational Initiatives

Until recently, the inclusion of content on violence in general, and elder abuse and neglect in particular, has not been a major focus of health care curricula. Increasingly, however, medical and nursing educators in particular are attempting to address elder abuse and neglect as a public health issue. Building on public health education approaches, medical and nursing educators are paying more explicit attention to the topic in their teaching. For example, the Ontario Medical Association has approved "Curriculum Guidelines for the Medical Management of Wife Abuse for Undergraduate Medical Students." The Department of Community Services in Halifax has developed "Procedures for a Co-ordinated Response for Victims of Family Violence." This document illustrates the work of a task force at Dalhousie University School of Medicine established to address the issue of abuse and violence in society as it relates to children, spouses and older adults. Its terms of reference include recommendations at the undergraduate, post-graduate and practising physician level for improving understanding, skills and attitudes. Although there is less evidence of such initiatives in dentistry, occupational therapy, physiotherapy, and other health professional programs, seminars and lectures are generally provided as the subject comes up (Hoff, 1995).

With respect to nursing, a curricular initiative at the University of Ottawa School of Nursing has resulted in the production of a "Curriculum Guide for Nursing: Violence Against Women and Children" (Hoff & Ross, 1993; Ross & Hoff, 1994). Within a framework of essential knowledge, skills and attitudes, the guide emphasizes the centrality of social, political and gender issues in shaping not only the experience of survivors of violence, including older adults, but also the professional response of nurses. Although funded by the Ontario Ministry of Colleges and Universities specifically for nursing, this document has been reviewed and extended for application by other health care professions under the auspices of the Family Violence Prevention Initiative of Health Canada. An interdisciplinary guide entitled "Violence Education for Health Professionals" (Hoff, 1994), developed from this project and directed to health professionals throughout Canada, underscores the central factor that violence in all its forms, and as it affects all age groups, is the business of all health care workers. This Guide provides curriculum direction for specific health care disciplines, as well as illustrations of how members of interdisciplinary teams work collaboratively on behalf of survivors of abuse. During the development of this Guide, it was revealed that one of the most demanding challenges of health care educators is to assist students in grounding themselves securely in their respective profession without losing sight of the increasingly important team approach to multi-faceted issues such as abuse and mistreatment of older adults. Also, survey and focus group data from these two curriculum projects revealed that the topic of elder abuse received the *least* systematic attention among all the categories of abuse addressed (Hoff & Ross, forthcoming). This finding mirrors the widespread neglect of issues affecting older Canadians in society at large. The following section focusses on two major characteristics of professional education that provide the context within which curriculum development and implementation related to abuse and neglect of seniors need to be addressed.

## Key Features of Professional Health Education

Professional education embodies features that make it unique among educational environments. These features, which provide the structure within which curriculum development and implementation occurs, include the centrality of experiential learning to teaching and learning and the integration of content from a variety of disciplines.

### The Centrality of Experiential Learning

Much of the knowledge associated with the health professions is generated from interaction with individuals, families and groups in a variety of institutional and community-based settings. Such knowledge, which is embedded in practice, accrues over time in the practice of an applied discipline (Benner, 1984). Students encounter patients and clients, engage in decision-making and carry out tasks and interventions under the supervision of specialists in education and practice. Expertise develops by testing and refining propositions, hypotheses and principle-based expectations in actual practice situations. Within the context of such experiential learning, it is crucial that students have the opportunity to learn the clinical culture and get to know the personnel involved. It is also crucial that the experiences selected for students have the potential of revealing the concepts that students are expected to learn and that they have the opportunity to test out in practice their knowledge and skill with respect to these concepts. Consequently, with respect to abuse of older adults, it is important that students have the opportunity to encounter in their practice older persons who are survivors of violence or are at risk of being abused. In this way, students in medicine, nursing and physiotherapy, for example, could learn about possible abuse histories if they implement routine screening for all injured and emotionally-distressed older patients whose explanations do not correspond with their symptomatology. Such encounters should move beyond traditional health care settings such as health departments, physicians' offices and acute care hospitals and include individuals' homes and institutions such as homes for the aged, nursing homes, dental offices and chronic-care facilities. Dental hygienists, visiting nurses and occupational therapists, for example, are in key positions to detect, intervene and/or refer in community-based settings. In situations where this extension of field experience is impossible, it would be appropriate for educators to invite older survivors of abuse to share their experience with students in classroom settings so students could learn about the dynamics and traumatic results of abuse by entering vicariously the lives of mistreated older Canadians. By doing so, they can empathically capture the realities of abuse from the perspective of abused seniors themselves. It would also be important for educators to use learning resources such as videos, films and self-directed learning packages that are increasingly appearing on the market.

### The Integration of Content from a Variety of Disciplines

Students bring to health care curricula knowledge from the biomedical and psychosocial sciences and the arts and humanities. They also bring varying levels of professional knowledge and degrees of critical analysis. Students are supported in their learning by peers, teachers, and health care personnel who help them relate to, and cooperate and collaborate with, others in the provision of care. Throughout their program of learning, selected courses, content or concepts from other disciplines are sequenced so as to be relevant to the dimensions of the health profession being studied at any point in the curriculum. Although it is beyond the scope of this chapter to discuss all the content required by health professionals to respond appropriately to older adults in actual or potentially abusive situations, suffice it to say that without a sensitivity to the political reality of devaluation of older adults and a knowledge of the health and social consequences of advancing age, students will be at a major disadvantage in their practice, and health care of older individuals will be severely compromised. In addition, given that abuse of older Canadians is in large measure, although not exclusively, a women's issue, students must have the opportunity to analyse and discuss gender issues. Finally, since no single discipline holds the key for solving the problems and meeting the needs of older adults who enter the health care system (Estes & Close, 1993), the principles of interdisciplinary training must continue to be integrated into curricular initiatives related to abuse of older adults (Hoff, 1995).

## ELEMENTS OF CURRICULUM DEVELOPMENT

This section focusses on issues that will ensure that abuse of older adults is considered in a manner that is systematic and comprehensive with respect to the education of health professionals. Discussion centres on the nature of curriculum change, the development of a conceptual framework, the determination of content, and the essential knowledge, attitudes and skills required for the provision of care to older adults who have been mistreated or are at risk of abuse.

### Curriculum Change

Curriculum change ideally is ongoing and reflects the fluctuation in problems, values, and issues among those who are served, in this case, older adults. The inclusion of content related to violence must be systematically included in health care curricula and at various levels of practice if future practitioners are to have the knowledge, attitudes and skills to better serve abused older adults. In most schools focussing on the education of health professionals (Hoff & Ross, forthcoming), societal violence is addressed in some way, ranging from reading journal articles to several hours of classroom instruction. Its coverage in clinical instruction to date, however, is more incidental than planned. In strategizing to move from incidental to systematic coverage of victimization and abuse of older adults in the context of already overcrowded curricula, it is important to consider the principles of academic freedom, including theoretical pluralism and diverse methods for achieving curriculum goals. Curricular change, however, cannot be legislated and can only occur to the degree that faculty members are committed to, and involved in, the change. Furthermore, it cannot be assumed that all faculty members will have the knowledge and skill to deal with content on abuse and neglect of seniors. Rather, experts in the field may have to play a key role in initiating inclusion of the content and in providing assistance to faculty members as they move toward increasing competence with the topic. Involving seniors, experts in gerontology and women's studies, and community activists who are, in large measure, responsible for the current attention being paid to violence against children, women and older adults, is an important strategy for bringing about curricular change that is relevant to the realities of older persons' lives.

## The Development of a Conceptual Framework

Curriculum design involves developing a framework within which disparate topics, empirical studies and theoretical explanations can be linked. The challenge lies in combining areas that reflect different degrees of abstractness, level of analysis, and sophistication in theory and practice. An analytical framework that is eclectic, interdisciplinary and draws on concepts from gerontology, sociocultural analysis, crisis theory, victimology, life event research and feminist scholarship is proposed. Such a framework will ensure that although the substantive focus will be dynamic and changing, a consistent theoretical approach will be applied. In addition, an inclusive framework ensures that issues are not seen exclusively from more traditional perspectives such as pathological models which focus their placement of abuse within the context of personality dysfunction. Abuse of older adults cannot be understood and responded to effectively until health professionals take into account such sociological and political factors as increased longevity, patterns of frequent migration across vast geographic regions, poverty, ageism, unequal access to care, and other social and political consequences of aging.

## The Determination of Core Content

The principles of relevance, applicability, integration and diversity provide guidance for the determination of content on the topic of abuse and neglect of seniors for students in the health professions.

### Relevance

Health care workers live in a pragmatic world. Concepts are useful, insofar as they provide direction and make a difference in one's ability to practice. For example, students must understand the dynamics of traumatic stress, the particular vulnerability of disabled or frail older persons, and the criteria and strategies for routinely assessing victimization trauma in clinical practice settings. Consequently, concepts that are selected for inclusion must be based on both theory and practice. While theoretical concepts contribute to knowledge of a phenomenon, practice-based concepts facilitate the application of knowledge. This is important with respect to the topic of abuse and neglect of seniors.

### Applicability

Concepts must be presented in ways that clearly demonstrate their application to practice. For example, when concepts related to power and control are presented with their empirical referents or dealt with by showing how power relationships are played out differently in different settings, their application to the clinical situation is more readily revealed. Thus, an abused senior who is dependent financially, physically and emotionally for care, will usually be reluctant to disclose or acknowledge abuse for fear of retaliation and further abuse in these unequal power relationships. Health professionals must have communication skills to elicit disclosure about these sensitive issues while also attending to issues of legal reporting and respect for privacy.

### Integration

Given the integrative nature of professional education, it is crucial that concepts related to violence against older adults be linked to other concepts from the biomedical and psychosocial sciences and the humanities. For example, the power disparity cited above must be grounded in sociological theory regarding age, class and gender relations and social change strategies. Such concepts cannot be dealt with in a vacuum and must also be considered within the context of social and political realities.

## Diversity

Professional education occurs in a variety of settings and at varying levels. For example, nurses are prepared in both community college and university settings and at the diploma, baccalaureate, master's and doctoral levels. Physicians are prepared in a variety of practice areas. In addition, in-service and continuing education programs for health care workers are on-going in most health care facilities. Consequently, curricular initiatives must include concepts, methodologies and resources that have utility for diverse programs and levels of professional practice. For example, dental hygienists and pharmacists are concerned primarily with detection, prevention and referral; whereas family physicians', nurse practitioners' and social workers' roles include follow-up treatment and family-based counselling as well.

## CORE CONTENT

Core content refers to the essential knowledge, attitudes and skills required to work with older persons who have experienced abuse or are at risk of violent events. A core curriculum encompasses those courses or learning units required of all students graduating from an educational institution, without which the educational goals would not be met. The content presented here is excerpted from the results of a consultation and review process with interdisciplinary panels across Canada (Hoff, 1995).

## Knowledge

There are two broad categories of essential concepts that health care professionals must master: 1) concepts explicitly concerned with violence against older adults and its physical and mental health implications, including the controversies surrounding research findings about abuse and neglect of older persons (Phillips, 1989; McDonald, et al., 1991); and 2) concepts related to violence that are already addressed in the curriculum, but which require explicit elaboration for their relevance to the prevention of abuse in later life and the appropriate response to such violence. For example, concepts like stress, trauma, primary prevention, crisis, social change, and cultural variation are not unique to specific disciplines or the care of abused older adults. Their inclusion here is to emphasize their particular importance to this population and to adapt established curriculum content to the specific needs of abused older persons who are affected by violence. Key concepts relate to the theoretical underpinnings of health status and health service delivery. These include the problem, incidence and sociocultural context of elder abuse, issues related to prevention and protection, and concepts related to clinical practice.

### The Problem, Incidence and Sociocultural Context

Epidemiological data and demographic correlates of violence and victimization such as age, sex, class, race, sexual identity, physical ability/disability, immigration status and geographic location are central to a comprehensive understanding of the phenomenon of elder abuse. It is also crucial that students learn about the intersection of violence with economic disparity and other disadvantages such as those based on age, ethnicity and gender relations. A knowledge of family dynamics, role theory, sex-role stereotyping, gender relations and power disparities including feminist analysis and social change theory is a pre-requisite for students to situate abuse of older adults within the larger context of power relationships underlying violent situations and episodes. Concepts related to multiculturalism, cultural relativism and cross-cultural patterns and differences in violence, victimization and healing are also needed to respond appropriately in situations that are different from those that health professionals bring to their learning and clinical practice. The phenomenon of stigmatization and bias, and its potential for creating a climate that activates violence potential toward people who are old is also an important aspect of knowledge related to the sociocultural context of elder abuse.

### Prevention and Protection

Knowledge of the principles of primary, secondary and tertiary prevention is central to the prevention of violence and protection of older persons from abuse as well as to the appropriate response of health professionals to older survivors of violence. In addition it is crucial that health professionals are well-versed in the ethical and legal issues (e.g., legal protections, limits of legal restraint, mandated reporting, duty to warn potentially abused seniors', rights and accountability of defendants) that serve as the underpinnings of health care practice aimed at the prevention and amelioration of elder abuse.

### Clinical Concepts

The prevention of, and response to, situations of elder abuse involves an understanding of the dynamics of abuse, including social, cultural, economic, psychological, behavioural and biophysical ramifications and an understanding of the intersection of violence and victimization with substance abuse, physical health status, depression, suicidal risk and other mental health sequelae. Students in the health professions must appreciate fully the experience of traumatic stress and its implications for self-esteem, health and well-being. They need to be knowledgeable about the criteria for identifying survivors of abuse in health and social service entry points (triage) and for assessing victimization trauma and the potential for episodes of violence to escalate to homicide. The theory behind crisis intervention and social support strategies for survivors of abuse, families and assailants, including appropriate referral to community-based resources is also central to appropriate action on the part of health care professionals in their response to older survivors of violence and abuse.

## Attitudes

Deeply embedded beliefs/attitudes regarding aggression create a context in which individuals facing conflict and stress can readily turn to violence as solutions to problems in diverse situations affecting the health and safety of older adults. If students in the health professions are expected to prevent abuse of older adults and intervene on behalf of abused seniors, a first step in education is to provide opportunities to deal with normal aging, as well as to develop a sensitivity to the political reality that older people in contemporary Western societies are generally devalued. Since health care professionals are influenced by the dominant values that have spawned and exacerbated the plight of survivors, values clarification is critical to their formation as professionals contributing to the care of society's abused seniors. A second underlying assumption is recognition by faculty members and clinical preceptors that the traditional stance assuming professional objectivity or neutrality in the face of issues like violence no longer hold. Feminist and multicultural critiques of the scientific enterprise make clear that scientists and health professionals are not immune from the values of the culture in which they reside, teach and practice (Hoff, 1988, 1991; Keller, 1985; Oakley, 1981; Rosser, 1986). The principle of acknowledging the influence of values and ideology applies in health care practice generally and with respect to societal violence, including that perpetrated against older adults. A survey of Ontario's Schools of Nursing, however, underscores the particular challenge of examining attitudes and values in regard to abuse of older adults. Survey findings revealed striking parallels between the topics addressed in nursing education and societal responses to abuse of older adults. Compared with child abuse and wife battering, abuse in old age had the least coverage and was the only topic covered by more than one respondent in "reading only" (Hoff & Ross, forthcoming). This finding parallels the more comprehensive response of society to abused children and battered women when compared with abused older adults. Compared with knowledge and skills, attitudinal content, which necessitates a major departure from deeply held values regarding older adults and elder abuse, presents the greatest challenge for both teachers and learners.

## Skills

Essential skills required in implementing strategies for the care of abused seniors include the techniques of crisis management, that is, identification, assessment (including victimization trauma and the risk of suicide and/or violence toward others), planning, implementation, and evaluation. Students, however, must be cautioned against the singular use of crisis intervention as a strategy, since older adults' problems tend to be multiple and interrelated, tend to take longer to solve and need to be monitored closely (Ledbetter & Hancock, 1990). Other skills required by students in the health professions working with elderly people who have been abused include communicating by listening actively, questioning discretely, responding empathetically, and advising and directing appropriately. In addition, teaching older adults how to assess assault/homicide potential in domestic and other situations; educating people how to recognize symptoms of abuse, name the problem and its source; and avoiding self-blame are important skills for health professionals. Furthermore, it is crucial that students in the health professions learn to advise abused older persons of their legal rights and link them to legal resources which will avoid the traditional practice of re-victimization. They also need to learn to mobilize safety, legal, and community resources effectively (e.g. arranging admission to a shelter; finding translators for immigrant older Canadians; providing support for caregivers as a means of preventing abuse of home-bound older persons) and to implement agency policy regarding mandated reporting, keep accurate records, so that records cannot be used against an abused senior, but rather can possibly aid later legal action and use the consultative process, i.e., knowing whom to call under what circumstances, and in fact doing it. Finally, students in the health professions need to learn to complete the steps of crisis management and follow-up referral while withholding judgment and not imposing values on the abused older person and her or his significant others; implement health promotion and illness prevention strategies and work with community organizations such as seniors' groups and women's groups.

The effectiveness of these strategies in preventing and detecting elder abuse and intervening in situations of actual abuse depends upon attention to three additional considerations for health professionals: 1) they must gain a comfort level in communicating with older people (as discussed above); 2) they must recognize the particular complexities of assessing mental competence in old age; and 3) they must realize that many older adults have legally placed their general welfare and financial assets in the hands of the people who may be the source of risk.

## IMPLEMENTATION ISSUES

It is one thing to acquire the knowledge, attitudes, and skills required to provide humane and effective care to abused older people. It is quite another for students to act effectively by applying the knowledge gained in their professional education to the workplace. This requires considering two related issues: the personal abuse or violence histories of students and health care workers, and inequity and violence in the workplace.

## The Personal Abuse or Violence Histories of Students and Health Care Workers

Since the incidence of physical and/or sexual abuse among the general female population is high (Russell, 1990; Statistics Canada, 1993), and since the majority of students in the health professions and health care workers are women, it is probable that abuse histories exist as well among students and faculty. In addition, there may be many of these individuals who are currently in abusive situations themselves. It is also probable that trauma from such abuse may never have been worked through and that potentially disturbing content may trigger unanticipated responses. For such individuals, barriers may surface that preclude their effective interaction with older adults who are in similar situations of abuse. Students in the health professions should receive, early in their education, an introduction to potentially disturbing topics such as violence and their possible connections to their own personal histories. Such an introduction may motivate a student to seek counselling for belatedly uncovered problems that have not been resolved. When such an approach fails, crisis intervention and referral by faculty for distressed students is appropriate; on-going counselling is not. Health educators must build into health service and other personnel programs for students, clinical staff and faculty members opportunities for disclosure of abuse histories and accountability for possible abusive behaviour. Such programs include peer support and self-care strategies as important pre-requisites for preparing people to provide service to older persons who are have been abused.

## Inequity and Violence in the Workplace

Another issue affecting the delivery of health care to abused older people concerns unequal power and status among workers within the health system. While women constitute the majority of health care workers, this majority is not reflected in their personal autonomy with respect to patient care and decision-making. It is certainly true, for example, that nursing as a profession has made remarkable gains during the past few decades. Nevertheless, there is considerable evidence that nurses are still regarded (and some regard themselves) as second-class citizens within the health care system (Cox, 1991a). A reality of the workplace that continues in large measure, is that others define the work of nurses and other women (Hall, 1993). These women workers are socialized to expect interruptions from patients, physicians and administrators and are expected to develop strategies for coping. They are ordered to care, but the structures and values, in fact, prevent them from caring as they are taught (Reverby, 1987). In caretaking situations for older adults, the majority of direct service providers are women with minimum levels of education and salaries, who are already stressed with the burden of most unpaid domestic work. Frail older persons may be at risk of physical and financial abuse by such over-stressed workers, who may be socially disadvantaged themselves. All health providers of older adults, whether technical or professional, regardless of explanations that may be offered, must be held accountable for their abusive behaviour while administrators and policymakers attend simultaneously to alleviate workplace conditions that place older adults at risk. Curriculum development should attend to these realities. A broad-based analysis in all professional education must recognize the inherent connections among the devaluation of women generally, women's work in particular, the traditionally subordinate status of female dominated occupations (Keddy, 1993) and the care of older adults.

There are increasing reports of violence in the workplace. Sexual harassment occurs at relatively high rates in health care settings, particularly among female health care workers (Grieco, 1987; Silverstein, 1991; Stockard, 1991), and students (McComas, Hebert, Glacomin, Kaplan & Dulberg, 1993). Physicians continue to be a source of verbal abuse of nurses (Cox, 1991b). In psychiatric settings, where the incidence of physical attacks by patients against staff is generally higher, and in nursing homes, the most vulnerable staff members are female nursing assistants, often women of colour, and definitely the lowest paid group among the hierarchy of direct care staff; professional nurses are the next most frequently injured, and traditionally higher-status staff least often injured. Despite an increase in programs to facilitate the management of aggressive and assaultive behaviour on the part of cognitively-impaired older adults and others, there is a lack of administrative attention paid to the prevention of assaultive behaviour, and protection and compensation for injuries incurred when such behaviour occurs. Health professionals cannot provide optimal care unless they themselves feel safe as they carry out their responsibilities on behalf of older adults.

## IMPLEMENTATION STRATEGIES

There is no best way to implement curricular change with respect to abuse and neglect of older people. It is important, however, that the introduction of the subject into the curriculum take place in concert with an exploration of students' own attitudes and readiness to cope with the content. It is also important that early in their education, students' attention is focussed on the prevailing social norms which tolerate, and perhaps legitimate, the forms of oppression that are manifested in physical and other acts of violence against older adults. This approach offers a counterbalance to courses which introduce students to violence as an aspect of mental illness or a by-product of alcohol and substance abuse. In addition, curricula should emphasize the goals of developing critical thinking and experiential learning (Bevis & Watson, 1989; Knowles, 1980).

Methods for curriculum implementation are varied and include the use of formal didactic sessions and small informal group seminars, workshops and tutorials. Traditional approaches involve the use of single and/or optional courses. While this method may be particularly attractive in situations where curricula are already overcrowded, it has disadvantages for students who do not have the theoretical or practical grounding to cope with the content. Furthermore, the use of optional courses does not address the need to ensure the systematic coverage of content with all students. The "curriculum thread" approach corrects some of the disadvantages of the single course, however, it presents a major requirement of total faculty involvement and vigilance to avoid "losing the thread" somewhere along the line. A series of short courses representing a middle ground between the single course and the curriculum thread, offers a compromise. These courses could focus on particular components of core content (knowledge, attitudes and skills), levels of practice (introduction, elaboration and synthesis), and setting of practice (community, hospital, nursing home). A problem-based learning approach, which is used in some Schools of Nursing, can present essential content in the form of required case studies that are dealt with in small groups with tutors and through clinical experience in diverse settings. This approach has the advantage of being learner-centred and interactive. In addition, problem-based learning is highly accessible for continuing education programs where time is at a premium. Discussion of actual cases of elder abuse is another method to expand exposure to assessment and intervention dilemmas. Medical rounds and case conferences with health care workers in hospitals provide opportunities for reviewing situations where older adults are being treated for abuse (Trilling, Greenblatt & Shepherd, 1987) and afford rich opportunities for learning. Whatever the methods, it is crucial that students be provided with a basic library of bibliographic, audio-visual and clinical protocol resources dealing with the best research and clinical material available on the topic. It is to be hoped that the next generation of health care providers will have the knowledge, attitudes and skills to effectively advocate on behalf of older adults, particularly those who have been abused or who are at risk of abuse or mistreatment.

## A FINAL NOTE

The issue of abuse or mistreatment of older adults is highly complex. So too are efforts to ensure that all health care workers have the knowledge, attitudes and skills required to prevent abuse and intervene sensitively and effectively where abuse has occurred. This chapter has taken the position that for health care curricula to be relevant and accountable, abuse must be situated within the context of the violence in our society which is rooted in deeply-embedded values and structures that are disempowering, particularly of women and older adults. The curriculum model presented focusses on experiential learning and the integration of content from a variety of disciplines. This model also details the essential knowledge, attitudes and skills required by health professionals who work with older adults. The chapter concludes with methods of curriculum implementation and a plea that systematic training regarding prevention, detection and effective intervention become a priority for all charged with the education of health care professionals who work with older adults in both community and institutionally-based settings.

# SECTION 4: RESEARCH

# INTRODUCTION:

## RESEARCH ISSUES AND FINDINGS IN THE ABUSE AND NEGLECT OF OLDER PEOPLE

*J.F. Kozak*

Violence between individuals in situations based on trust is all too common in North America. It has been estimated that one in eight women in a relationship is abused by her partner, and that Canadian physicians feel they identify only 50% of abused women in a family practice setting (Ferris & Tudiver, 1992). A recent study from the World Health Organization (Belsey, 1993) reported child (under 5 years old) abuse and neglect estimates to be between 13 and 20 per 100,000. Robinson (1981) reported that there are more than 8,000 cases of physical abuse of Canadian children every year, with child neglect involving more than 80,000. As in the early history of spousal abuse, professionals have been late in recognizing that abuse and neglect of seniors also occurs between individuals in a trusting relationship.

The purpose of this section is to explore research conducted in abuse and neglect of the elderly both in Canada and elsewhere. Its goals are:

1.  to evaluate the current status of Canadian research

2.  to understand Canadian research in the context of international research efforts

3.  to explore and recommend future directions of research.

The first chapter by Michael Stones explores the complexity behind the definitions of abuse and neglect. Stones argues that the definition is, in essence, phenomenologically-based; that is, we define the problem according to our own professional and personal perspectives. For research in this field to be meaningful, there must be consistency in the definitions of abuse and neglect.

In the second chapter, Albert Kozma and Michael Stones examine the measurement of abuse and neglect. Current assessment tools are divided into two large categories, clinical scales and survey instruments, and the authors stress the need to distinguish between the two. Their review points out that screening and assessment tools have typically been developed by practice-based workers, with little attention paid to establishing the psychometric properties (reliability, validity, and generalizability) of these instruments. Some promising work has started to address this problem in Canada. In reading the authors' discussion of qualitative and quantitative research, the reader should bear in mind that the definition of these terms is discipline-specific. For example, what a psychologist would define as qualitative research may be different from that defined by a cultural anthropologist.

The chapter by Kozak, Elmslie and Verdon examines the epidemiological research on abuse and neglect of seniors. In the first section of their work, the authors focus on the definition of prevalence and incidence as well as factors that greatly affect the validity, reliability and generalizability of research findings. The authors point out that the epidemiological research conducted to date is limited in establishing the magnitude of abuse and neglect of seniors in Canada and elsewhere.

The last chapter, by Charmaine Spencer, focuses upon the outcome evaluation research in abuse and neglect of seniors. The author notes that the development of abuse intervention programmes has relied on past experience and anecdotal evidence of success and failure. Severely impeding the development of intervention programmes and their evaluation of outcome is the lack of objective definitions and measures of success or successful intervention. As noted by the author, the removal from harm of an abused senior through hospitalization may be a "success" for the professional, but not for the senior. This may partially explain the findings that a relatively large number of seniors refuse assistance from agencies.

In all, Canadian research in the field of elder abuse and neglect is just as rigorous and problematical as in the United States and elsewhere. Our ability to progress depends on the sharing and marshalling of efforts by seniors, professionals, communities, governments, public and private funding agencies, and the mass media. The development of standards and guidelines for dealing with elder abuse and neglect, and the development of community-based models for the prevention of abuse and neglect of seniors is closely linked to research on this topic. These four chapters contribute significantly to our understanding of current research on abuse and neglect of seniors.

# 4-1

## SCOPE AND DEFINITION OF ELDER ABUSE AND NEGLECT IN CANADA

*M.J. Stones*

### INTRODUCTION

The purpose of a definition is to provide meaning. An impediment to progress in research on elder abuse and neglect is the imprecise or inconsistent use of definitions (Podnieks, 1990). The reason is that the meanings differ among vocational and interest groups. When the police speak of elder abuse, they mainly refer to violations against criminal law. Social workers and health professionals have a broader perspective, partly because of their work in administering the adult protective legislation enacted by Canadian provinces and American states. Workers in home care and homes for the aged (and other institutions) have policies and procedures intended to prevent the abuse of residents. Researchers and advocates for seniors have the widest frame of reference of all. Elder abuse for them is not limited to behaviour regulated by the law, or by professional ethics and workplace standards; instead, they include, within the scope of elder abuse and neglect both what the constructs *do* and *should* include. But what is the meaning of elder abuse to seniors—the only group directly at risk? Ironically, the professions often prefer to speak for seniors rather than allow them their own voice; at least, this is the impression a scan of the professional literature conveys. Journal articles are largely without reference to the wisdom of seniors about elder abuse.

The academic and professional literature contains three main approaches towards meaning and definition of elder abuse and neglect These approaches differ not only in intent but also in their products, which do not necessarily reflect the underlying intent. The first approach comprises *connotative* definitions that attempt to specify the full meaning of elder abuse. Such definitions ought to provide a conceptual base for the construct validation of tools. Second, *structural* definitions make reference to the different kinds of criteria used to evaluate abuse. Their main use is to promote effective communication among different professional and advocacy groups. Third, *denotative* definitions simply cite examples of abuse. They have the potential to guide the development of screening and survey tools.

This chapter will show that the products of the three approaches have different properties: (1) connotative definitions emphasize the consequences of abuse for the recipient; (2) those based on structural criteria cite the multiple meanings of abuse; (3) denotative definitions elaborate upon the behaviour of the instigator. The following pages review the three approaches.

## CONNOTATIVE DEFINITIONS

Connotative definitions attempt what proved difficult to accomplish: to provide a comprehensive meaning of elder abuse. This aim, although laudable, may be infeasible because the meanings differ depending on who does the defining and for what purpose. An outcome of trying to be too encompassing may be a product with diluted meaning and sacrificed precision. It is for such reasons that many researchers find connotative definitions to be unhelpful when developing tools for measurement.

Most connotative definitions include up to four components, only two of which are truly substantive. The components comprise (1) destructive behaviour, (2) against someone older, (3) within a trust relationship, (4) that causes unnecessary damage (Abdennur, 1990; Hudson, 1991; Johnson, 1986; O'Malley, Everitt, O'Malley & Campion, 1983; Phillips, 1983). The two substantive components, about which there is wide agreement, refer to the age of the recipient and the context of a formal or informal trust relationship (Hudson, 1991). The less substantive components refer to destructive behaviour and unnecessary damage. In contrast to the structural and denotative approaches, connotative definitions neglect to describe destructive behaviour in terms that are independent of the outcome. In other words, behaviour becomes classified as destructive *because* any resulting damage is unnecessary. It is the damage, rather than the precipitating action, upon which such definitions elaborate. Some examples follow:

- acts ... that jeopardized the well–being or safety of the elderly individual (Phillips, 1983);

- a state of ... suffering unnecessary to the maintenance of the quality of life of the older person (Johnson, 1986);

- destructive behaviour ... within the context of a relationship connoting trust ... of sufficient intensity and/or frequency to produce harmful ... effects of unnecessary suffering, injury, pain, loss and/or violation of human rights and poorer quality of life (Hudson, 1991);

- action/inaction jeopardizing health or well-being (British Columbia InterMinistry Committee, 1992).

If connotative definitions are neglectful about what destructive behaviour comprises, the notion of unnecessary damage is imprecise. Such imprecision creates more problems than it solves. First, allowance must be made for individual differences in damage thresholds—behaviour that damages one person may not harm another. Second, the different kinds of damage require reduction to a common metric when making assessments (e.g. physical injury, mental anguish, financial loss, loss of rights). Third, to show causation between abusive behaviour and damage is sometimes difficult. For example, although psychological abuse can cause misery, many people mentally suffer anguish before or without abuse. Fourth, harm may take overt or threatened forms, with threatening behaviour causing no overt damage but still being an offense in law. Issues such as these are difficult to resolve and relegate most connotative definitions to a category of impractical definitions.

## STRUCTURAL DEFINITIONS

Structural definitions provide answers to the following question: against what criterion is a behaviour judged to be abusive? Without criteria that are explicit, miscommunication may result. Take the example of cohabiting seniors, the dominant of whom swears regularly at a spouse under care. Such behaviour is unlikely to result in police action because cursing in the privacy of the home is not a crime. Social service workers may express concern, but any action taken will likely depend upon the limits imposed by adult protective regulations. Researchers appear to have no doubt that repeated swearing is abusive, with such behaviour incorporated into their survey tools (Pillemer & Finklehor, 1988; Podnieks, 1990). Advocates may similarly construe excessive swearing as violating socially-accepted standards.

Miscommunication can arise from a mixing of criteria. Pillemer and Finklehor (1988) reported a 14:1 discrepancy between abuse rates with a survey tool compared to cases opened by state agencies. The extent to which this discrepancy is due to differences in the criteria used *versus* underreporting to the authorities is an open question. Effective communication requires either the use of consistent criteria when making comparisons or acknowledgement that comparison may be inappropriate if the criteria differ.

Structural definitions are compatible with jurisprudence, which refers to the philosophy and logic—not the letter—of the law. The main categories of criteria include *laws*, *regulations*, and *beliefs* about abuse. Stones (1994) incorporated these standards into the definitional scheme reproduced as Table 2 in Kozma and Stones, this volume. The definition given for elder abuse is as follows: "Behaviour [by someone in a trust relationship] contravening legal standards, regulated professional or workplace ethics, and what are believed to be community standards of tolerable conduct" (p. 4). Pillemer and Bachman=Prehn (1991, p. 52) gave a similar but more restricted example for patient care: "Any deviation from socially accepted (including regulatory or legal) standards for patient care carried out with the intent of harming a patient".

Pillemer and Bachman–Prehn (1991) raise the difficult issue of intent, about the relevance of which connotative definers cannot agree (Hudson, 1991). The logic of the structural approach offers a resolution to this problem. The law specifies an offense to occur if a prohibited act is committed. However, different levels of offense include acts known or known likely to produce specific harm (e.g. striking, stealing), prohibited acts resulting in unanticipated harm (e.g. injury arising from neglect), and acts prohibited despite intent (e.g. exerting undue influence). These distinctions, respectively termed *primary*, *secondary*, and *tertiary* offenses, relate intent to the level of an offense, not to whether abuse took place. Consequently, abuse becomes defined simply as *a misdemeanour against acknowledged standards* (e.g. the law, vocational ethics, advocacy standards), while intent relates to *the severity of judging that misdemeanour.*

Compared to connotative definitions, structural definitions offer a more incisive rationale for identifying and classifying abusive behaviours. The approach is also consistent with what happens in practice, where the different professions (including advocates) often have their own criteria. Disagreement over what makes up abuse largely occurs when these criteria fail to coincide. However, providing rules is only a stepping stone towards developing tools. Subsequent progress requires a specification of those behaviours prohibited by the respective criteria. The scope of this task falls within a denotative framework.

## DENOTATIVE DEFINITIONS

Denotative definitions of elder abuse simply list examples. A problem with existing attempts to provide classification is that the main categories of abuse, and the examples within categories, lack uniformity. For example, Tomita (1982) included within a category of psychological abuse the examples of yelling, insulting, threatening, silence, social isolation, and infantization. Sengstock and Hwalek (1987) narrowed the range to include only verbal assault and threats not involving a weapon. Sengstock and Hwalek (1987), but not Tomita (1982), included within their definition a category of violation of personal rights. Clearly, any tools based on these two definitions would contain different content.

Stones (1994) reported the first systematic attempt to derive a denotative definition using both practitioners and seniors as respondents in a construct validation design. The first stage included the compilation of a comprehensive inventory of elder abuse and neglect items from the literature. Second, added to this inventory were further examples derived from thirty focus groups conducted with institutional and community-dwelling seniors. Third, the inventory was piloted using thirty seniors and the wording revised where necessary. Fourth, 572 representatively-sampled practitioners and seniors rated all 112 items of the revised inventory for severity of abuse. Fifth, those items rated by 80% or more of respondents as definite examples of abuse were retained for the final stages of the procedure. These stages included the classification of the retained items into content categories by a practitioner, a researcher, and a senior, and an independent check on the reliability of such classification. The product was termed the *Elder Abuse Survey Tool (EAST)*, comprising 71 items that were reliably assigned to nine categories. The content of the *EAST* provides a systematically derived denotative definition and is reproduced in Table 1.

## CONCLUSIONS

As stated previously, attempts to define elder abuse and neglect succinctly but comprehensively met with frustration (i.e. connotative definitions proved unsuccessful). Structural definitions more usefully convey the general meaning of abuse and neglect by acknowledging the diversity of the criteria against which abuse and neglect are evaluated. The simplest of such definitions is given by Stones (1994) as follows: *A misdemeanour against acknowledged standards by someone a senior has reason to trust.* However, structural definitions may not readily translate into tools for research. For such purposes, a denotative framework is required. The most systematically developed denotative framework is that given by the *EAST*, which contains 71 items grouped into nine categories.

# TABLE 1:    Examples of Elder Abuse and Neglect

| Content category | Exemplars of abuse by a person having a trust relationship with a senior | Content category | Exemplars of abuse by a person having a trust relationship with a senior |
|---|---|---|---|
| **Physical assault** | Causing pain or physical or emotional damage by: Hitting, Throwing something hard, Tripping, Burning or scalding, Bathing in cold water, Pushing or shoving, Rough handling, Unwanted sexual acts, Spitting | **Humiliating behaviour** | Forcing a senior to eat unappetizing/ unwanted food, Treating a senior like a servant, Treating a senior like a child, Withholding information of importance, Failure to check allegations of elder abuse |
| **Excessive restraint** | By means of: Alcohol or tranquilizers, Tying to furniture, Forcing a senior to remain in bed, Locking in a room | **Abuse in an institution** | Failure to: Provide a clean environment, Serve appetizing, nutritious food, Provide prerequisites for personal cleanliness, Provide sufficient bathroom space for privacy, Provide sufficient space for personal privacy, Provide adequate personal care, Treat residents of different financial status equally. Excessive: Use of physical restraints, Use of medication to control residents |
| **Putting health at risk** | By: Leaving an incapacitated senior alone too long, Withholding food or other necessities, Unnecessary or traumatic medical intervention, Incorrect administration of prescribed medicines, Overprescribing medications, Inadequate effort medical attention due to age, Exposing a senior to undue risk or danger, Buying alcohol for a senior who often gets drunk | **Material exploitation** | Theft, Selling property without permission, Controlling money matters against a senior's will, Charging excessively for goods or services, Refusing to move out of a senior's home if asked, Opening mail without permission, Failing to repay borrowed money when asked, Sharing a senior's home without paying fairly for expenses |
| **Failure to give care by someone acting as a paid or unpaid caretaker** | Failure to: Facilitate access to medical care, Enable access to aids or assisting devices, Provide personal care, Turn a bedridden senior frequently, Take a senior to necessary appointments, Remain with a senior who needs help, Provide necessary clothing, Take a senior on (at least occasional) outings, Provide adequate nutrition, Provide safe and comfortable conditions | **Verbal humiliation** | Excessive criticism, Lying, Swearing, insulting, calling names, Unreasonably ordering around, Telling a senior he/she is too much trouble, Talking unkindly about death to a senior, Unkind statements about a senior to other people, Statements that convey false beliefs about illness |
| **Undue pressure** | To sign legal documents or those poorly understood, To prevent access to legal help, To move from or relinquish ownership of the home, To buy alcohol or other drugs, To engage in paid work to bring in extra money, Not to seek help for abuse of alcohol/ drugs, To make or change a will, To change or not to change marital status, To give money to relatives or other caretakers, To do things the senior doesn't want to do | | |

# 4-2

# ISSUES IN THE MEASUREMENT OF ELDER ABUSE

*Albert Kozma and M.J. Stones*

## INTRODUCTION

Two sources of information were used in evaluating current measures of elder abuse and neglect: the level of consensus about the nature of the abuse construct and the psychometric properties of current measures. Our approach led to the identification of two conceptual frameworks with distinct implications for the evaluation of abuse measures.

Frequently used, published measures fell into two general classes: Clinical Scales and Survey Instruments. The former class was subdivided further into Screening and Classification Instruments. Screening measures were primarily evaluated on the basis of their ability to correctly identify abused individuals, while classification and survey instruments were also rated on their adequacy to represent postulated abuse components.

Threats to validity arise from inadequate standardization and unknown psychometric properties of the measures, and from differences in verbal comprehension among abused seniors, from fear of retaliation, and from an embarrassment over suffering abuse from a family member. The best way to improve current measures of abuse and neglect of seniors is to use adequate standardization procedures. For screening instruments, evidence must show that the measures can adequately discriminate between abused and non–abused individuals. For classification instruments (including surveys), an additional requirement is that the instrument is able to differentiate among types of abuse and neglect. In neither case should face validity (i.e. where the items "appear" to reflect abuse) be the sole criterion.

## GENERAL CHARACTERISTICS OF MEASURES OF ABUSE

Before proceeding with the evaluation of abuse measures, a brief discussion on the importance of measurement may be in order. Good measures ensure accuracy in screening and classification; such accuracy is necessary for effective treatment. They allow practitioners to reach the same conclusions about type and degree of abuse irrespective of where the problem occurs or who does the assessment. In order to qualify as a good measure, an instrument must have undergone adequate standardization by having been developed on a sufficiently representative sample under clearly specified conditions, and demonstrate acceptable reliability and validity. Classification instruments also must be able to discriminate effectively among types of abuse and neglect (Kozma, Stones & McNeil, 1990.)

Two approaches to an understanding of abuse and neglect of seniors can be identified. One stresses qualitative procedures while the other emphasizes quantitative techniques. "Qualitative approaches are concerned with describing patterns of behaviour and processes of interaction, as well as revealing the meanings, values, and intentionalities that pervade elderly people's experience...." (Reinharz & Rowles, 1988, p. 6). In our opinion, such an approach may be better suited to an evaluation of risk factors and the development of effective prevention and intervention strategies than to measurement of elder abuse.

Measurement, by its very nature, is quantitative. The concern is with the frequency or intensity of a characteristic. Most of the assessment strategies in the literature dealing with elder abuse assume a continuum from mere inconvenience to major physical or psychological harm. The instruments discussed in this chapter reflect this continuum.

From our perspective, qualitative and quantitative approaches are complementary. For instance, with some of the instruments, clients need to write in experiences of abuse not covered by checklists. With others, focus groups and clinical interviews are used to establish types of abuse. But, to achieve consistency in screening or in classification, the emphasis, in our opinion, must be on quantitative procedures.

To assess the potential usefulness of a measure, it is necessary to evaluate its psychometric properties. The primary ones are reliability, validity, and generalizability. Reliability is usually reported as the consistency of obtained test scores over time and/or across test items. Validity is an indication of the extent to which an instrument actually measures the construct (type of abuse, in this case) that it claims to measure. Construct validity, a major form, is concerned with determining the extent to which a measure adequately represents the properties of the construct being measured. Finally, whether results from an instrument are appropriate (generalizable) to other groups and locations depends on how well target populations were represented during the scale construction period (standardization). For measures of elder abuse, the question is how well all types of abuse are assessed by an instrument in the targeted population.

Before such a question may be answered, one must first establish whether there is consensus among researchers as to the properties of the elder abuse construct. Most, if not all, professionals involved in the assessment and treatment of elder abuse recognize the subjective nature of the construct (Fulmer, 1989; Reis, Nahmiash & Shrier, 1993). This recognition is reflected in the clinical instruments used to assess abuse. These instruments rely heavily on the subjective impressions of health care and social service workers and/or the verbal reports of informants and abused elders (Bloom, Ansell & Bloom, 1989; Reis et al., 1993). Such an approach to assessment may over-emphasize the face validity of items and thereby fail to determine whether such items do, in fact, discriminate between abused and non-abused people.

A second property of the construct of elder abuse for which there is a high degree of consensus is its multidimensional nature (Ferguson & Beck, 1983; Stones, 1993a). Types of abuse include physical/sexual abuse and neglect, psychological abuse and neglect, material abuse, and violation of personal rights (Sengstock & Hwalek, 1987). Clearly, one criterion in the evaluation of elder abuse measures is the extent to which types of abuse are adequately represented.

Unfortunately, an inspection of current measures indicates that item frequency for types of abuse is far from equal. A review by Sengstock and Hwalek (1987) revealed total item frequencies for seven measures ranging from 13 items for material abuse to over 100 items for physical neglect. In fact, the greatest number of items in current measures did not deal with types, but with predictors, or risk factors, of abuse. From a classification perspective, this diversity in item sampling raises doubt about the adequacy with which all types of abuse and neglect are adequately represented on any of the measures. Differences in frequencies for types of abuse obtained by different measures could reflect either a real difference in such frequencies in different populations, or it could reflect a greater emphasis on one type of abuse over another by different instruments.

Another problem for the evaluation of elder abuse instruments is the manner in which the types of abuse are operationalized by different researchers. There are differences in both the connotative (i.e. generalized statements about what constitutes abuse/neglect) and the denotative (i.e. selected instances of abuse/ neglect) definition. For instance, Podnieks (1985, p. 36) defines abuse as "Any act or behaviour by a family member...which results in physical or mental harm or neglect (of) an elderly person". In this definition, the emphasis is on the act. On the other hand, for Johnson (1986, p. 180), a defining property of abuse is "... inflicted suffering unnecessary to the maintenance of the quality of life of the older person." In this part of Johnson's definition the emphasis is on the unnecessary suffering inflicted by the act. According to the latter definition, one can inflict physical or mental harm as long as it is necessary. Moreover, Podnieks' definition narrows abuse to a family member, whereas Johnson's definition is broader and seems to include care—givers in general. These approaches would lead to differences in item selection and other assessment strategies to measure elder abuse.

Denotative definitions for a type or component of abuse also differ among researchers. Denotative definitions by Tomita (1982) and Sengstock and Hwalek (1987) will be used to illustrate these differences (Table 1). The least consensus appears to be for "psychological abuse and neglect". This lack of consistency in the way that elder abuse is operationalized creates difficulties for item selection and the assessment of construct validity.

To complicate matters further, Stones (1993b) has argued that an alternative classification system based on two criteria, "intent" and "harm", is more consistent with long–established jurisprudence. The main features of the classification system are summarized in Table 2. Although Stones' approach may overcome some of the problems arising from the way elder abuse is operationalized, all but one of the instruments reviewed in this chapter are based on the multi–dimensional approach mentioned earlier.

## CURRENT MEASURES OF ELDER ABUSE

Two broad approaches to the assessment of elder abuse can be identified. The Clinical approach is primarily concerned with detecting abuse or confirming it in suspected cases. The emphasis is on possible risk, individual problems of abuse, and on potential intervention strategies. Identification relies heavily on behavioural observations and reports of case workers and informants. Assessment techniques, whether they involve personnel from relevant disciplines such as nurses or social workers, or whether a multi-disciplinary approach is used, are normally limited to behavioural observation procedures, behavioural rating scales, and guided interviews. Behavioural observations provide an indication of the presence of a problem behaviour; conventional issues of validity and reliability do not apply, provided that the selected behaviours provide an exhaustive listing of all instances of the problem. Behavioural ratings and guided interviews, however, are closer to standardized tests, and issues of reliability and validity are similar to those associated with such inventories.

The Survey approach to the assessment of elder abuse is primarily concerned with the frequency and type of abuse in a specific population. Survey measures have all of the properties of standardized tests and the appropriate criteria of reliability and validity should be met.

# Clinical Measures

Clinical measures of elder abuse vary from simple "screening" instruments to detailed classification instruments. Different evaluation criteria apply to these measures, depending on whether the function of the instrument is to identify an abused individual or whether it is to provide a comprehensive profile of abuse for that individual. Screening instruments must be able to differentiate between positive (i.e. abused) and negative (i.e. non–abused) cases. Either high inter—rater agreement by judges, or a strong positive correlation with a more comprehensive, established measure is considered an acceptable criterion of concurrent validity in measures lacking a clearer objective criterion (Kozma & Stones, 1991).

A multi-dimensional behavioural measure requires the comprehensive representation of all types of elder abuse. Problems of validity and reliability are less important, and arise only if a construct is inadequately operationalized.

A major purpose of classification instruments is to provide accurate information to enable a differential diagnosis to be made. For measures of abuse/neglect, the result should provide a profile that reflects the level of abuse for all components (i.e. types of abuse) of the construct. These measures can be evaluated not only in terms of the number of types of abuse they assess, but also in terms of the adequacy with which the types are represented. A good measure must provide an extensive, if not exhaustive, listing of abuse for each component in a reliable and valid form.

## 1. Representative Screening Inventories

The purpose of screening inventories may be two–fold: to identify cases of abuse (Reis et al., 1993) and to identify the type of elderly person at risk of being abused (Ferguson & Beck, 1983). Screening measures of elder abuse are in their infancy. Evidence on reliability and validity is lacking, and little progress on measurement criteria is in evidence from early 1980s to the present. Although the measures share similar content, they differ in "focus, format, structure, and type of data generated..." (Ashley & Fulmer, 1989; p. 287). An evaluation of the most frequently cited screening protocols illustrates this conclusion only too well.

### (i) Screening Protocol for Identification of Abuse and Neglect of the Elderly (SPIANE)

The SPIANE (Johnson, 1981) is more of a guided interview procedure than a screening test. One part of the procedure involves obtaining interview data from the elderly person that include types of abuse and neglect. In a second part, similar information is obtained from the caretaker. The interview data are supplemented by observation of the elderly person, the caregiver, and the elder–caregiver interaction. Most of the observations centre on evidence of physical abuse and neglect in the elderly person (e.g. bruises and dehydration). The combined data from interviews and observations are then used to determine the presence of (a) neglect and/or inappropriate care, (b) material abuse such as theft, (c) psychological abuse, and (d) physical abuse. Although such a procedure can provide qualitative information, there is no apparent rule system on how these different data gathering procedures are to be combined in a quantitative manner.

Johnson fails to provide the needed evidence on the effectiveness of the SPIANE as a screening test for elder abuse. There is no information on inter—rater agreement or on numbers of correctly classified cases. Although four areas of abuse/neglect are subsumed by the SPIANE, it is impossible to determine how useful this measure of elder abuse is relative to other procedures.

## (ii) Elder Abuse Detection: Indicators (EADI)

The EADI (Bloom et al., 1989) was prepared as an elder abuse detection guide for physicians. It also qualifies as a guided interview procedure with observational overtones. Data are obtained from three sources: the patient's medical history (e.g. previous unexplained injuries), physical findings (e.g. fractures; poor personal hygiene), and observations (e.g. over–anxious or withdrawn). Physical abuse and neglect is emphasized more, and is more objectively assessed, than other forms of abuse and neglect.

As with the SPIANE, there is no discussion of the psychometric properties of the EADI. The content appears to have adequate face validity (i.e. the items appear to reflect abuse), and items in the "history" and the "physical findings" sections are moderately well operationalized and could yield reasonable inter–rater coefficients. However, no such coefficients are reported. Items under "observations" are not operationalized, and one would suspect poor inter–rater reliability for this section.

## (iii) H.A.L.F. (Health Status, Attitude Toward Living, Living Arrangement, Finances)

The H.A.L.F. (Ferguson & Beck, 1983) is used to assess family dynamics in four domains: health status, attitude toward aging, living arrangement, and finances. This measure is based on the premise that elder abuse is a symptom of family dysfunction caused by a variety of factors. Information on maladaptive functioning in several domains should be associated with abuse.

This 3–point Likert–type measure (almost always, some of the time, never) is used to assess frequency of the occurrence of abusive behaviour. The number and position of checks on the questionnaire are used to evaluate presence, absence, and severity of abuse. From a psychometric perspective, such a format is superior to a guided interview procedure since it normally leads to greater consistency in scoring. Another positive feature of the instrument is the inclusion of two examples on its use and interpretation. The authors claim that the tool "has been useful in identifying aged persons who are at risk for abuse or actually being abused" with over 50 families or individuals (Ferguson & Beck, 1983, p. 301). Except for such anecdotal evidence, there is no information on the psychometric properties of the H.A.L.F. (e.g. the number of correctly classified cases; internal consistency).

## (iv) A Brief Abuse Screen for the Elderly (BASE)

The BASE (Reis et al., 1993) is the only measure in this class for which the proponents make an effort to evaluate the instrument's psychometric properties. It uses a Likert–type format on questions of abuse and a "yes/no" format to identify the client as either a caregiver or a carereceiver. The one–page questionnaire requires health service personnel to make global judgments of abuse in four areas: physical, psychosocial, financial, and neglect. These areas are not defined. Evaluators must draw on personal experience and other sources of information to make their judgments.

In a study reported by Reis et al. (1993), one of three sources of information is employed: a ten–minute telephone interview with a caregiver, a two– to three–hour home interview with a caregiver, or information from a case conference. Agreement for BASE categories for the three sources of information (telephone, interview, case conference) range from 89% to 91%. These values are impressive and suggest that a good ten–minute telephone interview may be almost as good at detecting abuse as a two– to three–hour home interview. Of course, we have no indication just how good the home interview is at detecting abuse. Nevertheless, similar results for the three different information gathering sources suggest that these techniques measure the same underlying construct.

One problem with the BASE is its dependency on information obtained by other means. In order to employ this instrument, it would be advisable to use one of the three data gathering procedures employed by its inventors.

## Summary

Four potentially useful screening instruments were reviewed in this section. While the format used to obtain information varies (from behavioural observations to guided interviews to rating scales), the content appears to have face validity. What is lacking, however, is convincing information on how effectively the measures identify cases of elder abuse. It is imperative that such information is obtained by users of these instruments. The best effort in this direction has been undertaken by Reis et al.(1993) with regards to the BASE. If revalidation studies are as good as initial findings indicate, this instrument may turn out to be a very effective screening test.

## 2. Representative Classification Inventories/Protocols

The major purpose of Classification Inventories is to identify types of elder abuse in order to obtain an accurate picture of abuse patterns for purposes of diagnosis and treatment. Numerous community and state agencies have constructed their own classification measures. We will describe three of the more comprehensive instruments of this group. Such a sample is large enough to provide readers with a choice of instruments.

If the assessment procedure of such an instrument involves techniques other than behavioural observation, the instrument should be validated against an external criterion (judges' ratings, correlation with an established instrument, classification of groups with known properties). If a behavioural observation procedure is used, then the primary psychometric property of concern is inter–rater reliability. Unfortunately, no validation data of either type appear to have been published on this kind of instrument. Accordingly, comparison will have to be limited to the extent to which types of abuse are represented and how good the item pool is for an adequate assessment of each type of abuse.

The evaluation of each measure will be completed by three ratings, one for number of categories of abuse assessed by the measure (Construct: 1 to 6) one for the adequacy of content used to represent the category (Content: 1 to 6), and the third for length of administration (Time: 1 to 6). The higher the rating, the better the measure in the specified evaluation.

### (i) The Sengstock–Hwalek Comprehensive Index of Elder Abuse (SHCIEA)

The SHCIEA is the most comprehensive instrument of its type. It is 26 pages long and covers all six types of abuse discussed in Part II of this chapter: physical abuse, physical neglect, psychological abuse, psychological neglect, material abuse, and violation of personal rights. It also provides information on client and abuser characteristics. Responses are recorded as frequencies of observed or encountered events (1 to 8). On the surface, there is complete agreement between the multi–dimensional construct of elder abuse presented by Sengstock and Hwalek (1987) and the components assessed by the SHCIEA. However, it remains to be determined by such data reduction techniques as factor analysis, whether there is a match between the empirically derived components and the scale's factor structure.

The SHCIEA also does a relatively good job with item selection. It seems that every type of abuse/neglect is listed. Moreover, the instrument permits the write–in of un–itemized instances of abuse/neglect. Nevertheless, there are some potential problems with the procedure. It seems to us that the relationship between abuse/neglect and the items used to assess it is more direct for some types than others. For instance, it is easier to infer abuse from being "kicked" than from the presence of "bruises". Similarly, it is doubtful that one could get consensus on whether or not being "restrained because of confusion" constitutes physical abuse. In the absence of a clear criterion of abuse, the "ecological validity" approach (i.e. obtaining the necessary information by observation or interview procedures in the senior's own environment), used by Stones (1993a) may be a more fruitful strategy to item selection than the inclusion of every item ever to appear in a previous measure, or one deemed relevant by a group of judges.

*General Evaluation:* Construct 6; Content 6; Time 1.

### (ii) Older Adult Protective Services Investigation Report (OAPSIR)

The OAPSIR (Pennsylvania Department of Aging) is a five–page, seven–section inventory that covers all the types of abuse/neglect assessed by SHCIEA, although the specified types are not identical. Types of neglect assessed with this instrument consist of: evidence of physical abuse (e.g. bruises, welts), evidence of emotional abuse (e.g. threatened, disoriented), abusive actions (e.g. confined, pushed), evidence of neglect (e.g. skin rash, faecal/urine smell), neglect for actions (e.g. failure to provide adequate food, supervision), financial exploitation (e.g. stolen money, unusual financial arrangements), and inadequate environment (e.g. architectural barriers, pest problems). Item frequency for types of abuse/neglect range from five for "neglect for actions" to 13 for "evidence for emotional abuse". However, space is provided under "other" at the end of each section for listing observed/reported instances of abuse/neglect not included in the item pool. Each item is scored as "confirmed", "possible", "unknown", or "no"(absent).

The item pool of the OAPSIR is considerably smaller than that of the SHCIEA. It is possible, therefore, that not all instances of elder abuse and neglect will be noted. However, if the frequency of certain instances is very small, or if such instances are noted by "other", the much shorter OAPSIR may discriminate almost as well as the lengthy SHCIEA.

An interesting feature of the OAPSIR is the provision of space beside each abuse/neglect item into which information on the source and nature of abuse can be written. This information would make it easy to differentiate between accidental injuries and abuse.

*General Evaluation:* Construct 6; Content 4; Time 4.

### (iii) Protocol for Identification and Assessment of Elder Abuse and Neglect (PIAEAN)

The PIAEAN (Tomita, 1981) was designed to provide an assessment strategy to health care professionals for the detection of elder abuse/ neglect. It lists six types and provides between two and five instances or examples for each. Types of abuse/neglect targeted are: physical abuse, psychological/verbal abuse, material abuse, neglect/omission, sexual abuse/sexual assault, and medical abuse. Diagnosis is based on information obtained during a patient interview, from presenting symptoms on arrival, from a functional assessment and a physical examination, and from an interview with the caregiver. Clear instructions are provided on how to proceed and what to look for while carrying out each procedure. However, the assessor has to determine from a rather limited set of examples which type of abuse, if any, is suggested by the findings.

No evidence is provided on the accuracy of this protocol for detecting the types of abuse targeted for assessment. However, the dependence on an interview procedure to discover instances of abuse (as opposed to an exhaustive symptoms checklist), together with a limited number of examples for types of abuse, is bound to limit inter–rater agreement.

*General Evaluation:* Construct 5; Content 3; Time 3.

### Summary

Three of the most widely used Classification Measures of elder abuse were evaluated in the preceding section of this chapter. Since data on criterion validity and reliability were unavailable, construct validity and length of assessment were used as the criteria of evaluation. The SHCIEA and OAPSIR were more consistent with the 6–component (type) model of elder abuse described in the earlier parts of this chapter than the PIAEAN. The extent to which the three measures adequately sample the components (content) also varies. The SHCIEA has more items for each abuse type than either the OAPSIR or the PIAEAN. On the other hand, administration time is far lengthier for the SHCIEA than for either of the other two instruments. If a thorough assessment is required, the SHCIEA seems to be the measure of choice.

## Surveys

The primary purpose of surveys is to obtain information on the prevalence of a problem in the target population. In the case of elder abuse/neglect, the target population will normally be at least 65 years of age. Identification of cases of abuse depends on the adequacy of the survey instrument. All types of the construct must be represented, and normally, the larger the representative item pool is for each type, the more accurate the results will be.

The major problem with surveys has been a lack of consistency in the measures used. Instruments are designed to meet the construct requirements of the researchers. They will have face and, to some extent, construct validity. However, little attempt is made to achieve the necessary criterion validation, and some studies report only definitions and types of abuse, and not how these types were assessed. The procedure makes comparisons across studies difficult. It is not surprising, therefore, that reported frequencies of elder abuse/neglect vary by more than 500% from study to study (Hudson, 1986; Stones, 1993a).

One American and two major Canadian surveys, using the most extensive item array in the literature, have been carried out in the last three years. These studies are based on different conceptual frameworks of elder abuse/neglect, and differ in intent. A description of the assessment procedure employed in these studies follows.

### (i) Boston Survey Measures

The Boston study (Pillemer & Finkelhor, 1988) provides the first comprehensive assessment of three major types of elder abuse: physical, psychological and neglect. Information on abuse was obtained by means of a telephone interview procedure from 2020 community–dwelling people 65 years of age or older. A ten–item, modified Conflict Tactics Scale (CTS), was used to index physical abuse. A single occurrence resulting from the interaction with a spouse, a co–resident child, or a member of the person's social network since the elder turned 65, was classed as abusive. Psychological abuse was defined as "chronic verbal aggression" against the elder. Thus, being insulted, sworn at, or threatened at least ten times a year, was considered abusive. Neglect was determined by whether or not help was withheld for ten activities of daily living (using a modified section of the Older Americans Resources Scale—OARS). Ten or more occurrences of neglect in the preceding year, or a classification of "somewhat serious" or "serious", was deemed abusive.

The advantages of this study include a large, random sample and adequately operationalized constructs. Some of the disadvantages centre on limiting measurement of abuse to three areas and the failure to validate measures against a known group of abused elderly people. It is not clear that either the OARS or the CTS cover a large enough array of instances to adequately represent physical abuse and neglect. It is also difficult to determine whether ten instances of verbal aggression provide an adequate criterion for psychological abuse. Finally, there are validity problems associated with the use of telephone surveys involving elderly persons. These include low participation rates due to frailty, and misunderstandings due to hearing impairment.

### (ii) Ryerson Survey Measures

The Ryerson survey (Podnieks, Pillemer, Nicholson, Shillington, & Frizzel, 1990) used a modified version of the instruments employed by Pillemer and Finkelhor (1988). As in the former study, the information on elder abuse was obtained by means of a telephone survey; 2008 community dwellers over 65 years of age made up the sample. Four types of abuse and neglect were assessed: material abuse, chronic verbal aggression, physical violence, and neglect. These types appear to have been adequately operationalized, and the measure was pre-tested on a sub-sample of elderly people.

The major strengths of this study include the use of two widely–used scales to assess physical abuse and neglect (CTS and a modified version of the OARS) and the large modified random sample of elderly persons interviewed. The scales provide an acceptable means of operationalizing two types of abuse (i.e. physical abuse and neglect). The major weaknesses of the study include the assessment of only one manifestation of psychological abuse (repeated insults and threats), the limited item array represented by the OARS and the CTS, and the apparent failure to carry out criterion validation on a Canadian sample, especially when pre–testing was carried out. Moreover, it is not clear whether the six items used to determine financial abuse are sufficiently representative of that component.

### (iii) Senior Abuse Item Inventory (SAII)

Stones (1993b) administered 112 abuse/neglect items to 364 seniors and 204 professionals working with seniors. Participants were asked to rate each item on a 5–point severity scale, where a rating of 1 indicates "not abusive" and one of 5 indicates "severely abusive". The items were obtained from existing measures of abuse/neglect and were supplemented by items generated by several senior focus groups of elderly people. All items refer to behaviour within a trust relationship.

From a measurement perspective, the most interesting finding of this study is the high degree of agreement between professionals and elderly people on severity ratings for items. Accordingly, it should be easy to construct a measure of abuse/ neglect (termed "mistreatment" by Stones) that would adequately represent all types of abuse from the extensive array of items with mean group ratings greater than 3.

This might solve some of the difficulties faced by both Podnieks et al., and Pillemer and Finkelhor in obtaining an adequate criterion for psychological abuse. Of course, the construction of such a measure is only a preliminary step in the development of an adequate survey instrument. Stones would have to demonstrate that such a measure can effectively discriminate between a mistreated and a non–mistreated group of seniors.

### Summary

The approaches used in three surveys for determining the prevalence and/or type of elder abuse were evaluated in this section. Although samples sizes were quite adequate in these studies, the extent to which types of abuse were adequately operationalized, the limited types of abuse assessed, and in the Boston and Ryerson studies, the limited item array used to assess types of elder abuse poses problems in interpreting the results. The approach adopted by Stones appears to provide a good set of abuse items, but whether such an item array will be useful in differentiating between abused and non–abused elders remains to be determined.

## CONCLUSIONS AND SUGGESTIONS FOR FUTURE WORK

This chapter has reviewed three kinds of elder abuse/neglect measures: screening, classification, and survey measures. The major problem with screening measures is the lack of information on their accuracy. Such measures should be able to discriminate between abused and non–abused groups of elderly people. Work is required on the assessment of concurrent validity and test/retest reliability. It would be interesting to administer the four screening measures discussed above to an abused and non–abused elderly population to determine how effective each is in correctly classifying the two groups.

Developing a valid classification instrument may be more difficult. The major obstacle for instrument development is a lack of consensus as to the types of abuse such measures need to include. Without a clear operational definition of each type of abuse, the development of a general measure that adequately represents all components is impossible. Such an instrument may, of course, be developed within each conceptual framework. If such a procedure is adopted, the measure that will be most useful to clinicians will become the one most frequently used in the assessment of elder abuse/ neglect.

As with screening instruments, classification measures need to be validated. Again, the best procedure is to use known cases of various types of abuse, together with appropriate control cases, to determine how well such measures are able to identify and classify the selected participants. We would expect that both the SHCIEA and the OAPSIR to do well on such a test.

A more general concern for the standardization of clinical measures of abuse is obtaining an adequate criterion. At this time, the best criterion, for both screening and classification instruments, seems to be the measure based on a multidisciplinary case conference of experienced professionals.

Surveys require their own assessment tools. A direct adoption of clinical instruments is impossible because such instruments rely heavily on physical evidence and/or direct observation in classifying cases of abuse/neglect. Accordingly, item selection becomes an important concern for survey users. To date, we have not been able to find a survey instrument that has been adequately standardized. Items are selected and modified from existing measures and supplemented by ones representing the researchers' own conceptions of elder abuse/neglect. Findings are then treated as valid data. The problem with this approach is that we have no information on the reliability or validity of the constructed measure. It has been pointed out by several researchers (Hudson, 1986; Stones, 1993a) that this approach leads to widely discrepant findings across studies.

The approach in item selection and evaluation embarked on by Stones (1993b) helps to decide on critical items of elder abuse/neglect for survey instruments. However, item selection is only the first step in an effective standardization procedure. Next, the items need to be administered to known samples of abused and non–abused individuals to determine the discriminative powers of the newly–constructed instrument. Finally, the validated instrument should be used on randomly selected community samples of elderly people.

There have been important developments in the measurement of elder abuse/neglect in recent years. Screening, classification, and survey instruments are becoming more refined (e.g., the BASE and the EAII). Increased attention is being directed towards instrument validation. Nevertheless, we still have a long way to go before our measures meet adequate psychometric criteria. This chapter has presented some of the critical issues that need addressing before we gain an acceptable measure of elder abuse in Canada.

## Table 1:     Differences in Definitions of Elder Abuse/Neglect

### Example 1:     (Tomita, 1982)

a.     Physical Abuse: striking, shoving, beating, restraining
b.     Psychological Abuse: yelling, insulting, threatening, silence, social isolation, infantalization
c.     Material Abuse: theft or misuse of finances, property or possessions
d.     Neglect: withholding medical care, personal care daily needs; lack of necessary supervision

### Example 2:     (Sengstock and Hwalek, 1987)

a.     Physical Abuse: direct physical assault or threat with a weapon
b.     Psychological Abuse: verbal assault or threats not involving a weapon
c.     Material Abuse: theft or misuse of property
d.     Physical Neglect: failure to provide the necessities of life
e.     Psychological Neglect: including isolation or deprivation of companionship
f.     Violation of Personal Rights: the denial to choose a personal life style, marrying, etc.

**Table 2:** **Conceptual System of Elder Mistreatment Based on the Principle of Jurisprudence[1]**

| Level | Specification | Purpose |
|---|---|---|
| **Definition** | Behaviour contravening legal standards (L); regulated professional or workplace ethics (E); what are believed to be community standards of tolerable conduct (C). | To provide rules to differentiate mistreatment from tolerable behaviour |
| **Prerequisite Criteria** | Age over 65 years; the context of a formal or informal trust relationship | To differentiate elder mistreatment from crime by a stranger and self–violation |
| **Subclassification Criteria** | Legal; regulated by ethical and workplace norms; or by advocacy standards | To identify the type of standard violated |
| **Types of Evaluation Procedure** | Regulated (by law, or an agency, organization, or institution); formal (e.g. research procedures); nonformal | To indicate the thoroughness of the evaluation and implication for penalty |
| **Exemplar Sub–categories** | Criminal conduct, common law infringements, violation of professional ethics (L); dereliction of workplace duties (E); untoward conduct, abuse by an agency which contravenes standards of the conduct of an association in trust of care or service(C) | To provide exemplars of types of mis–treatment, so as to facilitate understanding, communication, and working definitions |

[1]  Adapted from Stones, 1993a

(L) = Legal Violation.
(E) = Ethical Violation.
(C) = Community Standards Violation.

# EPIDEMIOLOGICAL PERSPECTIVES ON THE ABUSE AND NEGLECT OF SENIORS: A REVIEW OF THE NATIONAL AND INTERNATIONAL RESEARCH LITERATURE

*J.F. Kozak, T. Elmslie and J. Verdon*

## INTRODUCTION

The goal of this chapter is to review and critique, from an epidemiological perspective, the national and, briefly, the international published research literature on abuse and neglect of elderly people. The first part of the chapter will explore methodological problems that researchers, practitioners, educators and policy analysts must be aware of, followed by a review of recent literature, identified risk factors and recommendations.

Since Burston's (1975) article on "granny-battering", little progress has been made in describing the prevalence and incidence of abuse and neglect among either community or institutional-dwelling seniors. Numerous factors have made it difficult to conduct proper epidemiological research on this topic, some of which are:

1.  problems in dealing with the highly sensitive nature of the phenomenon (Sengstock & Hwalek, 1986; Benton & Marshall, 1991);

2.  inconsistency of operational definitions (Wolf & Pillemer, 1989; Glendenning, 1993; Stones, 1994); and

3.  difficulty in obtaining representative samples (Brillon, 1987; McDonald, Hornick, Robertson & Wallace, 1991).

## METHODOLOGICAL ISSUES

### Definition of Prevalence and Incidence

A major problem encountered in the abuse/neglect literature is that it is difficult to discern if true prevalence and incidence were studied. Studies tend to confuse projection of abuse from prevalence as true incidence figures (e.g. Poertner, 1986). As prevalence and incidence require different methodologies, it is important that researchers, practitioners, educators and policy analysts understand the difference between the two concepts.

In epidemiology, the frequency of an event or its likelihood is described through the concepts of prevalence (point and period) and incidence. Point prevalence is a measure of the proportion of a group that either has or does not have the condition of interest at a *specific* time, whereas period prevalence is the total proportion of identified cases present *during* a period of time. Incidence, on the other hand, is a measure of the frequency of occurrence of new cases during a period of time among an at-risk group who are initially *free* of abuse/neglect. Where prevalence provides an indication of the extent of the current problem, incidence provides a projection of the future occurrence of new cases as time passes. Prevalence *cannot* be used to estimate future cases: because a study reports an abuse rate of 3.2% in 1989 does not mean that this figure can be used to project the number of cases to expect in later years.

The key to understanding the meaning of prevalence and incidence is in defining the two forms of information each must collect: the case (numerator) and the population (denominator). Case is defined as the basic unit under study, for example an individual or chart record. In prevalence, the numerator is the number of cases identified in the study and the denominator is the total number of individuals studied (the number of those with, plus the number of those without the identified condition). Prevalence estimates for a specific time period are then calculated by dividing the number of identified cases by the total number of cases studied. In incidence, the numerator is the number of *new* cases identified during a specific time period in a group of at-risk individuals who, at the start of the study, were free of the condition being studied (i.e. were not abused or neglected). The denominator is all of the at-risk, but abuse/neglect-free people monitored by the study. Incidence is then calculated by dividing the number of new cases by the total number of at-risk individuals studied.

Research designs used to obtain numerator and denominator information differ for prevalence and incidence. Prevalence is usually determined by using a cross-sectional design where a group of individuals are studied at a given point in time to determine who either has or has not the condition of interest. Although relatively easy to conduct in terms of time and cost, the cross-sectional design provides no information as to the temporal relationship (cause and effect) of variables nor does it include cases that fall outside of the time interval investigated. In contrast, incidence usually requires the use of cohort designs where the investigator must: 1) first determine that no abuse/neglect occurred, and then 2) follow the group prospectively. In abuse/neglect, the determination of whether or not it occurred is difficult as it depends on the investigator's time screen; for example, screening those where there was no incident of abuse/neglect over the past year versus those never experiencing abuse/neglect. Each can result in a totally different study sample, yielding different incidence estimates. In addition to this problem, incidence studies are costly and time-consuming to conduct because of their longitudinal approach.

Prevalence and incidence studies serve different purposes. Prevalence studies of abuse and neglect are needed for the planning of health and social service interventions. Incidence research is better suited to help explore causal models of abuse and neglect, and for evaluating the effectiveness of primary prevention programs.

## Threats to Validity

All research involves compromise between the desire for objective rigor and limitations imposed by: time, logistical factors, financial cost, ethical concerns, and unwillingness to report on sensitive topics. At best, the researcher attempts to either remove or control the various factors that are a major threat to the validity of the results. In reviewing recent studies, there are several common threats specific to the epidemiological research on abuse and neglect: operational definition; subject selection; sample size; and experimental bias.

## Operational Definition

There is a lack of agreement as to what constitutes abuse and neglect (Bennett, 1992; McCreadie, 1991). Definitions of abuse and neglect appear to be dependent more upon preferences of the individual, profession or agency studying the phenomenon than on any agreed-upon standard (see Stones, this volume). This lack of consistency makes it impossible to make any generalizations. Thus, for example, findings reported on abuse and neglect of elderly people in health-care settings (e.g. Ontario Nursing Association Report, 1993) do not clearly define when physical restraint constitutes abuse. As pointed out by Kozma and Stones (this volume), the lack of consensus in defining the phenomenon has also made it almost impossible to develop psychometrically valid and reliable measures of abuse and neglect.

## Subject Selection

To be valid, a study must specify its target population by using clear eligibility criteria and specify its sampling strategy. Only a small number of studies have attempted to take appropriate care in defining and sampling from the target population, either community-based (e.g. Pillemer & Finkelhor, 1988; Podnieks, Pillemer, Nicholson, Shillington & Fizzell, 1989) or institution-based (e.g. Pillemer & Moore, 1989). The majority of reported abuse and neglect studies describe the population as discovered through: chart audits (e.g. Cash & Valentine, 1987; Hall, 1989); recall by professionals (e.g. Holtzman & Bomberg, 1991; Hickey & Douglass, 1981); or on-site identification at an applied setting of respite care (e.g. Homer & Gilleard, 1990). Each of these approaches limits the generalizability of the findings because typically no denominator information is available: we know how many cases were identified, but not the type and size of population they were from. The use of convenience samples, such as cases admitted to an emergency ward, are frequently *not* representative of the type of abused or neglected senior seen either in the institution or community. Moreover, reliance upon recall by a health or social service professional is fraught with subjective error and difficulty in discerning unique cases; for example, several professionals may be reporting the same abused person to the researcher. To ensure true representation, studies need to employ a sampling strategy that will randomly select either individuals (e.g. random samples, stratified random samples) or families (e.g. cluster sampling) in a manner that will reduce selection bias.

## Sample Size

Few of the reported studies examining abuse and neglect of seniors contain adequate sample sizes. The researcher must ensure that there are enough subjects in the study to reduce chance error enough to allow accurate analysis of the data. Insufficient sample size makes interpretation of the data difficult. Moreover, the ability to make generalizations from research findings is directly related to how many people were selected for the study. Insufficient sample size reduces one's ability to interpret the results with any degree of accuracy. In addition to sample size, the ability to generalize study results depends on how *representative* the study sample is to the population the researcher is interested in. Thus, for example, findings based on a sample of cases seen in a hospital setting cannot be generalized to individuals living in the community. Only a random sample from the community can be said to be representative of that specific community.

The actual calculation of sample size depends upon two things:

1. the statistical level of confidence one wishes to obtain (prevalence and incidence studies most frequently use the 95% confidence interval); and

2. in the case of prevalence, an estimate of the number of cases one would expect to find in the community of interest.

Phenomena such as abuse and neglect of seniors with low or unknown prevalence levels require large sample sizes or carefully designed case-control studies with appropriate comparison or control groups. These requirements have not been met in the majority of published studies on abuse and neglect of elderly people. The reader interested in learning more about sample size estimation is referred to Assael and Keon (1982) and Freidman, Furberg and DeMets (1985).

## Experimental Bias

The last design issue to be raised is that of experimental bias. Regardless of the degree of sophistication of the researchers, all studies, whether observational or experimental in design, have one or another form of experimental bias that may underestimate or overestimate the results. It is important, therefore, that the researcher be aware of and control for the bias(es) that will most affect the results. The major biases related to abuse and neglect studies to be discussed briefly are: incidence-prevalence; volunteer; measurement; diagnostic suspicion; and nonresponse. For a more detailed discussion of this topic see Cook and Campbell (1979).

### Incidence-Prevalence Bias

Incidence-prevalence bias refers to the study's omission of individuals either because of the condition resolving itself prior to detection, or to the death of the individual. Retrospective studies of abuse and neglect conducted in clinical settings may underestimate the magnitude of the problem because of cases never reaching the investigator. For this reason, care must be taken to ensure that all known cases of abuse are detected or that any bias in case ascertainment is reduced or controlled.

### Volunteer Bias

Care must be exercised in establishing that subjects who volunteer are representative of the population of interest to the investigator. Social scientists and health care researchers have long been aware of the problem that people willing to identify themselves as abused are different from the assumed majority who remain silent (e.g. Hamberger, Saunders & Hovey, 1992; Sassetti, 1993). It is imperative that those who identify themselves as abused/neglected seniors are chosen for the research solely on the basis of the condition of abuse or neglect being present and not simply because of their willingness to participate in the study.

### Measurement Bias

In the abuse and neglect literature, measurement bias in questionnaire design results from the use of questions that encourage the subject to answer in either a positive or a negative manner. Great care is necessary when designing questions that deal with a threatening issue such as abuse and neglect. For example, questions that are threatening in nature need to be embedded in a questionnaire allowing the researcher to establish a rapport with the elderly person prior to the probing of sensitive issues. For an excellent practical treatment of this topic, the reader is referred to Sudman and Bradburn (1983). Techniques for overcoming survey-related problems in questionnaire design and response rate may be found in Dillman (1978) and Bradburn and Sudman (1979).

### Diagnostic Suspicion

There is the danger of bias when clinicians become sensitive to the relevance of a particular condition. This bias can either result in the underestimation or, more commonly, overestimation of the problem being investigated. Thus, for example, because of the prominence abuse and neglect is currently receiving, the investigator may unknowingly broaden his/her personal definition of abuse and "detect" cases that would have not been considered earlier as an abusive incident. To overcome this bias, care must be taken in operationally defining and detecting what is abuse and neglect prior to the start of any investigation. The definitions should be well-defined and not subject to change as the study is underway.

### Nonresponse

Care must be taken to ensure as high a response rate as possible (e.g. pilot testing, soliciting cooperation). Analysis of data in studies where the number of nonresponders is moderate or high presumes that there is no difference between those responding to the study and those who do not. Unless this presumption can be substantiated, the two cannot be viewed as being similar. Nonresponders reduce the ability of the researcher to say that the sample is representative of the population being studied; and, therefore, limits the generalizability of the study.

As is evident from the above sections, conducting research is extremely difficult. The investigator is faced with many decisions ranging from who should be studied (sample) to how should the study be conducted (methodology). Regardless of whether one is conducting a small case study using clinical records or a large scale epidemiological investigation, the researcher must continually ask her or himself: Are the sample and design appropriate and unbiased? A third problem, analysis of the data, is beyond the scope of this chapter. The following section examines the published literature on abuse and neglect with these questions in mind.

## RESEARCH LITERATURE

### Canada

Currently, there have been only a few reported prevalence studies conducted in Canada on abuse and neglect of seniors (see Table 1). Of these, only Podnieks et al. (1989) used a randomized sampling approach and thereby obtained a more truly representative sample of Canadian seniors. Most of the other studies are not available in the published literature and, therefore, must be examined through the use of secondary sources. To date, no incidence study has been conducted in Canada.

The first reported study in Canada was that of Bélanger (1981) who investigated the prevalence of senior abuse and neglect through mailed questionnaires to 140 professionals dealing with elderly people in the Montreal area. Although it is unclear on what sampling basis the 140 were chosen, the responding professionals reported the presence of physical abuse (25%), psychological abuse (34%), material abuse (30%) and rights violation (23%) among their older-aged clients. Relatively similar results were obtained by Shell (1982) who interviewed 105 professionals in several Manitoba health care settings.

Stevenson (1985) reported the presence of 498 cases of senior abuse and neglect as identified through a mail survey of service providers in Alberta. In a similar mail survey to service providers in Ontario, but with a disastrous return rate (9.3%), 213 cases of abuse and neglect among seniors were identified (Ministry of Community and

Social Services, 1985). The presence of either abuse or neglect in Canada has also been detected by chart reviews of social services in Montreal (Grandmaison, 1988) and hospital visits in Winnipeg (King, 1984), as well as by case-recall by other professionals (Lamont, 1985; Haley, 1984).

## TABLE 1: Abuse/Neglect in Canada

| Author | Sample | Method | Findings |
|---|---|---|---|
| Bélanger (1981) (Montreal) | 140 Professionals | Mailed Questionnaire | Physical (21.0%) Psychological (55.0%) Material (24.0%) Rights Violation (25.0%) |
| Shell (1982) (Manitoba) | 105 Professionals | Interview 402 Unique Reports | Physical (22.4%) Psychological (37.4%) Financial (40.2%) |
| King (1984) (Winnipeg) | Hospital Visits 1981-1984 | Screened by Staff | 19 Confirmed Cases |
| Haley (1984) (Nova Scotia) | Social Services Survey | 281 Seniors Studied | 48.7% Cases Reported |
| Stevenson (1985) (Alberta) | 422 Social Services Workers | Mailed Questionnaire 67% Return (1/3 Unusable) | 498 Cases |
| Lamont (1985) | 6 Service Workers | Interviews | 30 Cases of Abuse Reported |
| Ministry of Community and Social Services (Ontario) (1985) | Service Providers | 14,526 Mailed Questionnaires (9.3% Return, 7.6% Usable) | 213 Cases |
| Grandmaison (1988) (Montreal) | Centre of Social Services (CSSMM) | Review of Active Case Files | 5% Show Abusive Situation 73% Psychological |
| Podnieks et al. (1989) (Canada) | Telephone Interview | 2,008 Community Dwelling Seniors | 40/1,000 Cases |

The only conclusion one can derive from these findings is that abuse and neglect of seniors exists throughout Canada, with some regional variation. No information can be discerned regarding the extent of the existing problem (prevalence) nor can anything be said about the number of new cases (incidence). As well, no statements can be made about the nature and etiology of abuse and neglect of seniors in Canada. All of the studies are seriously flawed because of:

- poor mail survey techniques (e.g. Ministry of Community and Social Services, 1985).

- possible errors in recall (e.g. Shell, 1982; Bélanger, 1981).

- inability to identify duplicate cases reported by professionals (e.g. Bélanger, 1981; Stevenson, 1985; Lamont, 1985; Haley, 1984)
- lack of operational definitions of abuse and neglect (e.g. Bélanger, 1981)
- lack of information regarding possible reporting bias when identifying cases through social or health care agencies (e.g. Bélanger, 1981; Shell, 1982; King, 1984)
- no estimates of the accuracy and reliability of information found through retrospective chart reviews or patient identification (e.g. Grandmaison, 1988)
- poor description of experimental design and sampling procedure (e.g. no statement of the *total* number of charts reviewed or patients seen: Shell, 1982; Grandmaison, 1988)

As mentioned earlier, only the Podnieks et al. (1989) study was experimentally rigorous enough to provide us with what may be the actual prevalence of abuse and neglect among community-dwelling seniors in Canada. Using a structured telephone interview format that incorporated predetermined definitions of abuse and neglect, Podnieks and her team randomly selected 2,008 seniors stratified by geographical location. Her results, summarized in Table 2, indicate that the prevalence rate for abuse and neglect among seniors is 4% (95% confidence interval: 3.1-4.9) and it varies slightly across the country. Material abuse (2.5%), which included financial or property, and chronic verbal aggression (1.4%) accounted for most of the self-reported cases.

## TABLE 2: Podnieks et al. (1989) Study

| Type | Rate Per 1,000 | Estimated Victims in Canada | | |
|------|------|------|------|------|
| Material | 2.5% | 60,000 | B.C. | 5.3% |
| Chronic Verbal Aggression | 1.4% | 34,000 | Prairies | 3.0% |
| Physical Violence | 0.5% | 12,000 | Ontario | 4.0% |
| Neglect | 0.4% | 10,000 | Quebec | 4.0% |
| Total | 4.0% | 98,000 | Atlantic | 3.8% |
| Multiple Abuse | 0.8% | 19,000 | | |

*Podnieks (1992) p. 16 Journal of Abuse and Neglect.*

Differences can be seen in the risk profiles between types of abuse and neglect, though the number of abused seniors is relatively small. Thus, for example, material abuse is equally common among males and females who tend to live alone and whose abuser tends to be a distant relative or someone unrelated. Chronic verbal aggression is most common among spouses, with males and females being equally affected. Although males are more likely to be physically abused, physical abuse by males toward females tends to be more violent: a finding similar to that reported in the spousal abuse literature (e.g. Sonkin, Martin & Walker, 1985). The Podnieks et al. results, however, may be an under-estimation due to the use of telephone interviews to obtain highly sensitive, personal information; potential control of telephone contact by the abuser;

the use of quotas; and how complete their definitions of abuse and neglect were. For an excellent discussion of problems inherent to telephone-survey methods the reader is referred to Dillman (1978).

In Canada, there have been two reports dealing with abuse and neglect of seniors in institutions. In a task report by the Concerned Friends of Ontario Citizens in Care Facilities (1986), roughly one-half of the 56 detailed complaints were of sufficient grounds for criminal charges. Similarly, in a recent survey of its members, the Ontario Nurses Association (1993) reported that between 25 and 84% of nurses reported seeing either abuse or neglect. Because of the lack of a well-defined denominator (e.g. the total number of individuals over 65 years of age residing in Greater Toronto) and insufficient information regarding sampling strategy and operational definitions of abuse and neglect, these results are difficult to interpret. Additional problems such as the reluctance of the patient/caregiver and staff to report incidents, the lack of knowledge of the problem, and no consistent and valid definition of inappropriate care (e.g. O'Malley, 1987) make the interpretation of the findings even more problematic.

No Canadian study has been conducted on the role of ethnicity or culture in abuse and neglect of elderly people. Research is hampered by the lack of knowledge of how different ethnic groups define and demonstrate abuse and neglect of their seniors. In a recent report by the Research Study Group on Elder Abuse (Chappell, 1993), members representing the First Nation and Chinese communities stressed the need to redefine abuse/neglect from more culturally relevant perspectives. Thus, for example, abuse and neglect among First Nation seniors may involve issues around usefulness and freedom whereas for elderly Chinese people it may be disappointment or unhappiness in family matters.

## International

As with the Canadian research, the majority of reported senior abuse/neglect research in the international literature suffers from major methodological problems. The use of descriptive nonrepresentative samples, presence of case duplication, questionable and unclearly reported data collection procedures, low questionnaire return rates, nonresponders, and definitional problems are only a few of the problems. Problems that, as seen in the Canadian research, make it impossible to estimate the prevalence and incidence of abuse/neglect of seniors. The following is a brief presentation of some of the international studies. Because of the unavailability of primary sources, only the literature from United States, Great Britain, Europe and Australia will be discussed. For a more exhaustive description, the reader is referred to McDonald et al. (1991), Decalmer and Glendenning (1993) and Brillon (1987).

### United States

With respect to research on community-dwelling seniors, only two American studies were rigorous enough to warrant an in-depth discussion: Pillemer and Finkelhor (1988) and Gioglio and Blakemore (1983). Pillemer and Finkelhor conducted a stratified random survey of seniors, 65 years of age and older, in the Boston metropolitan area. Using a two-staged interview design—telephone interview followed up with a face-to-face interview—72% of 2,813 eligible seniors participated in the study. The authors reported a prevalence rate of 3.2% (95% CI: 3-3.4%), with physical abuse and chronic verbal aggression accounting for most of the reported incidents. The results are similar to the those reported by Podnieks et al. (1989).

The other important study by Gioglio and Blakemore (1983) involved surveying a stratified random sample of seniors 65 years of age and older residing in New Jersey. Based on the responses provided by 342 seniors (88.3% response rate), some form of abuse was found among 1% (95% CI: 0-2.1%) of the sample. The authors show that almost one-half of the cases were of financial abuse and the least reported was physical abuse. Compared with the Podnieks et al. (1989) and Pillemer and Finkelhor (1988) studies, Gioglio and Blakemore's findings appear to be under-estimated.

Although "incidence" rates have been reported in the American literature (e.g. Block & Sinnott, 1979; Poertner, 1986), these are *not* true incidences. As discussed earlier, the calculation of true incidence requires identifying new cases while following prospectively an identified at-risk sample which is, at the start of the study, free of any abuse/neglect. Incidence figures reported in the published literature have been calculated from projections based on prevalence studies. Thus Block and Sinnott (1979) and Steinmetz (1987) inappropriately report incidence figures based on current prevalence rates. Prevalence cannot be used to estimate incidence.

The remaining American studies tend to fall into the area of either non-representative descriptive case-finding in applied settings or non-representative descriptive surveys among professionals or seniors themselves. Although descriptive research yields a rich amount of information, especially in the area of complex social interactions as family violence, it is inappropriate for estimating the magnitude of a problem. Estimations of prevalence and incidence require the use of well-defined and constructed tests in individuals who are representative and randomly selected from the senior population. Analysis of the etiology of abuse/neglect and risk factors associated with it require the comparison of abused/neglected seniors against good control or comparison groups.

Methodological approaches used in American research can be divided into one of three categories: case/chart audits; survey of health care professionals; or a combination of both. Chart reviews of either consecutive visits (e.g. Fulmer, McMahon, Baer-Hines & Forget, 1992; Phillips, 1983) or past visits (e.g. Cash & Valentine, 1987; Lau & Kosberg, 1979) have indicated the presence of both abuse and neglect in a variety of applied health care and social service settings. Surveys of professionals indicate that hospital staff (e.g. Clark-Daniels, Daniels & Baumhover, 1990), dentists (e.g. Holtzman & Bomberg, 1991) and other service providers and practitioners (e.g. Poertner, 1986; Chen, Bell, Dolinsky, Doyle & Dunn, 1981; Hickey & Douglass, 1981) either are aware of the problem to a varying degree or have some personal knowledge of it. Studies combining both methods (e.g. U.S. House of Representatives Select Committee on Aging, 1981) report similar findings. These findings, however, are difficult to interpret because of possible methodological biases (e.g. recall errors, use of convenience samples, lack of chart information) and lack of denominator information.

Only one methodologically-sound study has been done on the type of abuse/neglect faced by seniors residing in American institutional settings. In a randomized sample of 577 nursing staff (RNs and RNAs) from 31 nursing homes, Pillemer and Moore (1989) studied the number of physical and psychological abuse cases reported by nursing staff. Physical abuse of patients was seen by 36% of the staff: use of restraints (21%), pushing, grabbing, shoving and pinching (15%), and slapping and hitting (15%). Eighty-one percent of the staff reported seeing psychological abuse. Again, the importance of this finding is hindered by possible reporting bias of the staff and the lack of clear numerator and denominator information - that is, the number of unique cases identified and the size of the populations from which the cases are obtained.

With respect to ethnicity, Sengstock and Liang (1983) reported that elder abuse and neglect occurs almost equally among whites and blacks whereas Fulmer et al. (1992) reported higher prevalence among non-white populations. Lack of specific sampling information and the inability to ensure that the white and non-white samples were equated on other factors (e.g. socioeconomic status) makes it difficult to generalize these findings.

### Great Britain, Europe and Australia

Partially because of poor description of methodology, there appears to have been no rigorous study on the prevalence or incidence of abuse/neglect outside of North America (McCreadie & Tinker, 1993). Tomlin (1988), in a case review of social services in England (actual number unknown), reported a 5% rate of abuse/neglect among seniors. Homer and Gilleard (1990) interviewed a small sample of older British patients and their caregivers in respite care at one hospital. Their findings indicated that caregivers tended to report abuse/neglect more often than did the patients. Ogg and Bennett (1992) described finding 27.6% incidents of abuse/neglect among a national survey of 2,130 seniors in England. Unfortunately, the report makes it impossible to determine either the validity of the finding or interpret its meaning.

Although abuse and neglect of seniors has also been reported in Ireland (O'Neill, McCormack, Walsh & Coakley, 1990), France (Hugonot, 1990) and the Nordic countries (Hydle, 1993), little detailed information is available to permit one to say more than that the phenomenon exits. For example, Hugonot (1990) reports that at least 20% of seniors experience abuse or "moral cruelty" in the home. No supporting information is provided as to how this figure was obtained other than it was mentioned in a panel discussion group.

The one published epidemiological study from Australia (Kurrle, Sadler & Cameron, 1991) reported an "abuse" rate of 4.6%. As this rate was based on a one-year retrospective chart review of geriatric and rehabilitation services in a hospital, with no information on the total number of charts reviewed, the results are difficult to interpret and are not generalizable outside of their specific hospital services.

## RISK FACTORS

Factors correlated with an increased likelihood of becoming abused/neglected are called risk factors. Risk factors are important for predicting who will become abused/neglected, identifying cause(s), and detecting the presence of abuse/neglect. However, the impact that a risk factor has, either causing or just being associated with a condition, can be difficult to determine because of: possible long latency periods; possible need for frequent exposure; low incidence (requiring large samples and time frames); occurrence of risk factors in other conditions (common presence); and dependency on the presence of other risk factors. In the case of abuse and neglect of seniors, this would mean that no single risk factor would be a good predictor of abuse and neglect because of its interaction with other variables such as family dynamics, caregiver stress, and social isolation to name but a few.

Because one generally cannot manipulate risk, this concept is usually studied using either observational or cohort designs. Although cohort studies are time consuming and expensive, they are perhaps the best method for establishing incidence and the relationship between risk factors and abuse/neglect. Appropriate case-control designs may also be used.

An ever-increasing body of literature exists on factors felt to place either elderly people or their caregivers at-risk for abuse and neglect (e.g. Wrigley, 1991; Pillemer & Finkelhor, 1989; Wolf, 1988). As summarized in Figure 1, the identified risk factors involve a complex interaction between socio-economic, psychological, and environmental dimensions. For example, recent research on seniors with Alzheimer's disease indicates that the risk for abuse by informal caregivers increased with caregiver depression, living arrangement, poor self-esteem of caregiver, and presence of spousal violence (e.g.

Pillemer & Suitor, 1992; Paveza, Cohen, Eisdorfer, Freels, Semla, Ashford, Gorelick, Hirschman, Luchins & Levy, 1992). Other factors, such as being mentally ill in rural areas, have also been identified as potential risk factors (Weiler & Buckwalter, 1992).

Abuse and neglect, depending upon the researcher's theoretical perspective, may be the result of: caregiver stress, personality characteristics or psychopathology of the abuser, and/or lack of community and family support. Although all of these and other factors undoubtedly can result in an abusive incident, case-control studies are required to understand their relative importance.

To date only two appropriate case-control studies have been conducted on the topic of risk factors in elder abuse (Pillemer & Suitor, 1992; Godkin, Wolf & Pillemer, 1989). The results clearly indicate that risk factors are not static dimensions whose presence or absence dictates the incident, but rather interact in a dynamic manner. Thus, for example, Godkin et al. (1989) reported that abused seniors were not more functionally dependent upon their caregivers than age-matched seniors who did not experience abuse/neglect. Rather, abusive incidents appeared when the abused senior and her/his caregiver became increasingly interdependent upon one another because of: a loss of family member support, increased social isolation, and increased financial dependency of the abuser.

Many of these factors are similar to those reported in the family violence literature (Sassetti, 1993; Block & Sinnott, 1979). Case studies with small samples have indicated a high degree of similarity between younger and older-aged battered women (Gesino, Smith & Keckich, 1982). Factors such as fear of reporting and professional reluctance to become involved in perceived family issues are common to both. It would appear that studies of risk factors would benefit by approaching the problem from a life cycle perspective where any of these factors can lead to either child abuse, spousal abuse, or elder abuse.

Overall, the role of risk factors cannot be understood until true incidence figures are established. In order to compare risk findings, research is necessary for establishing attributable risk (incidence following exposure above that of individuals not exposed to the risk factors) and relative risk (ratio of the risk of becoming abused/neglected among the exposed against the risk among the unexposed).

**FIGURE 1:    Associated Risk Factors**

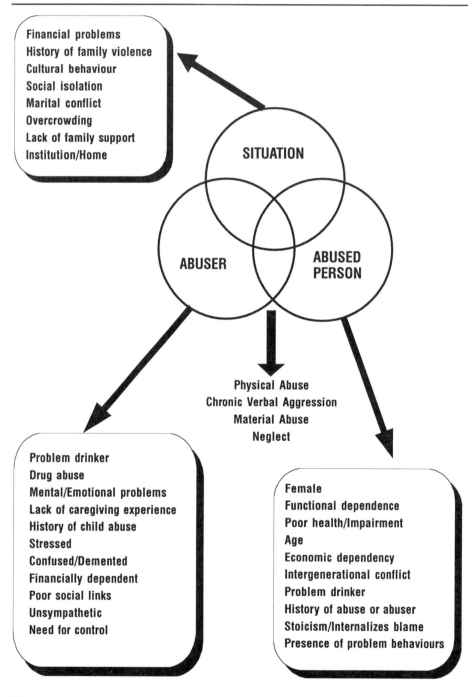

Financial problems
History of family violence
Cultural behaviour
Social isolation
Marital conflict
Overcrowding
Lack of family support
Institution/Home

SITUATION

ABUSER

ABUSED PERSON

Physical Abuse
Chronic Verbal Aggression
Material Abuse
Neglect

Problem drinker
Drug abuse
Mental/Emotional problems
Lack of caregiving experience
History of child abuse
Stressed
Confused/Demented
Financially dependent
Poor social links
Unsympathetic
Need for control

Female
Functional dependence
Poor health/Impairment
Age
Economic dependency
Intergenerational conflict
Problem drinker
History of abuse or abuser
Stoicism/Internalizes blame
Presence of problem behaviours

# RECOMMENDATIONS

It would appear that the prevalence rate of abuse/neglect among community-dwelling seniors in North America may be around 3 to 5 percent. This figure, however, is derived only from *self-reported* incidents. As for domestic violence, where victims tend not to report incidents and professionals are poor at detection (Sassetti, 1993), the actual prevalence of abuse and neglect among seniors is probably much higher.

Although abuse and neglect exist, there is little reliable information regarding the magnitude of the problem. Also, we do not have any reliable estimate of how many new cases we can expect in the future either in the community or in institutions. What is lacking is the application of appropriate research methodology for establishing the magnitude of the problem, both prevalence and incidence, and understanding the dynamic interplay between potential risk factors and triggering events. It is recommended that in research on the topic of abuse and neglect of seniors:

1. Appropriate prevalence (cross-sectional) and incidence (cohort) designs are used.

2. The sampling frame (target population) and case (person or chart from that population) are well defined. Studies based on the perception of the prevalence of abuse by a given professional group only tells us about the perception and not the rate.

3. Care be taken in the estimation of required sample size.

4. Agreement is reached as to the operational definition(s) of abuse/neglect as well as possible differences in the definitions because of external factors such as culture.

5. Methodological biases due to problems in recruiting strategies (e.g. convenience sample), measurement (e.g. reliance upon self-report), recall, and case ascertainment be minimized.

6. Appropriate research designs are employed in studying attributable and relative risk, as well as the dynamic roles of identified risk factors for abuse/neglect.

7. Cost-effective funding mechanisms for research into abuse and neglect be developed in partnership with funding agencies, service delivery agencies, and researchers.

Research must involve the establishment of trust among researchers, seniors-at-large, their caregivers, and professionals. Elder abuse and neglect research appears to be following a similar course to that taken by child and spousal abuse research: reports by front line workers preceding several studies, which are then followed by greater professional and public awareness leading to active interest by the research and policy-making communities. We are moving toward a greater awareness and interest in the topic of abuse and neglect of seniors. And finally, research in abuse and neglect has a social aspect. Epidemiological studies, either prevalence or incidence, must include in their design a mechanism for the possibility of having to deal with every case that is identified. Although this will be difficult because of numerous ethical and logistical reasons, to not do so would be a form of neglect.

# 4-4

# NEW DIRECTIONS FOR RESEARCH ON
# INTERVENTIONS WITH ABUSED OLDER ADULTS

*Charmaine Spencer*

## INTRODUCTION

The purpose of this chapter is to recommend a research agenda for evaluating interventions with abused older adults. The chapter introduces a brief discussion of the terms "effective" or "successful" intervention. It then reviews some of the Canadian and American research on interventions, highlighting the methods, briefly describing some of the findings, outlining limitations and setting out some considerations for conducting research in this area.

It should be noted that until recently American research in this area has been rudimentary, and Canadian research has been non-existent. As the abuse of older adults is a relatively new area of investigation (Shell, 1982), the lack of research on interventions might be expected: the emphasis, to date, has been more on mezzo or macro levels—educating, raising awareness of the social problem and developing procedures and policies (Hudson, 1988). The development of intervention programs (and subsequently research on their effectiveness) has been a lower priority. Existing intervention approaches have been designed primarily upon past experience, anecdotal evidence of successes and failures, and knowledge gained from other treatment programs (Stein, 1991). The lack of information on the relative effectiveness of intervention approaches creates a significant obstacle for organizations trying to address the problem in their community.

## EVALUATION RESEARCH

Intervention programs need to be evaluated for several reasons. Front-line workers need reliable information about which intervention practices are effective and why, in order to increase their knowledge and understanding of the problem, to understand the nuances of abuse or neglect and how it may manifest itself in various situations, and to break down personally and socially held stereotypes. Agencies also need the information to confirm or modify usage, to avoid replicating ineffective aspects of programs that others have initiated, and to avoid wasting resources (Synergy, 1992; Gallagher, 1993). However as Stein (1991, pp. 102-103) notes, "we still lack knowledge of what types of programs and delivery systems work effectively, given different sets of conditions and circumstances. Systematic testing of elder abuse intervention programs has been spotty at best, often relying upon simply designed evaluations. In essence, we still need to determine what 'works' and what doesn't 'work'."

Evaluation research is intended to find out "what works". Using social research methods, evaluation research appraises an intervention program on its effectiveness and efficiency. Evaluation research guides services agencies in improving the way their programs operate, and aids policy developers in distinguishing effective intervention programs from ineffective ones. Evaluation of intervention programs requires two distinct aspects. The first involves a preliminary analysis of the nature and scope of the problem, the target population, interventions used and the goals sought in terms of change. The second, containing the evaluation component, investigates whether the interventions reached the target population, whether they made a significant change in the problem, and at what cost (Rossi & Freeman, 1989).

## "EFFECTIVE" OR "SUCCESSFUL" INTERVENTIONS

As a society, we are struggling for a consensus on the proper extent of public involvement in the lives of abused older adults. The way in which we characterize interventions as "appropriate" or "inappropriate" and the manner in which we assess the effectiveness of specific types of interventions cannot be separated from personal values, as well as basic philosophical positions about aging and social responsibility to perceived vulnerable populations. In analyzing the effectiveness of particular interventions we must consider the rights of the abused individual, including the right to live at risk, to refuse help, and to stay in situations that others might deem unacceptable or not in the person's best interests (Gnaedinger, 1989). At the same time, we must also consider the balance between those individual rights and our social responsibilities to protect people from harm.

Whether or not an intervention is deemed to be effective is a matter of perspective. McDonald, Hornick, Robertson and Wallace (1991) note that intervention studies have typically focussed on effectiveness and success from the perspective of service providers or professionals, ignoring the abused person's view. This approach may tell us something about the values of the service providers or the agencies they work for, but, it may not inform us about the values, needs, or preferences of the person receiving the assistance. Often these two sets of values are significantly different. Service providers' perspectives can conflict with those of the abused person on whether there is a need for intervention and the form that it should take. Research in Canada and the United States has indicated that 30 to 45 % of older adults refuse help from agencies (McLaughlin, Nickell & Gill, 1980; Wolf, Strugnell & Godkin, 1982; Gallagher, 1993). Also, where service is given to an abused older adult, it can often be inadequate or inappropriate to the person's need, or the intervention chosen does not match the diagnosis of the situation (Hudson & Johnson, 1986). Professionals have stated that a large proportion of the cases they see are not satisfactorily resolved. Rates have varied from 36% (McLaughlin et al., 1980) to a high of 95% (Block & Sinnott, 1979). This raises two important research questions: What constitutes "resolution"? and, To whose satisfaction must a case be resolved? (Hudson & Johnson, 1986).

The values or principles used in accomplishing "successful" interventions are also important. What compromises are made, for what reasons, and by whom? In intervention research we need to consider whether other alternatives would have better helped the abused older adult at less personal cost (Mental Health Division, Health Services Directorate, 1993). For example, in one study, the most effective intervention reported by service providers was a change in the social or living situation, which usually meant placement in a nursing home or hospital (Wolf & Pillemer, 1989). Although removing abused older adults from their homes may stop the abuse, it may also sacrifice other important aspects of their lives.

Theoretical assumptions underlying particular intervention approaches also affect conclusions about the appropriateness and effectiveness of the intervention. For example, if a program is based on the assumption that abuse of older adults results from caregiver stress, and the researchers noted a reduction in caregivers' stress levels after the interventions, then they might conclude that the interventions were successful. However, if, from the researchers' perspective, stress had nothing to do with abuse, then its presence, absence or reduction would probably not be measured. Similarly, a perpetrator's acknowledging his/her actions as abusive is more likely to be considered as a measure of a program's success where the researcher or practitioner is assuming the person's culpability is an important factor.

## MEASURES OF EFFECTIVESS

Researchers have recognized that experimental designs involving a control group are ethically indefensible for abuse intervention research (Gallagher, 1993). Most agencies and researchers would find it untenable to not offer some form of assistance to a person who is being abused (Stein, 1991), and for that reason, researchers have relied on alternate methods of comparison.

In research, both qualitative and quantitative measures have been used to measure effectiveness of interventions with abused older adults. Measures of effectiveness vary across jurisdictions and among agencies. Many Canadian and American agencies measure the effectiveness of their interventions by indirect or informal means. For example, Dwelling Place, a New York City shelter for abused older adults, uses the criteria "when they are in crisis, do the people return to us?" (Cabness, 1989). In group counselling, effectiveness is sometimes measured by clients' continued willingness to come to the group. In both cases, the fact that people return is seen as demonstrating that they trust the program, the facility and its staff. Other agencies or centres consider clients telephoning to thank them for the help, or receiving renewed funding as positive support for their interventions.

Typical considerations for researchers and practitioners regarding effectiveness include: Does the intervention stop the abuse or neglect, or lessen its severity? Is there a change in the number of physical indicators (bruises, broken bones)? Is there a change in how often the abuse occurs, or how severe it is? Is there a change in the level of threat or the type of abuse or neglect? (Wolf & Pillemer, 1989; Penning, 1992). Some qualitative measures of effectiveness include: Does the abused adult feel there is an improvement in the situation? Does the older adult accept the intervention as a viable option? Does the older adult accept the options offered? Process-related measures may include: Do other agencies or professional bodies consider referring cases to the service provider using a particular intervention? If they do not, why not?

Measuring effectiveness is further complicated by the necessity of drawing comparisons among types of abuse of older adults. This creates theoretical, philosophical and legal difficulties for researchers and practitioners, as they try to gauge whether physical abuse is worse than psychological abuse, whether being assaulted once is equivalent to a week of verbal harassment, or whether financial abuse is better or worse than violation of personal rights. The issues are further compounded by the existence of both short and long term effects of abuse. While physical abuse may lead to a black eye or broken arm today, psychological abuse may lead to suicide six months from now.

Measuring effectiveness is further complicated by the changing dynamics of abuse. A perpetrator may shift from one form of abuse to another, or employ several different types simultaneously. The person who physically abuses often quickly learns that this is not socially acceptable, but then turns to more subtle forms, such as psychological abuse.  In these cases, if the intervention only deals with the abuse that first surfaces or only deals with one type of abuse, can the intervention be called "effective"?

Lastly, some effects of abuse or neglect sometimes can be manifested by other members of the family, but not necessarily by the abused person (Stein, 1991).  For example, a severely cognitively impaired older adult may have no idea that she or he is being sexually abused, or that her/his financial resources are being depleted.  On the other hand, other family members may show a range of stress reactions upon learning of, and dealing with, the abuse situation (Gallagher, 1993).

## MAJOR RESEARCH STUDIES ON INTERVENTIONS

This section briefly compares five projects to help illustrate the strengths and limitations of current research in examining interventions on abuse and neglect of older adults.  In project design and intervention research, interventions have typically been classified into three major models: adult protection, domestic violence, and advocacy (Wolf & Pillemer, 1989; McDonald et al., 1991).  More recently, two others have been added—the family systems model and the multidisciplinary model (Gnaedinger, 1989). There is considerable overlap among the terms, and "multidisciplinary approach", in particular, seems to be used loosely in connection with all the models.

The identified projects were selected because they represent some of the better research in this area: 1) Three Model Projects (Pillemer & Wolf, 1986), completed in the United States in the early 1980s, is considered a classic intervention research study.  It compared interventions used in three locations, Rhode Island; Syracuse, New York; and Worcester, Massachusetts. 2) Elder Abuse Resource Centre in Winnipeg, Manitoba was a one year demonstration project completed in 1992.  The project provided some direct services such as counselling to abused older clients, but also referred cases to other agencies. 3) Victoria Elder Abuse Project in Victoria, British Columbia, completed in 1993, focussed on a central case registry system and co-ordination of services.  One of the primary objectives of this project was to ensure uniformity in the way that abuse situations were described or recorded.  The interventions were delivered by different agencies, but the project aimed at co-ordinated service delivery.  4) Project Care in Montreal, Quebec is a study currently in progress, to be completed in 1995. This project utilizes a home care agency to help deliver services to abused older adults, focuses on caregiver/carereceiver  pairs and uses a multidisciplinary approach in assessing and addressing abuse and neglect cases. 5) Synergy II in Calgary, Alberta, is a study also currently in progress.  This project uses a "one-stop shopping approach" in which intervention services are located in a single location.  For the five studies, the services (counselling, referral) offered by an agency or project were often similar, but the ways in which the services were delivered may have differed. Table 1 compares the most salient features of each study:

## TABLE 1:    Comparison of Intervention Research Studies

| | Three Model Projects | Elder Abuse Resource Centre | Victoria Elder Abuse Project | Project Care | Synergy II |
|---|---|---|---|---|---|
| **Current status** | completed | completed | completed | in progress | in progress |
| **Sample size** | 328 cases at 3 sites | 163 cases (274 reports of abuse) | 147 clients (substantial evidence available for 117) | N=270 3 groups of 45 pairs (adult/ caregiver pairs) | approximately 60 clients |
| **Definitions used** | Pillemer & Wolf | Quinn & Tomita | Sengstock & Hwalek | National Advisory Council on Aging | Pillemer & Wolf |
| **Type of analysis** | • quantitative | • quantitative<br>• data collection tool specially designed | • quantitative<br>• B.C. version version of Sengstock-Hwalek Comprehensive Index | • quantitative<br>• validated tests, checklist, standardized questionnaire | • both quantitative and qualitative (ethnographic techniques)<br>• modifying scales and developing new scales |
| **Comparison group** | yes for one site, compared with other (non-abused) clients who used the home care agency | yes from general health survey | none identified in VEAP Report | yes-<br>1. (non-abused) home care clients<br>2. non-abused older adults from the community | no |
| **Multiple assessments** | yes:<br>1. initially<br>2. one reassessment | yes:<br>1. initially<br>2. three months later to assess EARC involvement<br>3. at 12 months | yes:<br>1. initially<br>2. six months later or at close of case | yes:<br>1. initial, monitoring throughout<br>2. at five months (at which time the intervention ceases)<br>3. follow-up six months later | yes:<br>1. initially<br>2. at conclusion of case, and<br>3. three follow-ups at 3 months, 6 months, and 12 months |
| **Time period** | two years | one year | 12 months | 3 years | 2 years and 3 months |
| **Information source** | • service providers; file information; but also directly interview a subsample of abused older adults | • 17% from abused older adults, 52% service providers, balance from friends, family others; on the two reassessments, information came from abused person less than half the time | • 1/3 clients; 2/3 from professionals<br>• considerable information missing because of refusal of services | • combination of sources (indirect from validated tests, checklists, and standardized questionnaires) | • combination of sources, including direct interviews with some older adults |

TABLE I:     Comparison of Intervention Research Studies (Continued)

| | Three Model Projects | Elder Abuse Resource Centre | Victoria Elder Abuse Project | Project Care | Synergy II |
|---|---|---|---|---|---|
| Age of subjects | 60+ | 54+ | initially 65+, but includes 57 | 60+ | 60+ |
| Major advantage | • large sample size<br>• compared three different models | • good sample size<br>• special designed data collection tool | • specially designed data collection tool | • length of the study<br>• participants surveyed at several points<br>• compares theories | • uses both quantitative and qualitative measures<br>• older adults interviewed on perspective |
| Major disadvantage | • definitions overlapped and imprecise<br>• no follow-up | • use of multiple informants (reliability)<br>• vague subjective measure of situation | • large amount of missing data | • large total populations, but few abused subjects<br>• questionable generalizeability outside of home care population | • definition overlap<br>• no comparison group |

As can be seen from Table 1, the five studies vary considerably in design and measures. To help identify the features of an ideal intervention research study, the five studies are compared below:

## Sample Size

For quantitative research, any intervention study must have an adequate sample size for researchers to determine whether there have been statistically significant changes in the abused older adults' situations. The appropriate number of subjects will depend, in part, on the type of questions being asked and the type of analysis being conducted. For an intervention study using quantitative methods an adequate sample will mean surveying a relatively large number of older adults who have been abused; the larger the group, the more comfortable we may feel about drawing conclusions from the results. Many types of quantitative analyses require at least 100 subjects. In the five studies cited here, the number of abused adults surveyed ranged from 45 to 328.

For an intervention study using qualitative methods, an adequate sample could be based on case studies of a few older adults who have experienced abuse or neglect; single-subject design could provide excellent information for intervention outcomes at the case study level. Synergy II uses ethnographic interview techniques with a small number of abused older adults (N=10) as part of its research design. With a qualitative approach such as ethnography, the smaller number of people interviewed reflects more detailed and intensive interviews, the special training required for interviewers in ethnographic techniques, the difficulty in recruiting willing subjects and the time taken to build rapport and trust with the interviewee.

Of equal importance with sample size is the need for detailed information coming from the most direct source possible, usually the abused older adult. Larger sample sizes have often been generated in studies by relying on file information, indirect sources such as service providers or families. In contrast, the researchers using smaller samples have often opted for more detailed information coming directly from the abused older adults. While sample size may affect the reliability of the conclusions, the source of the information may influence the quality of the conclusions. An ideal design will require a balancing of these two approaches.

Sample size for intervention research can be expanded in a number of ways: by increasing the length of time that the study continues, particularly the data collection component; or by combining information from a number of agencies. In urban centres, there is often more than one agency that has an intervention program in place, although not necessarily the same model. The primary advantage of involving more than one agency is the opportunity to compare the relative effectiveness of different approaches, while increasing the overall sample size. The primary disadvantage is that agencies seldom collect the same information.

## Comparison Groups

Ethical considerations make the use of control groups in abuse intervention studies impossible, but comparison groups are an option used by several of the studies to help ascertain whether changes in the abused clients' situations are related to the intervention, or to non-intervention factors, such as passage of time or idiosyncrasies of the clients involved. It is important to remember, however, that while the use of comparison groups creates an opportunity to determine whether there are characteristics peculiar to the abuse group, comparison groups do not provide us with empirical information about the effectiveness of the interventions. Although it may be intuitively satisfying to use a comparison group, it may be a better use of research resources to have a larger primary sample than to split resources between a primary sample and a comparison group.

## Pre-Test/ Post-Test

Any intervention study must be able to measure change. Current Canadian studies have recognized this. Studies typically undertake a detailed initial assessment, with a similarly rigorous comparative monitor several months later, or at the close of the case. More sophisticated studies have relied on follow-up interviews or surveys six months to a year after the intervention. These follow-ups are aimed at ascertaining whether or not the intervention had an enduring effect on the abused adult's situation, or whether changes were contingent on other factors (e.g. the presence of a person monitoring the situation might reduce the opportunity for abuse to occur undetected). Assessing individual client's situation over several intervals is resource-intensive; but when the data are aggregated, it has a significant potential to provide useful information.

Some studies have reported difficulties in obtaining follow-up information. For example, the Victoria study was able to obtain follow-up on fewer than half of the clients, and even then many questions were not answered. As a result, many of the statistical analyses the researchers would have liked to have done were not feasible. The difficulties in obtaining follow-up information were attributed in large part to the high number of competent clients who refused services.

The Victoria study raises an important issue for intervention research design. In a study of intervention service users, it is typical for those who refuse to use the services not to be studied at all. The fact they refuse the intervention option is recorded and appears as a passing note, usually on how it affects the sample size or the reliability of the study. By not attempting to follow-up on why some individuals refuse service, the researchers miss valuable opportunities to learn more about what services they should be offering and the manner in which they should be offered. Although the issue of follow-up interviews with older adults who refuse service raises a number of concerns about confidentiality, method and timing, it is an error to presume that people will refuse a follow-up interview simply because they refused an intervention in a crisis point in the past. Like many other presumptions in this area, the presumption that people who refuse services will not discuss their reasons needs to be investigated or, better still, avoided.

## Comparing Approaches

Most intervention studies to date have evaluated a single project. The two notable exceptions are the American Three Model Projects and a new Canadian national study called "Services for Abused Older Canadians". The latter was begun in late 1993 and may have preliminary information available in 1995 (University of Victoria Centre on Aging, 1994). The ideal intervention study would compare more than one intervention, and evaluate the relative effectiveness of each, thereby testing a wider range of variables or factors. Considering the heavy start-up costs for intervention studies, particularly for research design, evaluating more than one intervention program at a time may be more cost-effective than a series of single evaluations.

The Three Model Projects illustrates some of the strengths and limitations of multi-site analysis. All three sites had state or federal adult protection legislation in place, but used different intervention approaches, which were respectively identified as child abuse, advocacy, and legal models. In spite of differences in the general approaches the staff at each site took in their interventions, all three models recorded a large decrease in the manifestations of abuse/neglect and their severity, as well as a significant reduction in the level of threat to the abused older person. "Each of the projects also made headway in reducing the dependency of the victims on the abusers or family for companionship or daily needs, and the dependence of the perpetrator on the victim for financial resources" (Pillemer & Wolf, 1986, p. 226).

The different intervention approaches at the three sites all showed improvement for the clients. Although the lack of significant differences among the interventions might lead to the conclusion that providing any service is better than providing none, it is more likely that the categories or techniques used to measure effectiveness were not sufficiently defined or sensitive to measure differences among the projects. The researchers for the Three Model Projects noted that there was considerable difficulty in obtaining a consensus among the three agencies as to what information could or should be collected. In the end, the Three Model Projects used different collection methods at the sites, which may have confounded the analyses significantly.

## Case Resolution

None of the completed Canadian or American studies give detailed information on case resolution. The Three Model Projects recorded the average amount of time from initial intake to final assessment at each of the sites. On average, cases at Worcester took seven months, cases at Syracuse took eleven months, and cases at Rhode Island took nine months. The length of time may be a function of the relative complexity of the cases each agency saw. Two-thirds of the Worcester cases and three-quarters of Rhode Island and Syracuse cases were "resolved" or "resolved a lot". These are vague descriptions and, in particular, readers are left guessing as to what constitutes "resolved a lot". The terms "improved" or "somewhat improved" used in the Winnipeg study reflect similar vagueness. However, the Winnipeg study also attempted to ascertain specific ways in which the situation had changed for the person.

The Victoria study looked at changes in several measures, including prevalence, proportions of clients at low, medium and high risk, and the number of risk indicators. Relying on the change in the number of risk indicators has at least two drawbacks: 1) it only measures overall change (e.g. three indicators could worsen, three could improve, with no overall change in the number of risk indicators); and 2) some changes in risk indicators may be more important than others (e.g. changes in risk indicators such as the perpetrator's mental health or the severity of the exploitation, are likely more serious than changes in cleanliness of the older adult's residence).

The Project Care study, which is still in progress, takes a detailed approach to measuring case resolution. First, there is a three-tier screening process, part of which requires consensus by an admissions committee. In addition, a team assesses the situation at the close of the case. This consensus approach may help reduce some of the subjectivity in determining whether a case has been resolved. However, the one element that is lacking in each of these approaches is the client's input. By way of contrast, the Synergy II (1992, p. 20) project states that case resolution outcomes will be defined by the client:

> Some clients may simply want to protect themselves; others recognize that the abuse will not stop as long as they remain with the abuser; others may seek methods to control or limit abuse. Successful intervention will be judged by the client. It may be measured by the changes in the degree or levels of abuse experienced rather than the cessation of the abuse or by changes within the victim or in their skills to deal with the abuse.

Synergy's approach is a noticeable improvement over the simple definition of case resolution as "alleviation or elimination of maltreatment" used in the Three Model Projects. The latter was subsequently acknowledged by the researchers as inadequate, "especially when the victim does not wish to be separated from the perpetrator" (Wolf, Godkin & Pillemer, 1984, p. S13).

## Outcome Measures

In addition to client feedback, the Synergy II project will assess changes in the psychosocial state of the abused senior (e.g. changes in functional indicators, locus of control, self-esteem, assertiveness and the change in the type, degree and frequency of the abuse). Similarly, Project Care plans to use several quantitative scales to measure: a) general health; b) happiness/depression; c) burden; d) self-esteem; e) past and present relationship. The Winnipeg study had initially intended to use a psychosocial research tool with their counselling clients, but this was felt to be incompatible with a clinical encounter, so the component was discontinued.

## Individual Versus Global Measures of Outcome

Intervention studies typically take global measures of the effectiveness of the intervention. While a particular intervention may work well for the majority of cases, it is important for front-line workers and others to understand for whom or in what kinds of cases the intervention may not work. This may be particularly the case where special cultural or ethnic factors enter into the equation. Evaluation research analysis must highlight such differentiation.

## Quantitative Measures

To date, intervention studies have relied predominantly on quantitative analysis. Quantitative data are often used because they usually take less time to collect, and it takes less effort to recruit subjects. Some projects, such as Project Care, use a variety of standardized questionnaires, validated tests and piloted checklists. The use of quantitative measures raises three important questions: a) Are the tests sensitive enough? b) Do the tests really capture the information they are intended to measure? and c) Are indirect outcome measures better measures than directly asking the person if, and in what manner, the situation has changed?

### (a)  Are the tests sensitive enough?

Synergy II project researchers state that  many of the existing scales which have been applied to research on abuse and neglect of older adults have serious  limitations. The scales are often medically-oriented, generic, (i.e. designed for the adult population over the age of 18), or designed for very frail elderly people.  Others, such as the Conflict Tactics Scale (Straus, 1979) which is often used to measure physical abuse, are considered gender-biased. Few scales were considered sensitive enough to identify the predicted changes in seniors' psychological status or wellbeing in response to interventions or to confirm the existence of abuse in the first place. To overcome some of these limitations, Synergy II will be modifying the tests it will be using.  Project Care has designed a special screening test for similar reasons.

### (b)  Do the tests measure what they are supposed to measure?

One intervention study looked at changes in happiness as identified by a test called MUNSH (Memorial University Newfoundland Scale of Happiness). MUNSH is intended to measure happiness/depression.  Using an indirect measure such as MUNSH means we must be prepared to assume that a person who is in an abusive situation will report himself/herself as being 1) unhappy or unsatisfied with life, and 2) happy if he/she is no longer in an abusive situation. While we would certainly hope this to be true, human reactions, behaviours and feelings are more complex and, as a result, the test may not provide the answers we need.

### (c)  Are indirect outcome measures better than direct ones?

Researchers have sometimes been reluctant to directly ask abused older adults or perpetrators about their situation because they often feel that the people may minimize or deny the abuse; may not be able to express their feelings or  ideas; or may be reluctant to respond negatively, particularly when asked about the effectiveness of a service.  As a result, researchers may rely on indirect measures that they believe are more difficult for the abused older adult or the perpetrator to manipulate or circumvent. While people may be more willing to answer these indirect questions, the question still remains "Is this test or question measuring what it is supposed to be measuring?" Researchers must not only carefully consider, but must be able to clearly explain to others, why they are using specific indirect measures instead of direct measures.

## Qualitative Measures

A good intervention study will rely on both quantitative and qualitative analyses. The appropriateness of relying solely on quantitative data in researching interventions has recently come into question (Chappell, 1993). As Gallagher (1993) notes, quantitative data fail to capture the richness of the experiences of clients.  Quantitative analysis also only considers the client's situation at specific points of assessment, instead of capturing the process of change. To provide a more balanced approach of qualitative and quantitative measures, Synergy II has incorporated ethnographic interview techniques in its research design. These interviews and other qualitative measures have excellent potential to expand our understanding of abuse of older adults, particularly for intervention studies.

## Informants

The source of information about the abusive or neglectful situations has varied across the intervention studies, but in most cases the abused older adult has not been asked directly to provide information. In the Three Model Projects, the information came primarily from service providers and file information compiled on the case. In the Victoria project, information came directly from clients only one-third of the time. In addition, the assessment tool used in the Victoria study gathered information through observation, not direct questioning. The Victoria project report noted "greater reliability of findings could have possibly been achieved by requiring client validation of all observations. However, even that approach would be limited in cases of non-competent clients or persons experiencing strong denial" (p. 16). In the Winnipeg study, only 17% of the initial contacts came from the abused seniors themselves, 52% came from service providers, and the balance came from children, other relatives, friends or neighbours. At the second and third client assessment for the Winnipeg study, information was coming directly from the abused older person less than half the time.

Indirect information in intervention studies has many shortcomings, including potentially minimalizing the abusive situation and distorting the dynamics of the situation by having it filtered through the perspective of the person reporting (Tomita, 1990). For example, if the person giving the information was related to the abuser, the informant might side with the abuser; or if the abuser was seen by a service provider as a "stressed caregiver", the service provider might empathize with the caregiver and see the abusive behaviour as somewhat justified.

As the Winnipeg study has pointed out, the use of informants as sources is also dependent on how well they know the abused older adult's situation. Some informants may have had little or no contact with the person since the first referral. Use of key informants raises questions about the reliability of the information as well. In particular, researchers for the Winnipeg study found that the accuracy of longer term recall was at issue; for example, no spousal deaths were reported in the one year follow-up, whereas two cases had been mentioned in the three month follow-up. In these two cases, the informant had forgotten a very important detail like the abused adult's spouse dying. This oversight throws the reliability of their findings about other aspects of the person's life into question.

There are several possible explanations for the reliance on indirect sources of information about the abusive situation of older adults. It may result partly from untested and ageist assumptions about the reliability and validity of older adults' responses, or partly from assumptions that the older adult would not be willing to talk about the abuse. Pillemer (1985) has shown that direct interviewing can be successfully used in intervention studies. Many people who assist and support older adults trying to deal with abusive situations report that often older adults *are willing* to discuss the situations, given proper support. Indeed, in some cases the reluctance to talk openly about abuse comes more from the service provider than the older adult (Pay, 1993). Perhaps it is stating the obvious, but the answers that one gets will depend on the questions one asks and the way in which one asks them. Where the questions are posed with sensitivity and understanding, there may be more candour from abused older adults, substantially improving our knowledge base about the way interventions should be offered.

## Definitions

A well-designed intervention study should use clear and discrete definitions and terms. At a minimum, the definitions of "abuse" and "neglect" used should not overlap, as was the case in the Three Model Projects. As Hudson and Johnson (1986) note, this overlap subsequently made categorization unclear and confused the analysis. In the Three Model Projects, the researchers also noted that their simple classification system did not accurately characterize the nature of the abuse and neglect cases (Wolf et al., 1984). Project Care also faces difficulties with definitional overlap.

Among the five studies outlined in this chapter, only Project Care and the Three Model Projects used the same definitions for abuse and neglect. Although the use of different definitions affects the opportunity to draw comparisons across the studies, a global definition may not be the most important issue for attention at the present time. First, it is unlikely that everyone can agree on a global definition and efforts may be wasted in a protracted debate over whose definition will prevail. Second, even without a commonly accepted definition, as long as the definitions used are clear and consistently applied within each study, valuable information can be obtained. At any rate, evaluation research conducted independently of program design has no control over the definition used by an agency in the study being evaluated. However, there must be greater awareness in intervention research of the various definitions and some discussion of why particular definitions were chosen for the study. This may lead to a more meaningful comparison and analysis of intervention studies in the future.

Terms and categories also need to be clearly defined. For example, the category "safe and stable" used in the one study has been discounted as being of dubious value, either for research or clinical purposes, partly because abuse cases are highly volatile (Sengstock, Hwalek & Stahl, 1991). Abuse situations can become life-threatening for an older adult in a matter of minutes or days, depending on the abuser's mood.

## Ethics

Intervention studies pose peculiar ethical problems around soliciting abused older adults to participate in research. Some service providers have argued that counselling roles are incompatible with research roles, and that, in particular, clients should not be research candidates when they are still in crisis. This means that we need to consider at what stage of the intervention process it is appropriate to consider including an older person in a study on abused older adults. It has also been pointed out that there is often a difference in power between the service provider and the client. Even if the service provider does not intend it that way, asking clients about their willingness to participate in research may leave the clients with the impression that support or service is contingent on their participation. For this reason, among others, we need to give careful consideration to the ethical issues specific to intervention research on abuse of older adults.

A second ethical issue in intervention research is the inclusion of either abusers or abused older adults who have significant mental impairment. Should the researcher try to include these people in the research, and can the researcher get informed consent from these people to participate in the study? Are the tasks/scales used in the intervention study appropriate for people with mental impairment? Should proxies be used to gather the information instead? The issue becomes more complex, because the assessments are often conducted over a period of a year, which means a possible deterioration in the person's mental status. People who did not start off cognitively-impaired, could subsequently become impaired over the course of the study. For both researchers and program developers, to exclude this potentially high-risk group would leave a glaring gap in our knowledge. This raises the issue of whether we can conduct intervention research in a way that also protects these people's rights.

## SUMMARY AND CONCLUSION

To summarize, an ideal research design looking at interventions used for abused older adults should have the following: 1) sufficient sample size to answer the research questions; 2) definitions that do not overlap and terms that are clear and readily understood; 3) assessments of the abusive situation at several different points, including short and long term follow-up; 4) multiple frames to encompass a wider variety of abused older adults or abusive situations; 5) a combination of qualitative and quantitative methodology and analysis; 6) scales and tests that accurately measure changes in the abusive or neglectful situation and in the abused older adult's mental, physical or other status; 7) a comparison of programs from various agencies; 8) the abused older adult as an important information source; and 9) ethical guidelines.

In 1991, the National Aging Resource Center on Elder Abuse strongly recommended improvement in the way outcome research was designed and conducted (Stein, 1991), and recent Canadian research studies have shown an effort to improve the quality of research. The studies cited here all assessed the clients' situation at several points in time. Through the use of a follow-up assessment, some have attempted to see whether the intervention strategy has an enduring effect. Some studies have used comparison groups, although we can question whether the comparison group tells us anything about the effectiveness of the intervention. Some studies are trying to develop research measures specific to abusive situations.

All research is a compromise—and Canadian research is no exception. The compromises are usually between financial or organizational resources and research objectives. Researchers constantly make trade-offs between increasing sample size or length of the study and getting funding in the first place; and between developing more comprehensive tools/scales and getting people to use them. Each of the studies described here has offered unique strengths and opportunities for insights into interventions with abused older adults. By using the best qualities of these studies in future research on this topic, and by paying attention to the ethical, methodological and definitional issues which current studies have not yet addressed, we will achieve a greater understanding of what interventions contribute to a sense of security and wellbeing for abused older adults.

# CONCLUSION

# CONCLUSION

*Michael J. MacLean and Rosemary M. Williams*

Our purpose in undertaking this book was to assess current knowledge, to reflect on how to change the situation with regard to the abuse of older Canadians, and to share our findings with others in the hope of advancing our collective search for solutions to this complex and disturbing issue.

We have discovered that study and action on elder abuse and neglect is still at a relatively early stage. We lack a common definition of the term, and this has implications for practice as well as for research. Much of what we know needs testing out. We do have tools for detecting, assessing, and intervening with older persons in abuse and neglect situations, but the effectiveness of these tools has yet to be demonstrated. Moreover, our framework for understanding the problem needs to be broadened.

By a systematic focus on abuse and neglect of older persons from the four perspectives of practice, policy, education, and research, this book has been able to offer numerous recommendations for future action. The authors have highlighted gaps and problems, indicated areas for needed attention, and pointed to promising initiatives. A synthesis of their recommendations is to be found as Appendix A of this book.

We now turn these recommendations over to you, older and younger Canadians alike, all whose work brings you into contact with older persons, all whose awareness of the issue urges you towards doing something about it. We trust that these recommendations will indeed become the basis of collective strategies for changing the reality of abuse and neglect of older Canadians.

# LIST OF CONTRIBUTORS

# LIST OF CONTRIBUTORS

**ELAINE BAILLIE**, O.T.(C), is President of Elaine Kingsmill Baillie Associates, Educators and Consultants, Toronto. Previously, her roles have included: Director of Educational Services for the Ontario Association of Non-Profit Homes and Services to Seniors, member of the Task Force Reporting on Elder Abuse, Activation Consultant to the Ontario Ministry of Health and co-author of the publication "Prevention of Elder Abuse".

**MARIE BEAULIEU**, Ph.D., is a professor at the Université du Québec à Rimouski. Her undergraduate and graduate training is in the field of criminology and her doctoral work has dealt with the abuse of elderly people in long-term care facilities. Since 1987, she has been actively involved with issues relating to the abuse of elderly people, initially as a researcher for the Québec Ministry of Health and Social Services, and subsequently with the provincial coalition known as "Vieillir sans violence". Her expertise also comes into play with the training work she has been conducting in local health care service centres and in long-term facilities. She has been involved in the "Voix" project on prevention of elder abuse since 1992. She has also authored many conference presentations, news items, articles and reports on research activities conducted in her field.

**LISE BÉLANGER**, M.Sc., is Executive Director of four Long-Term Care Centres in Québec. Other important roles she has held with respect to elderly people include: Administrator, Québec Confederation of Long Term Care and Rehabilitation Centres; President, Québec Federation of Long-Term Care Centres; President, Regional Service Organization Committee on Planning for the Elderly; Elder Abuse Committee member, Québec Health and Social Services Department; and Founding Member, Québec Association on Gerontology. She is the author of a number of publications, particularly on aspects of institutional care for elderly people.

**JOHN B. BOND Jr**, Ph.D., member of the CAG Project Advisory Committee, is Professor and Head of the Department of Family Studies at the University of Manitoba. He received his B.Sc in Psychology from the University of Illinois and his M.Sc. and Ph.D in Child Development and Family Life from Purdue. For several years Dr. Bond served as Chair of the Project Management Committee of the Elder Abuse Resource Centre in Winnipeg. His recent research interests include the support provided by middle-aged offspring to their aging parents, and perceptions of effectiveness of legislation in Canada and the United States regarding abuse of elderly people.

**THOMAS J. ELMSLIE**, M.D., M.Sc., CCFP, FRCPC, is an Associate Professor of Family Medicine and of Community Medicine and Epidemiology at the University of Ottawa, and Director of the Clinical Epidemiology Unit, Élisabeth Bruyère Health Centre. He is active in the college of Family Physicians of Canada where he is a member of the National Research Committee; Chair of the planning committee of the National Research System (NaRes); and a member of the steering committee for the Clinical Practice Management Project.

**LORELEY GREENSLADE**, M.Sc., is the Project Coordinator for the Products and Services Research Group of CARNET: The Canadian Aging Research Network, at the University of Manitoba. She received her B.A.(Hons.) in Psychology from the University of Winnipeg, and her M.Sc. in Family Studies from the University of Manitoba. Her recent research interests include adaptive strategies (including the use of products and services) to enhance independence among community-dwelling elders, and service providers' perception of the prevalence, causes, and effective interventions in elder abuse and neglect cases.

**ADRIAN GREK**, MD, FRCPC, is an Assistant Professor in the Department of Psychiatry at McMaster University, Hamilton, Ontario, and Chief of Geriatric Psychiatry Services at Chedoke-McMaster Hospitals.

**SR. ST. MICHAEL GUINAN**, O.S.U., Ph.D., Professor Emeritus in Gerontology at Brescia College, London, Ontario, was born in 1904. A founding member of the Canadian Association on Gerontology, the Ontario Gerontological Association, and the Canadian Institute of Religion and Gerontology, a Fellow of the Gerontological Society of America and an Honorary Life Fellow of the Canadian Psychological Association, she has won many awards throughout her distinguished career, including the Canadian Silver Jubilee medal, the Papal Medal, and the Governor General's Medal. She was the first woman to receive a Canada Council grant in support of doctoral studies. She is listed in the World Who's Who of Women.

**LEE ANN HOFF**, R.N., Ph.D., is Adjunct Professor at the University of Ottawa, School of Nursing where she has been instrumental in bringing together individuals and groups to examine issues related to women and health, including violence against women and children of all ages. She holds a Doctorate in Social Science and a Masters in Nursing. Dr. Hoff has extensive expertise in the area of violence against women and has authored several texts, including the book *People in Crisis* and *A Curriculum Guide for Nursing on Violence Against Women and Children*, as well as many articles on this subject.

**ALBERT KOZMA**, Ph.D., is Professor of Psychology and Co-Director of the Gerontology Centre at the Memorial University of Newfoundland, with cross-appointments to the School of Nursing and Community Medicine faculties there. For the past fifteen years, Dr. Kozma has been collaborating with Dr. M. J. Stones in a substantial research program on the physical and psychological well-being of elderly Newfoundlanders. He received his Ph.D. from the University of Western Ontario and has published extensively.

**JEAN KOZAK**, Ph.D., member of the CAG Project Advisory Committee, is Associate Director of the University of Ottawa's Department of Family Medicine Clinical Epidemiology Unit and Director of Research of the Sisters of Charity of Ottawa's Élisabeth Bruyère Health Centre. He received his Ph.D from the University of British Columbia and is active in applied clinical research, particularly with respect to frail elderly people. Dr. Kozak is currently involved in developing assessment procedures for evaluating frailty, and the capacity for providing informed consent for health care decisions. He is one of the co-investigators in the current CSHA study and is involved with the CAG in developing a directory of Canadian researchers in gerontology and geriatrics.

**SHARON MACIBORIC-SOHOR**, M.S.W., a social worker at the Psychogeriatric Day Hospital at Seven Oaks General Hospital in Winnipeg, Manitoba, has been working with abused seniors for ten years. She was involved in the development of the institutional policy and protocol for management of abused seniors and their families. Past Chairperson of the Provincial Geriatric Social Work Advocacy Committee, she currently chairs the Educational Committee which explores issues that concern both social workers and their clients.

**MICHAEL MACLEAN**, Ph.D., Chair of the CAG Abuse and Neglect of Older Canadians Advisory Committee, is Professor of Gerontology and Social Work (part-time) at McMaster University, and President of the Canadian Association on Gerontology. He holds a doctorate in Social Psychology from the University of London, England. His teaching and research interests are in cultural diversity and aging, abuse and neglect of seniors, and social policy and practice issues in gerontology. He has held teaching and research positions at a number of Canadian Universities and at the Université du Troisième Âge in Toulouse, France. He has also been Executive Director of the Canadian Association of Schools of Social Work and Research Associate at the Institute for Research on Public Policy.

**LYNN MCDONALD**, Ph.D., member of the CAG Project Advisory Committee, is an Associate Professor and Academic Co-ordinator of the Centre for Applied Research in the Faculty of Social Work at the University of Toronto. She received her Ph.D. from the University of Calgary and is active in applied research in substance abuse and the elderly and retirement in Canada. Dr. McDonald is the first author of *Elder Abuse in Canada,* and is currently involved in a feasibility study for a shelter for older persons.

**PEARL McKENZIE** is an independent contractor and trainer. Until June, 1994, she was Executive Director of North Shore Community Services, Vancouver and has been actively involved in issues concerning abuse of women and people with disabilities since starting a community law office service at this agency in 1982. Pearl was a member of the B.C. Task Force on Family Violence, was on the Advisory Committee to the Federal Panel on Violence against Women, on the Federal Policy Circles on Abuse of Older Adults and Abuse in Institutions, and on the Joint Working Committee to Reform Adult Guardianship Legislation in B.C. Pearl has authored the manual *Legal Issues in Elder Abuse Intervention* and is currently working with the newly-formed B.C. Coalition to Eliminate Abuse of Seniors to build community networks, provide training in elder abuse issues, and ensure that there are accessible legal services for seniors.

**DAPHNE NAHMIASH**, member of the CAG Project Advisory Committee, leads a full and multifaceted career as a social worker, teacher, author, manager and research investigator. She received her M.S.W. degree from McGill University, where she is currently part-time Adjunct Professor at the School of Social Work. She is undertaking doctoral studies in social work at Laval University, and concentrates her considerable experience, energy and skills in the area of elder abuse. She has been Home Care Director of the CLSC Metro, has served on many boards and committees, and has provided consultant services to such government groups as the Quebec Elder Abuse Task Force and the provincial committee of Experts on Services to Seniors.

**SHEILA M. NEYSMITH**, D.S.W. is a Professor at the Faculty of Social Work, University of Toronto. Her research and writing has examined the effects of social policy on women as they age, and her current research is on the emotional and mental labour (invisible) done by homemakers who care for frail elderly persons. She has co-edited a book entitled *Women and Caring: Feminist Perspectives on Social Welfare.*

**CHRISTOPHER J. PATTERSON**, M.D., FRCPC, is a Professor in the Department of Medicine at McMaster University. He received his undergraduate medical training at the University of London, England, and immigrated to Canada in 1971. After several years in general practice he completed residency training in General Internal Medicine at Queen's University, Kingston, and in Geriatric Medicine at University of Western Ontario and McMaster University. He serves on the Canadian Task Force on the Periodic Health Examination. His research interests include prevention, health services effectiveness, and laboratory utilization.

**ELIZABETH DOW PITTAWAY**, D.S.W. is a graduate of the University of Western Ontario ('73) and Wilfrid Laurier University ('74,'90). She completed her doctorate in Social Work specializing in the field of gerontology. Dr. Pittaway is an assistant professor and a research affiliate with the Centre on Aging at the University of Victoria. She teaches in the School of Social Work, and in the Multidisciplinary Master's Program on Policy and Practice in the field of aging. Dr. Pittaway has conducted research in the area of elder abuse and is a co-principal investigator of a national study, "Services for Abused Older Canadians", sponsored by the British Columbia government and funded through Health Canada, Family Violence Prevention Division.

**ELIZABETH PODNIEKS**, M.E.S., member of the CAG Project Advisory Committee, is Professor at the School of Nursing, Ryerson Polytechnical Institute, Toronto. She is the Chair of the Ontario Network for the Prevention of Elder Abuse, and was Principal Investigator for the National Survey of Abuse of the Elderly in Canada. She is currently a doctoral student at the Ontario Institute for Studies in Education, University of Toronto.

**GERALD B. ROBERTSON** is Chair of the Health Law Institute at the University of Alberta and a Professor in the Faculty of Law there. He obtained his LL.B. degree at the University of Edinburgh and his LL.M. at McGill University and is a Barrister and Solicitor in Alberta. His research interests are in the areas of medical law and mental health law, and he is the author of two publications on these subjects, titled *Mental Disability and the Law in Canada*, and *Elder Abuse and Neglect in Canada*. Professor Robertson has also published extensively in legal and medical journals in Canada, the United States and Britain.

**MARGARET M. ROSS**, R.N., Ph.D., is currently an Associate Professor at the University of Ottawa School of Nursing and holds a Ministry of Health of Ontario Career Scientist Award. Dr. Ross received her B.Sc. Nursing at St. Francis Xavier University, her Masters in Education at Dalhousie and her Doctorate in Community Health at the University of Toronto. Her research interests lie primarily in aging and health, and in the provision of personal and professional care in the home. She has published extensively in scientific and professional journals and is co-author of a Curriculum Guide for Nursing on Violence Against Women and Children.

**CHARMAINE SPENCER**, LL.M. is a Research Associate with the Gerontology Research Centre at Simon Fraser University. Her work has focused on a range of abuse and neglect issues including financial abuse, institutional abuse and neglect, and ethical dilemmas facing professionals and business people in suspected abuse situations. She is currently writing on how native communities in Canada and the United States are addressing abuse and neglect of elders. Ms. Spencer is also a lawyer whose work has focused on disability and human rights issues. She was actively involved in a community-based law reform project developing alternatives to adult guardianship.

**MICHAEL STONES**, Ph.D., member of the CAG Project Advisory Committee, received his Ph.D. from the Faculty of Medicine at the University of Sheffield, England. He worked as a clinical psychologist at St. James University in Leeds and was the first clinical psychologist in the U.K. to work exclusively in a Geriatric Unit. He joined the Department of Psychology at the Memorial University of Newfoundland in 1974 and received the President's Award for Outstanding Research in 1984 for his work on physical fitness and happiness in elderly people. With Co-Director Dr. Al Kozma, he initiated the Gerontology Centre. He took up a new position in 1994 as Professor in the Dept. of Health Studies and Gerontology at the University of Waterloo. To balance his academic and research achievements, Dr. Stone is also a race walker who has competed internationally for Canada, and is also a "sometimes poet".

**LINDA TOD** is a Geriatric Social Worker and is Director, Social and Support Services, at the New Vista Society, Burnaby, B.C. Linda is Chair of the B.C. Coalition to Eliminate Abuse of Seniors. She chaired the Steering Committee of the North Vancouver Elder Abuse Project. She was a member of the Project to Review Adult Guardianship, and was involved in the new Adult Guardianship laws passed by the Province in July 1993.

**JOSÉE VERDON**, M.D., a specialist in internal medicine and geriatrics, is an active clinician in the field at the Hôpital Saint-Luc in Montreal. She is a clinical researcher at the Centre de recherche clinique André-Viallet and Centre de recherche Centre Hospitalier Côte des Neiges. Her research focuses on clinical and functional problems faced by elderly people and their families, and her specific interests are in dementia, comorbidities and epidemiological studies. Dr. Verdon is currently principal investigator in CSHA and an active collaborator in Project Image on the cause of Alzheimer's disease.

**ELIZABETH WATSON**, M.D., is a geriatrician at Seven Oaks General Hospital in Winnipeg and an Assistant Professor at the University of Manitoba. She received her medical training at the Royal College of Surgeons in Ireland, her rotating internship in Newfoundland, and her residency in Winnipeg and Hamilton. She was a member of the Project Management Committee of the Elder Abuse Resource Centre and is involved with the Domestic Violence Committee at Seven Oaks Hospital.

**ROSEMARY M. WILLIAMS**, M.S.W., is the Project officer with the Abuse and Neglect of Older Canadians project. She has studied at University of Toronto, l'Université de Strasbourg, Memorial University of Newfoundland, and Concordia University. Her master's research at McGill University focused on foster home care for elderly persons. She has coordinated a community-based respite program for frail elderly homebound people, and has a long history of active involvement with organizations such as Oxfam, Canadian Parents for French, International Programs of the YMCA, and several church-based social justice groups.

**PENNY YELLEN**, M.S.W., R.S.W., is the Manager of the Age & Opportunity Elder Abuse Resource Centre in Winnipeg. She was co-investigator of a research project "Relationship Between Laws and Elder Abuse" and has served on the Advisory Committee for "Community Awareness and Response: Abuse and Neglect of Older Adults" and on the National Advisory Committee for "Abuse and Neglect of Older Adults: Information Session for People in the Workplace". Penny is a Board Member of the Manitoba Research Centre on Family Violence and Violence against Women, and Past National President of the National Council of Jewish Women of Canada.

# REFERENCES

# REFERENCES

## A

Abdennur, A. (1990). *Elder mistreatment: Toward the development of a standardized definition*. Ottawa, ON: Department of Justice Canada.

Abel, E., & Nelson, M. (Eds.). (1990). *Circles of care: Work and identity in women's lives.* Albany, N.Y.: State University of New York Press.

Age and Opportunity Elder Abuse Resource Center. (1993). *Final report of the Demonstration Project, Appendix 1.* Winnipeg, MB: Author.

Alberta Law Reform Institute. (1990a). *Enduring powers of attorney* (Report for discussion No. 7). Edmonton, AB: Author.

Alberta Law Reform Institute. (1990b). *Enduring powers of attorney* (Final report No. 59). Edmonton, AB: Author.

Alexander, M. P. (1988). Clinical determination of mental competence: A theory and a retrospective study. *Archives of Neurology, 45,* 23-26.

Allred, G.B. & Dobson, J.E. (1987). Remotivation group interaction: Increasing children's contact with the elderly. *Elementary School - guidance and counselling, 21*(3), 216-220.

American Association of Retired Persons. (1990). *Toward the prevention of domestic mistreatment or abuse.* Washington, D.C.: Author.

American Medical Association, Council on Scientific Affairs. (1987). Elder abuse and neglect. *Journal of the American Medical Association, 257,* 966-971.

American Medical Association. (1992). *Diagnostic and treatment guidelines on elder abuse and neglect.* Chicago, IL: Author.

Anderson, T. (1989). Community professionals and their perspectives on elder abuse. In R. Filinson & S. R. Ingman (Eds.), *Elder abuse: practice and policy* (pp. 117-129). New York: Human Sciences Press.

Anetzberger, G. J. (1987). *The etiology of elder abuse by adult offspring.* Springfield, IL: Charles C. Thomas Publisher.

Anonymous. (1983). Elder abuse: The merit of mandatory reporting laws and the Minnesota response. *William Mitchell Law Review, 9,* 365-387.

Appelbaum, P. S., & Grisso, T. (1988). Assessing patients' capacities to consent to treatment. *New England Journal of Medicine, 319,* 1635-1638.

Ashley, J., & Fulmer, T. T. (1988). No simple way to determine elder abuse. *Geriatric Nursing, 9,* 286-288.

Assael, H., & Keon, J. (1982). Nonsampling vs. sampling errors in survey research. *Journal of Marketing, 46,* 114-123.

Association des Centres d'Accueil du Québec. (1991). *Les services gérontologiques en centre d'hébergement et de soins de longue durée pour adultes en perte d'autonomie: Un cadre de référence* (Gerontological services in residence and longterm care facilities for less-than-autonomous persons: A frame of reference). Montréal, QC: Author.

Association des Centres d'Accueil du Québec. (1993a). *Le code d'éthique: Une démarche et un outil de mobilisation* (The code of ethics: An approach and instrument of mobilization). Montréal, QC: Author.

Association des Centres d'Accueil du Québec. (1993b). *Guide sur la création d'un comité des usagers dans un établissement de santé et de services sociaux* (Guide to the creation of a users' committee in a health and social services agency). Montréal QC: Author.

Association des Centres d'Accueil du Québec. (1993c). *Guide sur l'examen des plaintes formulées par les usagers d'un établissement de santé et de services sociaux* (Guide to the review of complaints formulated by users in a health and social services establishment). Montréal, QC: Author.

**B**

Baines, C., Evans, P. & Neysmith, S. (Eds.). (1991). *Women's caring: Feminist perspectives on social welfare.* Toronto, ON: McClelland & Stewart.

Bane, S. D. (1991). *The rural elderly network, 3,* 3.

Baril, M., & Beaulieu, M. (l989). *Les personnes âgées se prononcent sur la vie en résidence* (The elderly comment on life in residence). Unpublished manuscript, Université de Montréal, Centre International de Criminologie Comparée, Montréal, QC.

Baycrest Centre for Geriatric Care. (1994, July). What constitutes abuse? Recognizing it can help prevent it. *Baycrest Bulletin, 6*(3), 5.

Beaulieu, M. (1992a). *Les cadres de centres d'accueil publics et les pratiques d'intervention face aux abus à l'endroit des personnes âgées.* (The management of public residences and intervention practices in the area of elder abuse). Unpublished doctoral dissertation, Université de Montréal, Montréal, QC.

Beaulieu, M. (1992b). La formation en milieu de travail: l'expression d'un besoin des cadres en ce qui concerne les abus à l'endroit des personnes âgées en centre d'accueil (The expression of a management need concerning abuse of the elderly in nursing homes). *Le Gérontophile, 14*(3), 37.

Beck, C., & Philips, L. (1983). Abuse of the elderly. *Journal of Gerontological Nursing, 9*(2), 97-102.

Bélanger, L. (1981, November). *The types of violence the elderly are victims of: Results of a survey done with personnel working with the elderly.* Paper presented at the 34th Annual Scientific Meeting of the Gerontological Society of America, Toronto, Canada.

Belsey, M. A. (1993). Child Abuse: Measuring a global problem. *World Health Statistics Quarterly, 46*(1), 69-77.

Benner, P. (1984). *From novice to expert.* Menlo Park, CA: Addison-Wesley.

Bennett, G. C. J. (1992). Elder abuse. In J. George & S. Ebrahim (Eds.), *Health care for older women* (pp. 120-132). Oxford, England: Oxford Medical Publications.

Benton, D., & Marshall, C. (1991). Elder abuse. *Clinics in Geriatric Medicine, 7*(4), 831-845.

Bevis, E. O., & Watson, J. (1989). *Toward a caring curriculum: A new pedagogy for nursing.* New York: National League for Nursing.

Bissett-Johnson, A. (1986). Domestic violence: A plethora of problems and precious few solutions. *Canadian Journal of Family Law, 5,* 253-276.

Block, M. R., & Sinnott, J. D. (1979). *The battered elder syndrome: An exploratory study.* Unpublished manuscript, University of Maryland, Center on Aging, College Park, MD.

Bloom, J. S., Ansell, P., & Bloom, M. N. (1989). Detecting elder abuse: A guide for physicians. *Geriatrics, 44,* 40-44.

Bond, J. B., Penner, R., & Yellen, P. (1992). *Final report: The effectiveness of legislation concerning abuse of the elderly: A survey of Canada and the United States.* Winnipeg,MB: University of Manitoba.

Bookin, D., & Dunkle, R. (1985). Elder abuse: Issues for the practitioner. *Social Casework, 66*(1), 3-13.

Bouvier, M. (l988). La gestion de la violence exercée à l'endroit des personnes âgées handicapées, hébergées en établissement (Managing violence against the physically challenged or institutionalized elders). *Administration Hospitalière, 34*(5), 32-29.

Bowker, L. H. (1982). *Humanizing institutions for the aged.* Lexington, DC: Heath

Bowker, L. H., Arbitell, M., & McFerron J. (1988). On the relationship between wife beating and child abuse. In K. Yllo, & M. Bograd (Eds.), *Feminist perspectives on wife abuse* (pp. 158-174). Newbury Park, CA: Sage.

Bradburn, N. M., Sudman, S., & Associates. (1979). *Improving interview method and questionnaire design: Response effects to threatening questions in survey research.* San Francisco, CA: Jossey-Bass.

Breckman, R. S., & Adelman, R. D. (1988). *Strategies for helping victims of elder mistreatment.* Newbury Park, CA: Sage.

Brillon, Y. (1987). *Victimization and fear of crime among the elderly.* Toronto, ON: Butterworths.

Bristowe, E., & Collins, J. (1989). Family mediated abuse of noninstitutionalized frail elderly men and women living in British Columbia. *Journal of Elder Abuse and Neglect, 1,* 45-64.

British Columbia InterMinistry Committee on Elder Abuse. (1992). *Principles, procedures, and protocols for elder abuse.* Victoria, BC: Ministry of Health & Ministry Responsible for Seniors.

British Columbia InterMinistry Committee on Issues Affecting Dependent Adults/The Project to Review Adult Guardianship. (1992). *How can we help?: A new look at self-determination, interdependence, substitute decision making and guardianship in British Columbia.* (Discussion paper by the Joint Working Committee), Vancouver, BC: Author.

Bunch, C. (1987). *Passionate politics: Feminist theory in action.* New York: St Martin's Press.

Burston, G. R. (1975). Granny-battering. (letter) *British Medical Journal, 6,* 592.

# C

Cabness, J. (1989). The emergency shelter: A model for building the self-esteem of abused elders. *Journal of Elder Abuse and Neglect, 1*(2) 71-82.

Caldwell, J. M., & Kapp, M. B. (1981). The rights of nursing home patients: Possibilities and limitations of federal regulation. *Journal of Health Politics, Policy and Law, 6,* 40-48.

Callahan, J. J. Jr. (1988). Elder abuse: Some questions for policymakers. *The Gerontologist, 28,* 453-458.

Canadian Association of Social Work Administrators in Health Facilities (CASWAHF). (1989). *Domestic violence protocol manual for social workers in health facilities* (Cat. No. H7221/111989E). Ottawa, ON: Supply and Services Canada.

Canadian Association on Gerontology (CAG). (1993). *Seniors' perspectives: Currently important issues within the province/territory.* Ottawa, ON: Author.

Canadian Task Force on the Periodic Health Examination. (1993). *Secondary prevention of elder abuse.* Halifax, NS: Dalhousie University.

Carniol, B. (1990). *Case critical: Challenging social work in Canada* (2nd ed.). Toronto, ON: Between the Lines.

Cash, T., & Valentine, D. (1987). A decade of adult protective services: Case characteristics. *Journal of Gerontological Social Work, 10*(3/4), 47-60.

Cassell, E. (1989, March). Abuse of the elderly: Misuses of power. *New York State Journal of Medicine, 89,* 159-162.

Chang, C., & White-Means, S. (1991). The men who care: An analysis of male primary caregivers who care for frail elderly at home. *The Journal of Applied Gerontology. 10*(3), 343-357.

Chappell, N. L. (1993, March). *Research Study Group on Elder Abuse: Final Report.* Unpublished manuscript, University of Victoria, Centre on Aging, Victoria, BC.

Chen, P. N., Bell, S. L., Dolinsky, D. L., Doyle, J., & Dunn, M. (1981). Elderly abuse in domestic settings: A pilot study. *Journal of Gerontological Social Work, 4*(1), 3-17.

Chichin, E. (1991). The treatment of paraprofessional workers in the home. *Pride Institute Journal of Long Term Care, 10,* 26-35.

Clark-Daniels C.L., Daniels, R. S., & Baumhover, L. A. (1990). Abuse and neglect of the elderly: Are emergency department personnel aware of mandatory reporting laws? *Annals of Emergency Medicine, 19*(9), 970-977.

Comer-Calder, N. (1992). The learning channel. *Adults Learning, 4,* 2.

Cook, T.D. & Campbell, D.T. (1979). *Quasi-experimentation: Design & analysis issues for field settings.* Boston, MA: Houghton Mifflin.

Council on Aging of Ottawa-Carleton. (1988). *Enhancing awareness of elder abuse: Three educational models.* Ottawa, ON: Author.

Couture, M., & Beauvais, D. (1987). Violence aux personnes âgées (Violence toward the elderly). *Nursing Québec, 7*(2), 32-36.

Cowell, A. (1989). Abuse of the institutionalized aged: Recent policy in California. In R. Filinson & S. R. Ingman (Eds.), *Elder abuse: practice and policy* (pp. 242-253). New York: Human Sciences Press.

Cox, H. (1991a, February). Verbal abuse nationwide, Part I: Oppressed group behaviour. *Nursing Management, 22*(2) 32-35.

Cox, H. (1991b, March). Verbal abuse nationwide, Part II: Impact and modifications. *Nursing Management, 22*(3), 66-69.

Coyne, A. C., Reichman, W. E., & Berbig, L. J. (1993). The relationship between dementia and elder abuse. *American Journal of Psychiatry, 150*, 643-646.

Crawford, M., & Gartner, R. (1992). *Woman killing: Intimate femicide in Ontario 1974-1990.* Toronto,ON: Women We Honour Action Committee.

Culver, C. M., & Gert, B. (1982). *Philosophy in medicine: Conceptual and ethical issues in medicine and psychiatry.* New York: Oxford University Press.

## D

Davies, M. (1993). Recognizing abuse: An assessment tool for nurses. In P. Decalmer & F. Glendenning (Eds.), *The mistreatment of elderly people* (pp. 102-116).     London: Sage.

De Beauvoir, S. (1970). *La vieillesse I* (Old age I). Paris: Idées/Gallimard.

Decalmer, P. (1993). Clinical presentation. In F. Glendenning & P. Decalmer (Eds.), *The mistreatment of elderly people* (pp. 35-61). London: Sage.

Decalmer, P., & Glendenning, F. (Eds.). (1993). *The mistreatment of elderly people.* London: Sage.

Decalmer, P., & Marriott, A. (1993). The multidisciplinary assessment of clients and patients. In F. Glendenning & P. Decalmer (Eds.), *The mistreatment of elderly people* (pp. 117-135). London: Sage.

Dellman-Jenkins, M., Lambert, D. & Fruit, D. (1986).  Old and young together: Effect of an educational program on preschoolers' attitudes towards older people. *Childhood Education, 62*(3), 206-212.

Diamond, T. (1990). Nursing homes as trouble. In C. Abel & M. Nelson (Eds.), *Circles of care.* Albany, NY: State University of New York Press.

Diessenbaker, H. (l989). Neglect, abuse and the taking of life in old people's homes. *Aging and Society, 9*, 61-71.

Dillman, D. (1978). *Mail and telephone survey: The total design method.* New York: Wiley and Sons.

Dobash, R. E., & Dobash, R. P. (1992). *Women, violence and social change.* London: Routledge.

Dobash, R. P., Dobash, R. E., Wilson, M., & Daly, M. (1992). The myth of sexual symmetry in marital violence. *Social Problems. 39*(1), 71-91.

Dolan, R., & Blakely, B. (1989). Elder abuse and neglect: A study of adult protective workers in the United States. *Journal of Elder Abuse and Neglect, 1*(3), 31-49.

Donovan, R., Kurzman, P., & Rotman, C. (1993). Improving the lives of home care workers: A partnership of social work and labor. *Social Work. 38*(5), 579-584.

Doty, P., & Sullivan, E. (1983). Community involvement in combatting abuse and neglect and mistreatment in nursing homes. *Health and Society, 61*(2), 222-251.

Douglass, R.L. (1989). *Domestic mistreatment of the elderly.* Washington, D.C.: American Association of Retired Persons.

Drane, J. F. (1984). Competency to give an informed consent: A model for making clinical assessments. *Journal of the American Medical Association, 252*, 925-927.

Driedger, L., & Chappell, N. L. (1987). *Aging and ethnicity: Toward an interface.* Toronto, ON: Butterworths.

Dwyer, J. W., & Coward, R. T. (Eds.). (1992). *Gender, families, and elder care.* Newbury Park, CA: Sage.

**E**

Edinberg, M. A. (1986). Developing and integrating family-oriented approaches in care of the elderly. In K. Pillemer & R. S. Wolf (Eds.), *Elder abuse in the family* (pp. 267–281). Dover, MA: Auburn House.

Eichler, M. (1988). *Families in Canada today: Recent changes and their policy consequences* (2nd ed.). Toronto, ON: Gage.

Elliott C. (1991). Competence as accountability. *Journal of Clinical Ethics, 2*(3), 167-171.

Esping-Andersen, G. (1989). The three political economies of the welfare state. *Canadian Review of Sociology and Anthropology, 26*(1), 10-36.

Estes, C. L., & Close, L. (1992, March). *Long term care: The challenge to education.* Paper presented at the annual meeting of the Association for Gerontology in Higher Education (AGHE), Louisville, KY.

**F**

Falcioni, D. (1982). Assessing the abused elderly. *Journal of Gerontological Nursing, 8*(4), 208-212.

Faulkner, L. R. (1982). Mandating the reporting of suspected cases of elder abuse: An inappropriate, ineffective and ageist response to the abuse of older adults. *Family Law Quarterly, 16,* 69-91.

Fiegener, J., Fiegener, M., & Mezaros, J. (1989). Policy implications of a statewide survey on elder abuse. *Journal of Elder Abuse and Neglect, 1*(2), 39-58.

Ferris, L. E., & Tudiver, F. (1992). Family physicians' approach to wife abuse: a study of Ontario, Canada practices. *Family Medicine, 24*(4), 276-182.

Ferguson, D., & Beck, C. (1983). H.A.L.F.: a tool to assess elder abuse within the family. *Geriatric Nursing, 4,* 301-304.

Filinson, R., & Ingman, S. R. (1993). An evaluation of a program of volunteer advocates for elder abuse victims. *Journal of Elder Abuse and Neglect, 5*(1), 77-93.

Foekler, G., Holland, J., Marsh, M., & Simmons, B. (1990). A community response to elder abuse. *The Gerontologist, 30*(4), 560-562.

Folmar, S., & Wilson, H. (1989). Social behaviour and physical restraints. *The Gerontologist, 29*(5), 650–654.

Fraser, N., & Gordon, L. (1994). A genealogy of dependency: Tracing a keyword in the U.S. welfare state. *Signs: Journal of Women in Culture and Society. 19*(2), 309-336.

G. A. Frecker Association on Gerontology. (1983). Summary report on aging and victimization including 1983 St. John's survey results, St. John's, NF: MUN Extension Service.

Friedman, L. M., Furberg, C. D., & DeMets, D. L. (1985). *Fundamentals of clinical trials.* Littleton, MA: PSG Pub.

Friedan, B. (1993). *The fountain of age.* New York: Simon and Shuster.

Friedrich, J. (1988). A model program for training religious leaders to work with abuse. In A. Horton, & J. Williamson (Eds.), *Abuse and religion* (pp. 181-187). Lexington, DC: Heath.

Fulmer. T. (1989). Mistreatment of elders: Assessment, diagnosis, and intervention. *Nursing Clinics of North America, 24,* 707-716.

Fulmer, T. (1991). Elder mistreatment: Progress in community detection and intervention. *Family and Community Health, 14,* 26-34.

Fulmer, T., & O'Malley, T. A. (1987). *Inadequate care of the elderly: A health care perspective on abuse and neglect.* New York: Springer.

Fulmer, T. T. (1984). Elder abuse assessment tool. *Dimensions of Critical Care Nursing, 3,* 216.

Fulmer. T., McMahon, D.J., Baer-Hines, M. & Forget, B. (1992). Abuse, neglect, abandonment, violence and exploitation: An analysis of all elderly patients seen in one emergency department during a 6 month period. *Journal of Emergency Nursing, 18,* 505-510.

# G

Galan D. H., & Mayer L. L. (1992). *Elder abuse and the dentists' awareness and knowledge of the problem.* Winnipeg, MB: University of Manitoba, Faculty of Dentistry.

Gallagher, E. (1993). *Victoria Elder Abuse Project: Final Report,* Victoria, BC: British Columbia Health Research Foundation.

Gallagher, S., & Gerstal, N. (1993). Kinkeeping and friend keeping among older women: The effect of marriage. *The Gerontologist. 33*(1), 675-681.

Gelfand, D., & Yee, B. (1991). Trends & forces: Influence of immigration, migration, and acculturation on the fabric of aging in America. *Generations, 15*(4), 7-10.

Gelles, R., Steinmetz, S., & Straus, M. (1980). *Behind closed doors: Violence in the American family.* New York: Doubleday.

Gelles, R., & Straus, M. (1988). *Intimate violence.* New York: Simon and Shuster.

Gesino, J. P., Smith, H. H., & Keckich, W. A. (1982). The battered woman grows old. *Clinical Gerontologist, 1*(1), 59-67.

Gilbert, D. A. (1986). The ethics of mandatory elder abuse reporting statutes. *Advances in Nursing Science, 8,* 51-62.

Gioglio, G. R., & Blakemore, P. (1983). *Elder abuse in New Jersey: The knowledge and experience of abuse among older New Jerseyans.* Unpublished manuscript, New Jersey Department of Human Services.

Giordano, H., & Giordano, J. (1984, August). *Domestic violence: Profiles and predictors of five types of elder abuse.* Paper presented at the Second Family Violence Research Conference, Durham, NH.

Glendenning, F. (1993). What is elder abuse and neglect? In P. Decalmer, & F. Glendenning (Eds.), *The mistreatment of elderly people* (pp.1-34). London: Sage.

Glendenning, F., & Decalmer, P. (1993). Looking to the future. In F. Glendenning & P. Decalmer (Eds.), *The mistreatment of elderly people* (pp. 159-168). London: Sage.

Gnaedinger, N. J. (1989). *Elder abuse: A discussion paper,* Ottawa, ON: National Clearinghouse on Family Violence.

Godkin, M. A., Wolf, R. S., & Pillemer, K. A. (1989). A case-comparison analysis of elder abuse and neglect. *International Journal of Aging and Human Development, 28*(3), 207-225.

Gold, D., & Gwyther, L. (1989). The prevention of elder abuse: An educational model. *Family Relations, 38,* 8-14.

Gordon, L. (1988) *Heroes of their own lives: The politics and history of family violence.* New York: Penguin Books.

Gordon, R. M. (1992). Material abuse and powers of attorney in Canada: A preliminary examination. *Journal of Elder Abuse and Neglect, 4,* 173-193.

Gordon, R. M., & Tomita, S. (1990, December). The reporting of elder abuse and neglect: Mandatory or voluntary? *Canada's Mental Health, 38,* 1-6.

Gordon, R. M., & Verdun-Jones, S. N. (1992). *Adult guardianship law in Canada.* Toronto, ON: Carswell Thomson.

Gordon, R.M., Verdun-Jones, S.N., & MacDougall, D.J. (1986). *Standing in their shoes: Guardianship, trusteeship and the elderly Canadian.* Burnaby, B.C.: Simon Fraser University, Criminology Research Centre.

Gottlieb, B. (1991). Social support and family care of the elderly. *Canadian Journal on Aging, 10*(4), 359-375.

Gouvernement du Québec. (1989). *Growing old remaining free.* Québec, QC: Department of Health and Social Services.

Grams, A. (1992). Editorial. *Newsletter of the Association for Gerontology in Higher Education, 16,* 1.

Grandmaison, A. (1988). *Protection des personnes âgées: Étude exploratoire de la violence à l'égard de la clientèle des personnes âgées* (Protection of the elderly: An exploratory study regarding elderly clients). Unpublished manuscript. Montréal , QC; Centre de Services Sociaux du Montréal Métropolitain (CSSMM).

Grieco, A. (1987). Scope and nature of sexual harassment in nursing. *Journal of Sex Research, 23,* 261-266.

Groombridge, B. (1989). *Education and later life, human aging and later life: Multidisciplinary perspectives.* London: Hodder & Stoughton.

Guberman, N., Maheu, P., & Maille, C. (1992). Women as family caregivers: Why do they care? *The Gerontologist, 32*(5), 607-617.

## H

Halamandaris, V. (1983). Fraud and abuse in nursing homes. In J. Kosberg (Ed.), *Abuse and maltreatment of the elderly: Causes and interventions* (pp. 104-114). Boston, MA: John Wright PSG.

Haley, R.C. (1984). *Elder abuse/neglect.* Halifax, NS: Department of Social Services.

Hall, B. (1993). Time to nurse: Musings from an aging nurse radical. *Nursing Outlook, 41*(6), 250-251.

Hall, P. A. (1986). Minority elder mistreatment: Ethnicity, gender, age, and poverty. *Journal of Gerontological Social Work, 9*(4), 53-72.

Hall, P. A. (1989). Elder maltreatment items, subgroups, and types: Policy and practice implications. *International Journal of Aging and Human Development, 28*(3), 191-205.

Hamberger, L. K., Saunders, D. G., & Hovey, M. (1992). The prevalence of domestic violence in community practice and rate of physician inquiry. *Journal of Family Medicine, 24,* 283-287.

Hamilton, J. (1989). Hospitalized chronically ill. *Journal of Gerontological Nursing, 15*(4), 28-33.

Hamlet, E. (1992). *Training professionals to deal with elder abuse.* (Cat. No. H7221/ 801992E). Ottawa, ON: Health and Welfare Canada.

Harshbarger, S. (1993). From protection to prevention: A proactive approach. *Journal of Elder Abuse and Neglect, 5*(1), 41-55.

Health and Welfare Canada/Santé et Bien-Être Canada. (1986). *Les mauvais traitements à l'égard des personnes âgées.* (Elder abuse). National Clearinghouse on Family Violence, Ottawa, ON: Author.

Health & Welfare Canada. (1987). *Aging: Shifting the emphasis.* Working paper, Health Services and Promotion Branch, Ottawa, ON.

Health and Welfare Canada. (1990). *Seniors Independence Program: Today's projects enhancing the future, 1988-1989, 1989-1990* (Cat. H7430/1990E). Ottawa, ON: Supply and Services Canada.

Health and Welfare Canada. (1991). *Family Violence in Canada.* National Clearing House on Family Violence, Ottawa, ON: Author.

Health and Welfare Canada. (1992). *A shared concern: An overview of Canadian programs addressing the abuse of seniors* (Cat. H883/121991E). Ottawa, ON: Supply and Services Canada, Family Violence Prevention Division.

Health and Welfare Canada. (1993a). *Older Canadians and the abuse of seniors: A continuum from participation to empowerment.* Ottawa, ON: Supply and Services Canada.

Health and Welfare Canada. (1993b). *National Clearinghouse on Family Violence Annual Report 1992-93.* Ottawa, ON: Supply and Services Canada.

Hickey, T., & Douglass, R. L. (1981). Mistreatment of the elderly in the domestic setting: An exploratory study. *American Journal of Public Health, 71*(5), 500-507.

Hinrichsen, G., & Niederehe, G. (1994). Dementia management strategies and adjustment of family members of older patients. *The Gerontologist, 34*(1), 95-102.

Hoff, L. A. (1988). Collaborative feminist research and the myth of objectivity. In K. Yllo & M. Bograd (Eds.), *Feminist perspective on wife abuse* (pp. 269-281). Newbury Park, CA: Sage.

Hoff, L. A. (1991). Human abuse and nursing's response. In P. Holden & J. Littlewood (Eds.), *Nursing and Anthropology* (pp. 130-147). London: Routledge.

Hoff, L. A. (1995). *Interdisciplinary curriculum guide.* Ottawa, ON: Health and Welfare Canada.

Hoff, L. A., & Ross, M. M. (1993). *Curriculum guide for nursing: Violence against women and children.* Toronto, ON: Ontario Ministry of Colleges and Universities.

Hoff, L. A., and Ross, M. (forthcoming). Violence against women of all ages and children: Collaboration with community activists and curriculum implications. *Journal of Advanced Nursing.*

Hogg, P. W. (1992). *Constitutional law of Canada* (3rd ed.). Toronto, ON: Carswell Thomson.

Holt, M. (1993). Elder abuse in Britain: Meeting the challenge in the 1990's. *Journal of Elder Abuse and Neglect, 5,* 1, 33-39.

Holtzman, J. M., & Bomberg, T. (1991). A national survey of dentists' awareness of elder abuse and neglect. *Special Care in Dentistry, 11*(1), 7-11.

Homer, A. C., & Gilleard, C. (1990). Abuse of elderly people by their carers. *British Medical Journal, 301*(6765), 1359-1362.

Hornick, J. P., McDonald, L., & Robertson, G. B. (1992). Elder abuse in Canada and the United States: Prevalence, legal and service issues. In R. D. Peters, R. J. McMahon, & V. L. Quinsey (Eds.), *Aggression and violence throughout the life span* (pp. 301-335). Newbury Park, CA.: Sage.

Horowitz, A. (1985). Sons and daughters are caregivers to older parents: Differences in role performance and consequences. *The Gerontologist, 25,* 612.

Hudson, B. (1992). Ensuring an abuse-free environment: A learning program for nursing home staff. *Journal of Elder Abuse and Neglect, 4*(4), 25-36.

Hudson, J. E. (1988). Elder abuse: an overview, In S. Schlesinger & R. Schlesinger (Eds.), *Abuse of the elderly: Issues and annotated bibliography* (pp. 13-31). Toronto: University of Toronto Press.

Hudson, M. F. (1986). Elder mistreatment: Current research. In K. Pillemer and R. S. Wolf (Eds.), *Elder abuse: Conflict in the family* (pp. 125–167). Dover, MA: Auburn House.

Hudson, M. F. (1991). Elder mistreatment: A taxonomy with definitions by Delphi. *Journal of Elder Abuse and Neglect, 3,* 1-20.

Hudson, M. F., & Johnson, T. F. (1986). Elder abuse and neglect: A review of the literature. *The Annual Review of Gerontology and Geriatrics, 6,* 81-134.

Hughes, M. E. (1988). Personal guardianship and the elderly in the Canadian common law provinces: An overview of the law and charter implications. In M. E. Hughes & E. D. Pask (Eds.), *National themes in family law* (pp. 138-156). Toronto, ON: Carswell.

Hugman, R. (1991). *Power in caring professions.* London: Macmillan Press.

Hugonot, R. (1990). Abus et violences contre les personnes âgées (Abuse and violence against the elderly). *Bulletin de l'Académie Nationale de Médecine, 174*(6), 813-821.

Hydle, I. (1989). Violence against the elderly in Western Europe - treatment and preventive measures in the health and social services fields. *Journal of Elder Abuse & Neglect. 1,* 75-86.

Hydle, I. (1993). Abuse and neglect of the elderly—a Nordic perspective: Report from a Nordic research project. *Scandinavian Journal of Social Medicine, 21*(2), 126-128.

## I

Information London. (1990). *Community services directory.* London, ON: Author.

## J

Johns, S., Juklestad, O., & Hydle, I. (1992, November). *Developing elder protective services in Norway.* Paper presented at the Adult Protective Services Conference, San Antonio, TX.

Johnson, T. F. (1986). Critical issues in the definition of elder mistreatment. In K. Pillemer & R. Wolf (Eds.), *Elder abuse: Conflict in the family* (pp. 167-196). Dover, MA.: Auburn House.

Johnson, T. F. (1989). Elder mistreatment identification instruments: Finding common ground. *Journal of Elder Abuse and Neglect, 1,* 15-36.

Johnson, D. (1981, January). Abuse of the elderly. *Nurse Practitioner, 6*(1), 29-34.

## K

Kahana, E., & Young, R. (1990). Clarifying the caregiving paradigm: Challenges for the future. In D. E. Biegal & A. Blum (Eds.), *Aging and caregiving: theory, research and policy* (pp. 204-210). Newbury Park, CA: Sage.

Kane R. S., & Goodwin J. S. (1991). Spontaneous fractures of the long bones in nursing home patients. *American Journal of Medicine, 90,* 263-266.

Kassel, V. (1982). A geriatrician's view of health care of elderly. In C. G. Warner & G. Braen (Eds.), *Management of the physically and emotionally abused: Emergency assessment, intervention and counselling* (pp. 172-183). CA: Capristano Press.

Katz, K. D. (1980). Elder abuse. *Journal of Family Law, 18,* 695-722.

Keddy, B. (1993). *Feminism and patriarchy in university schools of nursing: An unsettling dualism.* Paper presented at the Women's Issues and Nursing Education Conference of the Canadian Association of University Schools of Nursing, Atlantic Region. Moncton, NB.

Kellaher, L. (1986). Determinants of quality of life in residential setting for old people. In Department of Health and Social Security (Ed.), *Residential Care for Elderly People* (pp. 127-137). London, England: Her Majesty's Stationery Office.

Keller, E. F. (1985). *Reflections on gender and science.* New Haven, CT: Yale University Press.

King, N. R. (1984). Exploitation and abuse of older family members: An overview of the problem. In J. J. Costa (Ed.), *Abuse of the Elderly: A Guide to Resources and Services* (pp. 56-68). Lexington, MA: Lexington Books.

Kingson, E., Hirshorn, B., & Harootyan, L. (1987). *The common state: The interdependence of generations.* Washington, DC: Gerontological Society of America.

Kinney, J., & Stephens, M. (1989). Assessing the daily hassles of caring for a family member with dementia. *The Gerontologist, 29,* 328-332.

Korbin, J. E., Anetzberger, G., Thomasson, R., & Austin, C. (1991). Abused elders who seek legal recourse against their adult offspring: Finds from an exploratory study. *Journal of Elder Abuse and Neglect, 3*(3), 1-18.

Korpi, W. (1989). Power, politics and state autonomy in the development of social citizenship. *American Sociological Review. 54,* (3), 309-328.

Kosberg, J. (1988). Preventing elder abuse: Identification of high risk factors prior to placement decisions. *The Gerontologist, 28*(1), 43-50.

Kozma, A., Stones, M. J., & McNeil, J. K. (1991). *Subjective well-being in later life.* Toronto,ON: Butterworths.

Kratcoski, P. C. (1990). Circumstances surrounding homicides by older offenders. *Criminal Justice and Behavior, 17*(4), 420-430.

Krauskopf, J. M., & Burnett, M. E. (1983). The elderly person: When protection becomes abuse. *Trial, 19,* 61-67.

Kurrle, S. E., Sadler, P. M., & Cameron, I. D. (1991). Elder abuse: An Australian case series. *Medical Journal of Australia, 144,* 150-153.

## L

Lamont, C. (1985). La violence à domicile faite aux femmes âgées. In Yves Brillon (1987) *Victimization and fear of crime among the elderly.* Toronto, ON: Butterworths, p. 83.

Langley, A. (1981). *Abuse of the Elderly.* (Human Services Monograph Series). Washington, DC: United States Government Printing Office, Department of Health and Human Services.

Lau, E., & Kosberg, J. I. (1979). Abuse of the elderly by informal care providers. *Aging, 299-301,* 11-15.

Law Reform Commission of Canada. (1984). *Working paper on assault.* (Working Paper No. 38). Ottawa, ON: Law Reform Commission of Canada.

Ledbetter Hancock, B. (1990). *Social work with older people* (2nd ed.). Englewood Cliffs, N.J.: Prentice Hall.

Lee, D. (1986). Mandatory reporting of elder abuse: A cheap but ineffective solution to the problem. *Fordham Urban Law Journal, 14,* 723-771.

Lee, G. R. (1992). Gender differences in family caregiving: A fact in search of a theory. In J. W. Dwyer and R. T. Coward (Eds.), *Gender, families and elder care* (pp. 120-131). Newbury Park, CA: Sage.

Lemke, S., & Moos, R. (1989). Ownership and quality of care in residential facilities for the elderly. *The Gerontologist, 29*(2), 209-215.

Lindgren, C. (1993). The caregiver career image. *Journal of Nursing Scholarship, 25,*(3), 214-219.

Lucas, E. T. (1991). *Elder Abuse and its recognition among health service professionals.* New York: Garland.

## M

MacLeod, L., & Picard, C. (1989). *Toward a more effective criminal justice response to wife assault: Exploring the limits and potential of effective intervention.* Ottawa, ON: Department of Justice Canada, Research and Development Directorate.

MacLeod, L. (1989). *Wife battering and the web of hope: Progress, dilemmas and visions of prevention.* Ottawa, ON: Health and Welfare Canada, National Clearinghouse on Family Violence.

Maddox, G.L. (1988). The future of gerontology in higher education: Continuing to open the American mind about aging. *The Gerontologist, 28,*(6), 748-752.

Maxwell, E. K., & Maxwell, R. J. (1992). Insults of the body civil: Mistreatment of elderly in two Plains Indian tribes. *Journal of CrossCultural Gerontology, 7*(1), 3-23.

McComas, J., Hebert, C., Glacomin, C., Kaplan, D., & Dulberg, C. (1993). Experiences of student and practising physical therapists with inappropriate patient sexual behaviour. *Physical Therapy, 73*(11), 732-770.

McCreadie, C. (1991). *Elder abuse: An exploratory study.* London: King's College, Age Concern Institute of Gerontology.

McCreadie, C., & Tinker, A. (1993). Review: Abuse of elderly people in the domestic setting: A UK perspective. *Age and Aging, 22,* 65-69.

McDonald, P. L., Hornick, J. P., Robertson, G. B., & Wallace, J. E. (1991). *Elder abuse and neglect in Canada.* Toronto, ON: Butterworths.

McLaughlin, P. (1979). *Guardianship of the person.* Downsview, ON: National Institute on Mental Retardation.

McLaughlin. J. S., Nickell, J. P., & Gill, L. (1980). An epidemiological investigation of elder abuse in southern Maine and New Hampshire. In U.S. House of Representatives Select Committee on Aging (Ed.), *Elder Abuse* (pp. 111-147). (Publication No.68463) Washington DC: U.S. Government Printing Office.

Mental Health Division, Health Services Directorate (1993). *Community awareness and response: Abuse and neglect of older adults.* Ottawa, ON: Health and Welfare Canada, Health Services and Promotion Branch.

Mercer, S. (1983). Consequences of institutionalization of the aged. In J. Kosberg (Ed.), *Abuse and maltreatment of the elderly: Causes and interventions* (pp. 84-103). Boston, MA: John Wright PSG.

Metcalf, C.A. (1986). A Response to the problem of elder abuse: Florida's Revised Adult Protections Act. *Florida State University Law Review, 14:* 745-777.

Miller, B. (1990). Gender differences in spouse management in the caregiver role. In E. Abel & K. Nelson (Eds.), *Circles of care: Work and identity in women's lives.* Albany, NY: State University of New York Press.

Miller, D. B. (1991). *Handbook of research design and social measurement* (5th ed.). Newbury Park, CA: Sage.

Ministry of Community and Social Services. (1985). *Report of a survey of elder abuse in the community.* Standing Committee on Social Development, Government of Ontario, Toronto, ON.

Ministry of Native Affairs. (1990). *The aboriginal peoples of British Columbia: A profile* (Canadian Cataloguing Publication No. ISBN 0772610916). Ottawa, ON: Supply and Services Canada.

Moamai, N. (1988). *Psychogériatrie: Les problèmes psychiatriques du 3e âge.* Montréal, QC: Les éditions La Presse.

Montraynaud, F., Pierron, A., & Suzzoni, F. (1989). *Dictionnaire de proverbes et dictons (Dictionary of Proverbs and Dictums).* Paris: Les Dictionnaires Le Robert.

Moon, A. & Williams, O. (1993). Perceptions of elder abuse and help-seeking patterns among African-American, Caucasian-American, and Korean-American elderly women. *The Gerontologist, 33,* 386-395.

Myers, J. (1993, March). Personal empowerment. *Aging International, 20,* 3-9.

**N**

Nahmiash, D., & Reis, M. (1992). *An exploratory study of private homecare services in Canada.* (Cat. No. H39-24811992E). Ottawa, ON: Supply and Services Canada.

Nahmiash, D., & Shrier, M. (1992). *Program designed to prevent abuse and mistreatment of the elderly in the community.* Montreal, QC: CLSC NDG/Montreal W.

National Advisory Council on Aging (NACA). (1991). *Elder abuse: Major issues from a national perspective.* (Cat. No.H71-2/3-2-1991). Ottawa, ON: Supply and Services Canada.

Nerenberg, L., & Garbuio, S. (1985). *The San Francisco consortium for elder abuse prevention: A history and description.* United States Department of Health and Human Services, Administration on Aging.

Nerenberg, L., & Garbuio, S. (1987). Organizing an elder abuse prevention network in your community. In L. Nerenberg (Ed.), *Serving the victim of elder abuse: A "How-to" manual for practitioners and program planners.* San Francisco: San Francisco Institute on Aging at Mount Zion Hospital and Medical Centre.

Newquist, D., Berger, M., Kahn, K., Martinez, C., & Burton, L. (1979). *Prescription for neglect: experiences of older Blacks and Mexican Americans with the American health care system.* Los Angeles, CA: Ethel Percy Andrus Gerontology Center.

Neysmith, S., & Aronson, J. (1993, July). *Homemakers define their work.* Paper presented at the World Congress on Aging. Budapest, Hungary.

Nolan, M. (1993). Carer-dependent relationships and the prevention of elder abuse. In P. Decalmer and F. Glendenning (Eds.), *The mistreatment of elderly people* (pp. 148-158). London: Sage.

Noone, J. F., Decalmer, P., & Glendenning, F. (1993). The general practitioner and elder abuse. In F. Glendenning & P. Decalmer (Eds.), *The mistreatment of elderly people* (pp. 136-147). London: Sage.

Novak, M. (1993). *Aging and society: A Canadian perspective.* Scarborough, ON: Nelson Canada.

## O

O'Malley, T. A., Everitt, D.E., O'Malley, H.C., & Campion, E.W. (1983). Identifying and preventing family-mediated abuse and neglect of elderly persons. *Annals of International Medicine, 98,* 998-1005.

O'Malley, T. A. (1987). Abuse and neglect of the elderly: The wrong issue? *Pride Institute Journal of Long Term Health Care, 5,* 25-28.

O'Neill, D., McCormack, P., Walsh, J. B., & Coakley, D. (1990). Elder abuse. *Irish Journal of Medical Science, 159*(2), 48-49.

Oakley, A. (1981). Interviewing women: A contradiction in terms. In H. Roberts (Ed.), *Doing feminist research.* London: Routledge.

Office for Senior Citizens' Affairs. (1992). *A review of community/program responses to elder abuse in Ontario.* Toronto, ON: Ministry of Citizenship, Government of Ontario.

Ogg, J., & Bennett, G. (1992). Elder abuse in Britain. *British Medical Journal, 305,* 998-999.

Ogg, J., & Munn-Giddings, C. (1993). Researching elder abuse. *Aging and Society, 13,* 389-413.

Ontario Advisory Council on Senior Citizens. (1989). *Aging together: An exploration of attitudes towards aging in multicultural Ontario.* Toronto, ON: Queen's Printer.

Ontario Association of Professional Social Workers. (1992). *Elder Abuse: A practical handbook for service providers.* Toronto, ON: Author.

Ontario Nursing Association College (1993). *Report on Abuse of the Elderly.* Unpublished report, Toronto, ON: Author.

Opperman, D. S. (1981). Michigan's bill of rights for nursing home residents. *Wayne Law Review, 27,* 1203-1227.

Orloff, A. (1993). Gender and the social rights of citizenship: The comparative analysis of gender relations and welfare states. *American Sociological Review, 58*(3), 303-328.

## P

Pagelow, M. (1988). Abuse of the elderly in the home. In A. Horton, & J. Williamson (Eds.). *Abuse and religion* (pp. 30-37). Lexington, Massachusetts: DC Heath.

Pal, L.A. (1992). *Public policy analysis: An introduction* (2nd ed.). Scarborough, ON: Nelson Canada.

Pascall, G. (1986). *Social policy: A feminist analysis.* New York: Tavisock Publications.

Paveza, G. J., Cohen, D., Eisdorfer, C., Freels, S., Semla, T., Ashford, W., Gorelick, P., Hirschman, R., Luchins, D., & Levy, P. (1992). Severe family violence and Alzheimer's disease: Prevalence and risk factors. *The Gerontologist, 32*(4), 493-497.

Pay, D. (1993). *Ask the question: A resource manual on elder abuse for health care personnel.* Vancouver, BC: Institute on Family Violence.

Pearson, L. (1991). *Toward the prevention of abuse.* Washington, DC: American Association of Retired Persons.

Penning, M. J. (1992). *Elder Abuse Resource Centre: Research Component Final Report*, Winnipeg, MB: University of Manitoba, Centre on Aging.

Pennsylvania Department of Aging. (1988). *Older Adult Protective Services Investigation Report*. Pittsburgh, PA: Author.

Phillips, L. R. & Rempusheski, V. F. (1985). A decision making model for diagnosing and intervening in elder abuse and neglect. *Nursing Research, 34*(3), 22-26.

Phillips, L. R. (1983). Abuse and neglect of the frail elderly at home: An exploration of theoretical relationships. *Journal of Advanced Nursing, 8*, 379-392.

Phillips, L. R. (1989). Issues involved in identifying and intervening in elder abuse. In R. Filinson & S. R. Ingman (Eds.), *Elder abuse: Practice and Policy* (pp. 86-93). New York: Human Science Press.

Phillips, N. M. (1980). Ohio's bill of rights for nursing home patients. *University of Dayton Law Review, 5*, 507-525.

Pillemer, K. (1993). The abused offspring and dependent: Abuse is caused by the deviance and dependence of abusive caregivers. In R. Gelles & D. Loeske (Eds.), *Current controversies on family violence* (pp. 237-249). Newbury, CA: Sage.

Pillemer, K. (1985). The dangers of dependency: New findings on the domestic violence against the elderly. *Social Problems, 33*(2), 146-158.

Pillemer, K., & Bachman-Prehn, R. (1991). Helping and hurting: Prediction of maltreatment of patients in nursing homes. *Research on Aging, 13*, 74-95.

Pillemer, K., & Finkelhor, D. (1985, October). *Domestic violence against the elderly: A discussion paper.* Paper presented at the Surgeon General's Workshop on Violence and Public Health, Leesburg, VA.

Pillemer, K., & Finkelhor, D. (1988). The prevalence of elder abuse: A random sample survey. *The Gerontologist, 28*, 51-57.

Pillemer, K., & Finkelhor, D. (1989). Causes of elder abuse: Caregiver stress versus problem relatives. *American Journal of Orthopsychiatry, 59*, 179-187.

Pillemer, K., & Hudson, B. (1993). A model abuse prevention program for nursing assistants. *The Gerontologist, 33*, 128-131.

Pillemer, K., & Moore, D. W. (1989). Abuse of patients in nursing homes: Findings from a survey of staff. *The Gerontologist, 29*(3), 314-320.

Pillemer, K., & Moore, D. W. (1990). Highlights from a study of abuse of patients in nursing homes. *Journal of Elder Abuse and Neglect, 2*(12), 5-29.

Pillemer, K., & Suitor, J. (1992). Violence and violent feelings: What causes them among family caregivers? *Journal of Gerontology, 47*(4), S165-S172.

Pillemer, K., & Wolf, R. S. (1986). Major findings from three model projects on elderly abuse. In K. Pillemer & R. Wolf (Eds.), *Elder abuse: Conflict in the family* (pp. 212-238). Dover, MA.: Auburn House.

Pillemer, K., & Wolf, R. S. (Eds.). (1986). *Elder abuse: Conflict in the family.* Dover, MA.: Auburn House.

Pittaway, E. D. (1993). *Ethnicity and elder abuse: practice issues.* Paper presented at the CAG preconference workshop of the 22nd Annual Scientific and Educational Meeting of the Canadian Association on Gerontology, Montreal, QC.

Pittaway, E. D., & Westhues, A. (1993). The prevalence of abuse and neglect of older adults who access health and social services in London, Ontario. *Journal of Elder Abuse and Neglect, 5*(4), 77-93.

Podnieks, E. (1985). Elder abuse: It's time we did something about it. *The Canadian Nurse, 81*(11), 36-39.

Podnieks, E. (1988a). Définitions, facteurs et profils (Definitions, factors and profiles). *Vis-à-vis, 6*(3), 4 & 8

Podnieks, E. (l988b). Comprendre la dimension du phénomène des mauvais traitements aux personnes âgées (Understanding the dimensions of elder abuse). *Vis-à-vis, 6*(3), 1 & 8.

Podnieks, E. (1992). The lived experience of abused older women. *Canadian Women's Studies, 12*(2), 38-44.

Podnieks, E., Pillemer, K., Nicholson, J. P., Shillington, T., & Frizzel, A. F. (1989). *A national survey on abuse of the elderly in Canada: Preliminary findings.* Toronto, ON: Ryerson Polytechnical Institute, Office of Research and Innovation.

Podnieks, E., Pillemer, K., Nicholson, J. P., Shillington, T., & Frizzell, A. F. (1990). *National survey on abuse of the elderly in Canada.* Toronto, ON: Ryerson Polytechnical Institute.

Poertner, J. (1986). Estimating the incidence of abused older persons. *Journal of Gerontological Social Work, 9*(3), 3-15.

Poirier, D. (1988). Models of intervention for the guardianship and protection of elderly persons in Canada. In M. E. Hughes & E. D. Pask (Eds.), *National themes in family law* (pp. 157-178). Toronto, ON: Carswell.

Pollick, M. K. (1987). Abuse of the elderly: A review. *Holistic Nursing Practices, 2*, 43-53.

Pratt, C. C., Koval, J., & Lloyd, D. (1983, March). Service workers' responses to abuse of the elderly. *Social Casework, 64*, 142-153.

**Q**

Quinn, M. J., & Tomita, S. K. (1986). *Elder abuse and neglect: Causes, diagnosis and intervention strategies.* New York: Springer.

**R**

Rappaport, J. (1985, Fall). The power of empowerment language. *Social Policy, 16*, 15-21.

Reinharz, S., & Rowles, G. D. (Eds.). (1988). *Qualitative gerontology.* New York: Springer.

Reis, M., Nahmiash, D., & Shrier, R. (1993, October). *A brief abuse screen for the elderly (BASE): Its validity and use.* Paper presented at the 22nd Annual Scientific and Educational Meeting of the Canadian Association on Gerontology, Montreal, QC.

Reis, M., & Nahmiash, D. (1994). *When seniors are abused: An intervention guidebook on research.* Unpublished manuscript.

Reuveni, U. (1985). The family as a social support group now and in 2001. *Journal for Specialists in Group Work, 10*(2), 88-91.

Reverby, S. (1987). *Ordered to care.* Cambridge, MA: Cambridge University Press.

Roberge, R., & Beauséjour, R. (1988). L'usage des contentions en milieu d'hébergement pour les personnes âgées (Use of restraints in hospitals and nursing homes) *La Revue canadienne du vieillissement, 7*(4), 372-376.

Robertson, G. B. (1994). *Mental disability and the law in Canada* (2nd ed.). Toronto, ON: Carswell Thomson.

Robinson, S. C. (1981). Preventing child abuse: The obstetric responsibility. *Bulletin of the Society of Obstetrics and Gynaecology of Canada, 2*(2), 1-2.

Roche, T., & Doumkou, A. (1990). *Seniors' needs assessment.* London, ON: London Intercommunity Health Centre.

Ross, M. (1988a). Abuse of the elderly. *The Canadian Nurse, 81*(2), 37-39.

Ross, M. (1988b). *Violence against older adults: Implications for professional practice.* Ottawa, ON: Ottawa-Carleton Council on Aging.

Ross, M. & Hoff, L.A. (1994, June). Teaching nurses about abuse. *The Canadian Nurse, 90,* 33-36.

Ross, M., Ross, P., & Ross-Carson, M. (1985, February). Abuse of the elderly. *The Canadian Nurse, 81,* 36-39.

Rosser, S. V. (1986). *Teaching science and health from a feminist perspective.* New York: Pergamon Press.

Rossi, P. H., & Freeman, H. E. (1989). *Evaluation: A systematic approach* (4th ed.). Newbury Park, CA: Sage.

Rozovsky, L. E. (1980). *The Canadian patient's book of rights.* Toronto, ON: Doubleday.

Rozovsky, L. E., & Rozovsky, F. A. (1987). Why the patient's bill of rights is not a good thing. *Health Care,* p.38.

Russell, D. (1990). *Rape in marriage* (rev. ed.). New York: Collier Books.

## S

Sadler, P. M., & Kurrle, S. E. (1993). Australian service providers' responses to elder abuse. *Journal of Elder Abuse and Neglect, 5*(1), 55-75.

Santé et Bien-Être Canada. (1986). *Les mauvais traitements à l'égard des personnes âgées.* (Elder abuse). National Clearinghouse on Family Violence. Ottawa, ON: Author.

Sassetti, M. R. (1993). Domestic violence. *Primary Care, 20*(2), 289-305.

Saunders, D. (1988). Wife abuse, husband abuse or mutual combat? In K. Yllo & M. Bograd (Eds.), *Feminist perspectives on wife abuse* (pp. 90-113). Newbury Park, CA: Sage.

Schlesinger, B., & Schlesinger, R. (Eds.). (1988). *Abuse of the elderly.* Toronto, ON: University of Toronto Press.

Scogin, F., Beall, C., Bynum, J., Stephens, G. Grote, N., Baumhover, L., & Bolland, J. (1989). Training for abusive caregivers: An unconventional approach to an intervention dilemma. *Neglect, 1*(4), 73-85.

Secretary of State (1988). *Ethnicity and aging.* Ottawa, ON: Supply and Services Canada.

Sengstock, M. C., & Hwalek, M. (1986a). A critical analysis of measures for the identification of physical abuse and neglect in the elderly. *Home Health Care Quarterly, 6*(4), 27-39.

Sengstock, M. C., & Hwalek, M. (1986b, September). Domestic abuse of the elderly: Which cases involve the police. *Journal of Interpersonal Violence, 3,* 335-349.

Sengstock, M. C., & Hwalek, M. (1987). A review and analysis of measures for the identification of elder abuse. *Journal of Gerontological Social Work, 10,* 21-36.

Sengstock, M. C., & Hwalek, M. (1988). *Sengstock-Hwalek comprehensive index of elder abuse.* Detroit, MI: SPEC Associates.

Sengstock, M. C., & Hwalek, M. (1990). Identification of elder abuse in institutional settings: Required changes in existing protocols. *Journal of Elder Abuse and Neglect, 2*(1,2), 31-50.

Sengstock, M. C., Hwalek, M., & Petrone, S. (1989). Services for aged abuse victims: Service types and related factors. *Journal of Abuse and Neglect, 1*(4), 37-56.

Sengstock, M., Hwalek, M., & Stahl, C. (1991). Developing new models of service delivery to aged abuse victims: Does it matter? *Clinical Sociology Review, 9,*142-161.

Sengstock, M. C., & Liang, J. (1983). Domestic abuse of the aged: Assessing some dimensions of the problem. *Interdisciplinary Topics in Gerontology, 17,* 58-68.

Sergerie, M. (1991). *L'abus et la négligence envers les personnes âgeés vivant en milieu naturel: Une recension d'écrits* (Abuse and neglect of the elderly living in natural surroundings: An inventory of writings). Rimouski, QC: Service de Gérontogériatrie et Département de Santé Communautaire, Rimouski.

Sharpe, G. S. (1988). The protection of elderly mentally incompetent individuals who are victims of abuse. In B. Schlesinger & R. Schlesinger (Eds.), *Abuse of the elderly: Issues and annotated bibliography* (pp. 64-74). Toronto, ON: University of Toronto Press.

Shell, D. J. (1982). *Protection of the elderly: A study of elder abuse.* Report of Manitoba Council on Aging, Association on Gerontology, Winnipeg, MB.

Silverstein, L. A. (1991). A case of threatened violence in the female therapist/male patient relationship. *Women and Therapy, 11*(2), 13-23.

Social Planning and Research Council of British Columbia. (1989). *Elder abuse and neglect: A guide to intervention.* Vancouver, BC: Author

Solomon, K. (1983). Victimization by health professionals and the psychological response of the elderly. In J. Kosberg (Ed.), *Abuse and maltreatment of the elderly: Causes and interventions* (pp. 150-171). Boston, MA: John Wright.

Sonkin, D. J., Martin, D., & Walker, E. A. (1985). *The male batterer.* New York: Springer.

Sprey, J., & Matthews, S. (1989). The perils of drawing policy implications from research: The case of elder mistreatment. In R. Filinson & S. R. Ingman (Eds.), *Elder abuse: Practice and policy* (pp. 51-61). New York: Human Sciences Press.

Stannard, C. (1973). Old folks and dirty work: The social conditions for patient abuse in a nursing home. *Social Problems, 20*(3), 330-342.

Stathopoulos, P. (1982). Consumer advocacy and abuse of elders in nursing homes. In C. G. Warner & G. Braen (Eds.), *Management of the physically and emotionally abused: Emergency assessment, intervention and counselling* (pp. 335-354). CA: Capristano Press.

Statistics Canada. (1993, November 18). The violence against women survey. *The Daily,* Ottawa: Author.

Steel, F. (1988). Financial obligations toward the elderly: Filial responsibility laws. In M. E. Hughes & E. D. Pask (Eds.), *National themes in family law* (pp. 99-116). Toronto: Carswell.

Stein, N., (1991). A national agenda for elder abuse and neglect research: Issues and recommendations, *Journal of Elder Abuse and Neglect, 3*(3), 91-104.

Steinmetz, S. K. (1981). *Abuse of the elderly.* Ottawa, ON: Health and Welfare Canada, National Information Centre on Violence in the Family.

Steinmetz, S. K. (1987). Elderly victims of domestic violence. In C. D. Chambers, J. H. Lindquist, O. Z. White, & M. T. Harter (Eds.), *The elderly: Victims and deviants* (pp. 126-190). Toledo: Ohio University Press.

Steinmetz, S. K. (1988). *Duty bound: Elder abuse and family care.* Newbury Park, CA: Sage.

Stevenson, C. (1985). *Family abuse of the elderly in Alberta.* Report of Government of Alberta Social Services and Community Health, Senior Citizens Bureau.

Stockard, S. (1991, November). Caring for the sexually aggressive patient: You don't have to blush and bear it. *Nursing, 21*(11), 72-73.

Stoller, E. (1990). Males as helpers: The role of sons, relatives and friends. *The Gerontologist, 30,* 228-235.

Stoller, E. (1992). Gender differences in the experiences of caregiving spouses. In J. Dwyer & R. Coward (Eds.). *Gender, families, and elder care* (pp. 49-64). Newbury Park, CA: Sage.

Stone, R., Cafferata, G., & Sangle, J. (1987). Caregivers of the frail elderly: A national profile. *The Gerontologist, 27,* 616-626

Stones, M. J. (1993a, October). *Defining senior mistreatment.* Paper presented at the 22nd Annual Scientific and Educational Meeting of the Canadian Association on Gerontology, Montreal.

Stones, M. J. (1993b, October). *Measuring perceptions of elder abuse.* Paper presented at the 22nd Annual Scientific and Educational Meeting of the Canadian Association on Gerontology, Montreal.

Stones, M. J. (1994). *Rules and tools: The meaning and measurement of elder abuse.* St. John's, NF: Milestones.

Stordeur, R., & Stille, R. (Eds.). (1989). *Ending men's violence against their partners.* Newbury Park, CA: Sage.

Straus, M. A. (1979). Measuring intra-family conflict and violence: The conflict tactics (CT) scales. *Journal of Marriage and the Family, 47,* 75-88.

Sudman, S., & Bradburn, N. M. (1983). *Asking questions: A practical guide to questionnaire design.* San Francisco, CA: Jossey-Bass.

Synergy (1992). *Synergy II: A demonstration project to address the issues of violence in older families.* Calgary, AB: Kerby Assembly.

**T**

Tarbox, A. R. (1983). The elderly in nursing homes: Psychological aspects of neglect. *Clinical Gerontologist, 1*(4), 39-51.

Tatara, T., & Rittman, M. M. (Eds.). (1991). *Findings of five elder abuse studies from the NARCEA research grants program.* Washington, DC: National Aging Resource Center on Elder Abuse.

Tellis-Nayak, V., & Tellis-Nayak, M. (1989). Quality of care and the burden of two cultures: When the world of the nurses' aide enters the world of the nursing home. *The Gerontologist, 29,* 307-313.

Tomita, S. (1982). Detection and treatment of elder abuse and neglect: A protocol for health care professionals. *Physical and Occupational Therapy in Geriatrics, 2,* 37-51.

Tomita, S. K. (1990). The denial of elder mistreatment by victims and abusers. *Violence and Victims, 5*(3), 171-184.

Tomlin, S. (1988). *Abuse of elderly people: An unnecessary and preventable problem.* London: British Geriatrics Society.

Toupin, C. (1990). *Rapport d'activités 1989-1990 et une rétrospective des plaintes des trois années précédentes* (1989-1990 activity report and a look back at complaints of the previous three years). Montréa, QC: Conseil de la santé et des services sociaux de la région de Montréal métropolitain.

Trilling, J. S., Greenblatt, L., & Shepherd, C. (1987). Elder abuse and the utilization of support services for elderly patients. *Journal of Family Practice, 24,* 581-587.

## U

Ungerson, C. (Ed.). (1990). *Gender and caring: Work and welfare in Britain and Scandinavia.* London: Harvester Wheatsheaf.

United States House Select Committee on Aging. (1981). *Elder abuse: An examination of a hidden problem.* Committee Publication No. 99-502, Washington DC, U.S. Government Printing Office.

University of Victoria Centre on Aging. (1994). A National study on services for abused older Canadians. *Bulletin, 2*(3), 2.

## V

Vinton, L. (1991). Abused older women: Battered women or abused elders? *Journal of Women and Aging, 3*(3), 5-19.

## W

Walker, A. (1980).The social creation of poverty and dependency in old age. *Journal of Social Policy, 9*(1), 49-75.

Walker, G. (1990). *Family Violence and the Women's Movement: The conceptual politics of struggle.* Toronto, ON: University of Toronto Press.

Watson, C., Kelley, M. L., MacLean, M., & Meredith, S. (1992). *Gerontology content in graduate social work curriculum across Canada.* Hamilton, ON: McMaster University, Educational Centre for Aging and Health.

Watson, W. H. (1991). Ethnicity, crime, and aging: Risk factors and adaptation. *Generations, 15*(4), 53-57.

Webber, P., Fox, P., & Burnette, D. (1994). Living alone with Alzheimer's disease: Effects on health and social service utilization patterns. *The Gerontologist, 34*(1), 8-14.

Weiler, K., & Buckwalter, K. C. (1992). Abuse among rural mentally ill. *Journal of Psychosocial Nursing and Mental Health Services, 30*(9), 32-36.

Weisstub, D. N. (1990). *Enquiry on mental competency: Final report.* (ISBN 0-7729-7282-6). Toronto, ON: Queen's Printer for Ontario.

Wilcox, B. (1983). Social support in adjusting to marital disruption. In B. Gottleib (Ed.), *Social networks and social support.* Newbury Park, CA: Sage.

Williams, F. (1989). *Social policy: A critical introduction.* Cambridge, MA: Polity Press.

Wolf, R. S. (1988). Elder abuse: Ten years later. *Journal of the American Geriatric Society, 36,* 758-762.

Wolf, R. S. (1992). Victimization of the elderly: Elder abuse and neglect. *Reviews in Clinical Gerontology, 2*(3), 269-276.

Wolf, R. S., Godkin, M. A., & Pillemer, K. (1984). *Elder abuse and neglect: Final report from three model projects.* Worcester, MA: University of Massachusetts Medical Centre, University Centre on Aging.

Wolf, R. S., & Pillemer, K. A. (1989). *Helping elderly victims: The realty of elder abuse.* New York: Columbia University Press.

Wolf, R. S., & Pillemer, K. A. (1994). What's new in elder abuse programming? Four bright ideas. *The Gerontologist, 34,* 126-129.

Wolf, R. S., Strugnell, C. P., & Godkin, M. A. (1982). *Preliminary findings from three model projects on elderly abuse.* Worcester, MA: University of Massachusetts Medical Centre, University Centre on Aging.

Wray, L. A. (1991). Public policy implications of an ethnically diverse elderly population. *Journal of Cross-Cultural Gerontology, 6*(2), 243-257.

Wrigley, M. (1991). Abuse of elderly people—"pathological" carers. *Irish Medical Journal, 84*(1), 31-32.

## Y

Yllo, K., & Bograd, M. (Eds.). (1988). *Feminist perspectives on wife abuse.* Newbury Park, CA: Sage.

Young, I. (1990). *Justice and the politics of difference.* Princeton, NJ: Princeton University Press.

## Z

Zarit, S., & Toseland, R. (1989). Current and future directions in family caregiving research. *The Gerontologist, 29,* 481-483.

Zay, N. (1981). *Dictionnaire-manuel de gérontologie sociale* (Dictionary-manual of social gerontology). Québec, QC: Les Presses de l'université Laval.

# LEGAL REFERENCES

*Adult Guardianship Act,* S.B.C. 1993, c.35.

*Adult Protection Act,* S.N.S. 1985, c. 2, now R.S.N.S. 1989, c.2.

*Adult Protection Act,* S.P.E.I. 1988, c.6, now R.S.P.E.I. 1988, c.A-5

Bill 74, The Advocacy Act, *An Act respecting the Provision of Advocacy Services to Vulnerable Persons,* S.O. 1992, c.26.

Bill 108, The Substitute Decisions Act, *An Act to provide for the making of decisions on behalf of Adults concerning the Management of their Property & concerning their Personal Care,* S.O. 1992, c.30-108.

Bill 120, *An Act to amend the act respecting health services & social services & amending various legislation,* R.S.Q. 1991, c.42, now R.S.Q. 1993, c.S-4.2.

*Canadian Charter of Rights and Freedoms,* Part I of the *Constitution Act,* 1982, Schedule B of the *Canada Act 1982* (U.K.), 1982, c. 11.

*Criminal Code,* R.S.C. 1985, c.C-46.

*Family Services Act,* S.N.B. 1980, c.F-2.2.

*Health Care (Consent) & Care Facility (Admission) Act,* S.B.C. 1993, c.48.

*Manitoba Mental Health Act,* R.S.M. 1987, c.M110

*Neglected Adults Welfare Act,* S.N. 1973, No. 81, now R.S.N. 1990, c.N-3.

*Nova Scotia (Ministry of Community Services) v. Carter* (1988) 89 N.S.R. (2d) 275 (Fam.Ct.).

*Nursing Homes Act,* now R.S.O. 1990, c.N-7.

Ontario Bill of Rights, *Human Rights Code,* R.S.O. 1990, c.H-19.

*Powers of Attorney Act,* S.A. 1991, c. P-13.5.

*Public Guardian & Trustee Act,* S.B.C. 1993, c.64.

*Re Eve* (1986), 31 D.L.R. (4th) 1 at 6.

*Representation Agreement Act,* S.B.C. 1993, c.67.

*The Dependent Adults Act,* S.S. 1989-90, c.D-25.1.

# APPENDICES

# APPENDIX A

## SYNTHESIS OF RECOMMENDATIONS

### 1. FOR BROAD APPLICATION

#### AUTHORS HIGHLIGHT AND RECOMMEND:

* including older Canadians in all aspects of work on this issue: in developing models for intervention, and in certain kinds of interventions such as peer support programs; in presenting educational programs; and in developing policies and research studies
* developing strategies that are feasible within the current context of economic restraint
* recognizing that analysis and understanding of the issue will have limited effectiveness without commitment on the political level towards eliminating abuse
* placing abuse and neglect of older persons within the wider context of societal violence, rather than within the more restricted domain of family violence
* encouraging positive imaging of older persons in the media, and responsible media coverage of issues surrounding the abuse and neglect of older people

### 2. FOR THE FIELD OF PRACTICE

#### AUTHORS IN THE PRACTICE SECTION HIGHLIGHT AND RECOMMEND:

* developing broad-based community responses rather than setting up special teams or relying on experts
* consulting seniors regarding the delivery of services
* including senior volunteers in providing services
* providing services that are sufficient, affordable, and accessible for older persons
* designing and delivering services with sensitivity to cultural barriers
* paying more attention to publicizing services, with efforts to ensuring that they are perceived as appropriate by the persons they are intended to serve
* providing follow-up counselling to abused seniors, and support for them through criminal justice proceedings
* paying attention to the ethical dimensions of interventions with abused seniors
* practitioners' engaging in advocacy for needed services, both on the individual level and on the community level

### AUTHORS IN THE OTHER SECTIONS HIGHLIGHT AND RECOMMEND:

* using multidisciplinary teams for dealing with elder abuse in the health-care field
* providing for better and quicker follow-up after detection
* training seniors in peer support programs for abused older persons
* initiating partnerships among practitioners, researchers, and funders
* developing a sense of trust among researchers, practitioners, seniors, and caregivers
* building follow-up on identified cases into the design of any research study on abused older persons

## 3. FOR THE FIELD OF POLICY

### AUTHORS IN THE POLICY SECTION HIGHLIGHT AND RECOMMEND:

* giving priority to providing services for abused older people, not just to detection and screening
* establishing shelters for abused older persons
* appreciating the particular effectiveness that seniors may provide with regard to follow-up and support services
* recognizing that the legal route, both criminal law and adult protection legislation, is an insufficient mode of response to the problem of elder abuse and neglect
* paying attention to the new Vulnerable Adults legislation in British Columbia, which offers a promising balance between protection (of abused persons) and respect for (the older person's) autonomy
* developing and implementing policies in all health care institutions regarding elder abuse and neglect
* giving priority to developing detection and screening tools; the need for protocols to address the outcomes of specific interventions
* involving multi-disciplinary teams when developing policies and protocols
* having sensitivity to cultural diversity and linguistic barriers when developing these tools and in all dealings with abused older people
* encouraging at all levels in health care institutions that suspected abuse and neglect be reported
* collecting data for all suspected cases of elder abuse or neglect

### AUTHORS IN THE OTHER SECTIONS HIGHLIGHT AND RECOMMEND:

* developing broad-based community responses rather than setting up special teams or relying on experts
* providing services for seniors, designing them creatively, ensuring that they are appropriate, known, available, accessible, affordable, and sufficient to meet the need
* consulting and involving seniors in the design and implementation of services for them
* extending analysis and strategizing about abuse and neglect in health care institutions to include all units, and not only nursing and care staff

* sharing and consolidating knowledge for effectively dealing with elder abuse and neglect; adapting existing programs and launching new ones for use in institutional settings
* reaching out to all members of society, young and old alike, as essential for the prevention of abuse and neglect of older persons

# 4. FOR THE FIELD OF EDUCATION

## AUTHORS IN THE EDUCATION SECTION HIGHLIGHT AND RECOMMEND:

* including seniors in developing and presenting educational programs on abuse and neglect of older persons
* reaching out to all members of society through educational programs aimed at developing awareness and sensitivity about elder abuse and neglect
* designing preventive education programs for children, knowing that attitudes toward seniors are formed from early childhood
* directing educational efforts in particular to older persons, caregivers, persons likely to be able to detect cases of elder abuse and neglect, and to health care professionals, both in their initial training and through continuing education programs
* extending concerted efforts to ensure that older persons and caregivers for older persons are informed about resources available to them
* using content from many disciplines in developing educational programs on elder abuse and neglect
* including experiential learning in educational programs on elder abuse and neglect

## AUTHORS IN THE OTHER SECTIONS HIGHLIGHT AND RECOMMEND:

* educating members of the public as well as service providers about abuse and neglect of older persons; aiming for them to assist in early detection and prevention of suspected and/or potential abuse and neglect
* educating practitioners and policy-makers about aboriginal and ethno-cultural communities in order to provide for better intervention and better provision of services
* educating health and social service practitioners with regard to the criminal justice system and how to work within it
* educating seniors about their legal rights and about existing legislation applying to situations of abuse and neglect
* highlighting gaps in resources and programs as a basis for increased lobbying by practitioners for more and better services for older persons
* including seniors in educational endeavours about elder abuse and neglect
* promoting sensitivity to older persons, culturally, linguistically, and with regard to their right to autonomy and self-determination
* recognizing that education on elder abuse and neglect (e.g. about risk factors, resources, and case management) is an essential requirement for the development of policies and protocols in health care institutions

## 5. FOR THE FIELD OF RESEARCH

### AUTHORS IN THE RESEARCH SECTION HIGHLIGHT AND RECOMMEND:

* seeking a common definition of elder abuse in order to overcome problems for research and for practice that arise from differing definitions

* recognizing that no general measure of abuse and neglect of older persons is possible without developing a clear operational definition

* recognizing the impracticality of definitions which define elder abuse in terms of resulting harm, without reference to behaviour or intent

* recognizing that definitions which define elder abuse in terms of criteria for judging abusive behaviour, while most comprehensive and succinct, are problematic where standards are not explicitly articulated

* recognizing that definitions which specify abusive and neglectful actions are needed in research studies (The EAST tool, specifying 71 items in 9 categories, is recommended.)

* further testing to establish the validity and reliability of the screening measures and classification instruments which are currently in use, and of measurement tools used in surveys

* developing an adequate criterion for standardizing screening measures and assessment tools

* attending to the use of appropriate research designs in studies of abuse and neglect of older persons

* attending to careful defining of the target population when conducting prevalence studies

* taking care with regard to estimations of the required sample size

* attending to developing an agreed-upon operational definition of elder abuse and neglect, and awareness of differences according to culture

### AUTHORS IN THE OTHER SECTIONS HIGHLIGHT AND RECOMMEND:

* undertaking more research about the needs of abused seniors and of abusers, evaluation of the effectiveness of intervention models and of services and resources

* investigating shelters as an option for abused older people

* researchers and health-care institutions collaborating in action-research on the issue of abuse and neglect of older persons

* giving priority to developing effective screening tools for use by health and social service practitioners and administrators

* ongoing review and analysis of policies, tools, and data collected on elder abuse and neglect in health-care institutions

* studying the relationship of dependency, stress, and isolation with regard to elder abuse and neglect in home-care as well as health care institutions

* collecting data on all suspected cases of elder abuse and neglect

* developing tools for evaluating the effectiveness of both formal and informal educational programs

# APPENDIX B

## COMMUNITY AGENCIES AND PROGRAMS

**Advocacy Centre for the Elderly (ACE)**
120 Eglinton Avenue East, Ste. 902, Toronto, Ontario M4P 1E1
Telephone: 416-487-7157          Fax: 416-487-1342

**American Association of Retired Persons (AARP)**
601 E Street N.W., Washington, D.C. 20049, U.S.A.
Telephone: 202-434-2222          Fax: 202-434-6474

**Bernard Betel Centre for Creative Living**
1003 Steeles Ave. West, Toronto, Ontario M2R 3T6
Telephone: 416-225-2112          Fax: 416-225-2097

**Canadian Association of Broadcasters**
P.O. Box 627, Station B, Ottawa, Ontario K1P 5S2
Telephone: 613-233-4035          Fax: 613-233-6961

**Church Council for Justice and Corrections**
507 Bank St., Ottawa, Ontario K2P 1Z5
Telephone: 613-563-1688          Fax: 613-237-6129

**Concerned Friends of Ontario Citizens in Care Facilities**
170 Merton St., Toronto, Ontario M4S 1A1
Telephone: 416-489-0146

**Council on Positive Aging**
148 North May St., P.O. Box 9, Thunder Bay, Ontario P7C 5V4
Telephone: 807-622-9393          Fax: 807-622-0040

**Deer Lodge Centre**
2109 Portage Ave., Winnipeg, Manitoba R3J 0L3
Telephone: 204-837-1301          Fax: 204-888-1805

**Educational Centre for Aging and Health**
Health Sciences Centre-1M7, McMaster University,
Chedoke Campus, Bldg. 74, Hamilton, Ontario L8N 3Z5
Telephone: 905-521-4986          Fax: 905-318-6556

**Elder Abuse Resource Centre, Age and Opportunity**
309-323 Portage Ave., Winnipeg, Manitoba R3B 2C1
Telephone: 204-942-6235          Fax: 204-946-5667

**Halton Regional Police Force, Community Relations Bureau**
P.O. Box 2700, Oakville, Ontario L6J 5C7
Telephone: 905-825-4777

**Kerby Centre**
1133-7th Ave., S.W. Calgary, Alberta T2P 1B2
Telephone: 403-265-0661          Fax: 403-264-7047

**Maison Jeanne Simard**
C.P. 35, Succ. M., Montréal, Québec H1V 3L6
Telephone: 514-259-7712          Fax: 514-259-7712

**National Film Board of Canada**
P.O. Box 6100, Station Centre-ville, Montreal, Quebec H3C 3H5
Telephone: 1-800-267-7710

**North Shore Community Services**
1060 Roosevelt Cres., North Vancouver, British Columbia V7P 1M3
Telephone 604-985-7138          Fax 604-985-9528

**Northern Educational Centre for Aging and Health**
Health Sciences Resources Centre, Lakehead University,
Thunder Bay, Ontario P7B 5E1
Telephone: 807-343-2126          Fax: 807-343-2104

**Older Women's Long-term Survival Project (OWLS)**
400-119 14th St. N.W., Calgary, Alberta T2N 1V6
Telephone: 403 283-6112          Fax: 403-244-4701

**Older Women's Network**
St. Paul's Centre, Box 12, 427 Bloor St. W., Toronto, Ontario M5S 1X7
Telephone: 416-924-4188

**Ontario Network for the Prevention of Elder Abuse**
Centre for Studies of Aging, 305-455 Spadina Ave., Toronto,
Ontario M5S 1A1 Telephone: 416-978-2197          Fax: 416-978-4771

**Project Care**
c/o Myrna Reis, Psychology Dept., Concordia University,
7141 Sherbrooke St. W., Montreal, Quebec H4B 1R6
Telephone: 514-848-2236          Fax: 514-848-2815

**Ryerson / CJRT Open College**
150 Mutual St., Toronto, Ontario M5B 2M1
Telephone: 416-595-0485          Fax: 416-595-9602

**Seniors Assisting Seniors**
SAS Confederation Park, 2212-13th St.N.W., Calgary, Alberta T2M 4P7
Telephone: 403-284-5575          Fax: 403-289-2028

**Seniors Education Centre**
University of Regina, College Ave. & Cornwall St.,
Regina, Saskatchewan S4S 0A2
Telephone: 306-779-4816          Fax: 306-779-4825

**T.M.D. Promotions Ltd.**
3600 Billings Court, Ste. 2020, Burlington, Ontario L7N 3N6
Telephone: 905-637-8018

**Texas Department of Protective Services**
El Paso Elder Abuse Project, P.O. Box 149030, Austin, Texas 78714-9030,
U.S.A.

**Victoria Elder Abuse Project**
Rm. 452 - 2251 Cadboro Bay Rd., Victoria, British Columbia V8R 5H3
Telephone: 604-370-6652          Fax: 604-598-3486